NOT MY GURU

NOT MY GURU

Living Inside The Osho International Ashram

By
Parvati Hill

Ralston Store Publishing
P.O. Box 4513
Durango, Colorado 81302

ISBN 978-0-9822585-5-2

Printed in the USA

Prologue

If Osho wasn't my guru, why did I go to his ashram? The answer is simple. I had been hoping for a transition away from my unsatisfactory life.

When the opportunity presented itself to spend three months at the Osho International Ashram in India, I jumped at it. Living in a foreign country at this controversial ashram was an adventure I couldn't resist. This was the perfect transition for me.

Before I arrived in India, I felt I had adequate information about my upcoming life at the ashram. I knew I had to wear a maroon robe. I knew I had to work seven days a week for the entire three months. And, I knew I had to watch a video showing of Osho every night. It was what I didn't know and didn't expect that affected me the most.

Living among strangers whose viewpoint was so different from mine created challenges I hadn't anticipated. Their blind devotion to this dead, Indian mystic both surprised and entertained me. When I arrived at the ashram, I knew almost nothing about Osho. When I left, I felt I knew him very well.

If you presume this book will prove how evil, dangerous, or phony Osho was, it will disappoint you. Or, if you presume this book will revere and glorify Osho, it will disappoint you. I believe I give a fair portrayal of his strengths and weaknesses. He was a wise and holy man, but he had his share of flaws. He was a human being like the rest of us.

Although there are times I speak of him with great respect, at other times I speak of him with disdain. And, I'm not spoiling anything by telling you that by the end of the book, Osho is still *NOT MY GURU*.

Day Zero – Arriving in India

After a four hour stretch between flights, I finally board the plane to India. I'm on my way! I sit in the aisle seat next to two Indians from Cleveland. Cleveland Indians! They are going north of Mumbai to visit relatives and will stay in India for six or eight weeks. They are friendly, and we talk for a while. I confess to them how worried I feel that my driver won't be there to get me. They offer to stay with me to make sure he does. How kind of them to offer.

When we arrive, construction reins at the Mumbai Airport. All the different paths confuse me, and I am glad I can follow my new friends. We get through customs with no problem, and I follow them to the luggage claim area. The airport has minimal or nonexistent signage. I would not have known where to go without asking many questions. Meeting them is a blessing.

When we get to the luggage claim area, my luggage comes quickly. I have my big, heavy suitcase, and another smaller carry-on-size suitcase. Although I worried about the little one, it arrives without issue. Their luggage is more of a problem.

Mrs. Cleveland Indian asks me to watch her purse because they are missing some of their luggage. It makes me feel uncomfortable. After what feels like forever, they finally retrieve their luggage.

Then we have to stand in another long line so they can x-ray the luggage. While standing there, an Indian official from the airport approaches me. He points to my luggage and says, "Is this all you have?"

When I say, "Yes," he points me out the door! I leave, but then sit on a bench and wait for the Cleveland Indian couple. When I see Mrs. Cleveland Indian struggling with her luggage, I start to drag my stuff over there to help her. Another airport official stops me. It would have been a problem, but Mr. Cleveland Indian comes over and says that I am with them.

When it comes time for me to meet my ride, there is a barrier; the Cleveland Indians can't get past it! They have to catch another flight. If they go out, they can't get back in. After all that, I am still on my own to hope that my ride awaits me. Mr. Cleveland Indian offers to come with me, but I assure him that I will be fine. The prospect of leaving them scares me. They are my connection with my old life. I step away from them into my new adventure.

I had arranged for someone to pick me up outside the airport door. The problem is that if I step out the door, I'm not sure I can get back in. I

1

don't know if there is a phone outside. On my way to the door of no return, I walk past a window and see a man holding a sign with my name on it. He must have seen my recognition, because he stands right there as I come through the door. What a relief! The moment I had dreaded, and it works out perfectly.

Outside the door, I see people packed together shoulder to shoulder. Not beggars like I thought, but people waiting for their rides or waiting for flights to arrive. I notice palm trees and a parking lot full of cars.

It is a long walk to the car, but maybe it only feels that way after being in a cramped plane for so long. My driver puts my luggage into the trunk of an American-type luxury car, and I settle into the front seat.

Once we get going, most of the cars are small and there are auto rickshaws and motorcycles all over the road. I see cars driving everywhere paying no attention to lanes, near misses constantly, and pedestrians barely avoided. It is like a virtual adventure at Disneyland: too bizarre to be real. It amazes and scares me. The sound of horns honking fills the air. One could describe the streets of Mumbai as, "A whole lotta honkin' goin' on." It surprises me how many people are on the street after midnight.

The drive to Pune is an adventure that takes three hours. My driver is good, but he swerves and honks his way all the way home. He drives excessively fast. When he goes through a red light, I ask, "Why don't you have to stop at red lights?"

He says, "There are no police around, so it's okay to go through." Once we are on the main highway, he asks, "Do you like Indian music?"

I say, "Yes." Although I imagine flutes and sitars, when he puts it on, it is Indian rock and roll. It isn't bad, just different with a familiar sound.

Halfway to Pune we stop at what must be a truck stop. The driver says he'll be back in five minutes. Five minutes pass, and then ten, and he doesn't return for fifteen minutes. I don't know what I would have done if he hadn't returned, because I don't even know his name.

I am glad to see him when he returns. We are on our way again. Next, we find ourselves stuck in bumper-to-bumper traffic on the expressway at two o'clock in the morning. Unreal. Finally, I arrive safely at the ashram hotel at three o'clock in the morning, India time.

While still on the plane, I had asked the Indian couple how much I should tip the driver. They said two hundred rupees, but I thought it should be more. When the driver drops me off at the ashram, naïve and unworldly person that I am, I ask, "What is your normal tip?"

He says, "Whatever you want, madam," in an obsequious voice.

I say, "Please, I don't know how much to tip you. Just tell me what a normal tip is."

He replies, "It's whatever you want, madam." His voice grows higher and even more obsequious. Finally, I give him two hundred rupees, but feel unsure that it's the correct amount.

Now at the hotel, when I ask the desk clerk how much to give the bellboy, he says one hundred rupees. Immediately, I realize I should have given more than two hundred to the driver. I have a hard time going to sleep because it upsets me so much. I hope to find a way to make it right.

Day One – A Room With a Loo

Although I set my clock early so I can make the eight-thirty orientation, I miss it. After taking the AIDS test and buying a maroon robe, it is too late. I'll have orientation tomorrow.

This morning I receive my room at the ashram. Up a steep, narrow, cement spiral staircase, I walk eighteen steps to the top. The room has a sliding door, which locks with a padlock. It is small and Spartan with few furnishings and a wonderful ceiling fan that makes it feel Hemingway-esque. Besides the single bed, the room has a stand-alone wardrobe, a set of narrow shelves, two bedside tables, and a stool with a cushion on top.

I like the room. As my husband, Sam, says, "A Spartan room is easier to clean." My ex-husband, really. Since our divorce will be final in a month, I should start calling him that.

The cyber cafe is around the corner from my room, and the laundry is close. The food in the restaurants is cheap, but it will take me awhile to figure everything out.

When I try meditating in my room, I hear music outside my closed window. I put in earplugs and turn on the noise cancellation headphones. It eliminates most of the sounds except the deep drumming. The music stops shortly after that. If there is a party out there at night, I'm in trouble. However, this is all part of being flexible, so I'll deal with it.

The bathroom that I share locks on the inside, so no one can enter while it's occupied. Before going to bed, I use it and forget to unlock the other door. An hour later, I'm not asleep yet and I hear the woman in the next room trying to get into the bathroom. A few minutes later, she knocks on my door. I know immediately what it is about.

Her name is Chandra, which she tells me means moon in Sanskrit. She stands there and gives me a lecture about us both being women, and she walks around nude, and we can share the bathroom at the same time. After all, it is a commune. She explains about the curtain over the toilet, and yadda yadda yadda. I tell her that I have no problem with any of that. The reason I locked the door is that I didn't know the protocol.

I ask, "Why is there a bucket of water in the shower?"

"I'm soaking my dirty clothes," Chandra says. "The laundry has shrunk some of my clothes and lost or stolen others. I don't trust them, so I wash the clothes that are important to me."

It strikes me as negative. Maybe I only feel that way because of her anger with me for locking her out of the bathroom. I can't blame her

4

for that.

I made a mistake with the electric heating pad that I brought. It's old, and I can't plug it into my converter. The electric toothbrush works, however, so I'm sure the computer will, too. The two items that will keep me sane while I'm here: my iPod and my computer.

I'm still shocked at the reality of all of this. Here I am, in India!

I miss my dog, Sheba, and Sam in a way. Although, I'm glad to be away from his energy; and glad to give him the freedom to be away from mine. The day I left, we finally cried together. I'd waited a month for that, and he was emotionless the entire time. On the day I left, we hugged and cried. He said, "Nineteen years has come to this." Then he said he wanted to find someone who would look at him like they wanted him - - the way I used to look at him.

That makes me so sad. I feel bad that's how it all worked out. Why did he stay so long? I know it took a toll on his self-esteem. I'm glad he's free now. I'm glad I'm free now.

There is a party in the plaza tonight, right outside my window. Chandra says that it goes on two nights a week, from nine thirty to midnight. I put in earplugs with my noise cancellation headphones and listen to Christmas music. It helps, but I still can't sleep.

Day Two - Orientation

When it is time to go to orientation, I assemble with the others at Osho plaza. A man there shows everyone where to wait. He is older and attractive, but he looks at women like a wolf looking at sheep. The predatory look on his face takes away his good looks.

I think about Osho called the sex guru, which makes me wonder if the ashram is still the free love type place it used to be. I didn't take part in the sixties free love and I won't now, either. Although I have to admit, I am sorry that I didn't participate back then! No AIDS to worry about, few diseases, I was young, healthy, and attractive. Why did I hold out? Too late to change it now, and I'm not interested in making up for lost time at this place.

I thought orientation was about the ashram, but it is about the different meditations. Osho thought that sitting meditations didn't suit today's individuals because everybody is so busy doing, doing, doing that asking them to sit and meditate was asking too much. Therefore, he created moving meditations.

We learn how to do the meditations and then we practice them all for a short time. Maybe it is because I haven't had much sleep, but they drain me. So much of it is dancing and moving around. There is one where you raise your arms in the air and shout, "O-SHO!" Then the music stops and you freeze where you are, with your arms still in the air. It's painful to have your arms in the air so long. When we go from an active part to a quiet part, I hear other people breathing hard, also.

I don't like these meditations. I'm an active person and I prefer my meditations quiet and uncomplicated. The mandatory nightly meeting has some dancing in it, but I hope not too much. I'll soon find out. I wonder what would happen if I skip it.

During the orientation, the facilitator, a guy named Anugyan, talks about how our culture and our religion condition us. There are people here from all over the world: Brazil, Argentina, Greece, Holland, France, Switzerland, Germany, Canada, and more countries I can't remember. There are only two or three Americans including me.

While Anugyan describes how to do each meditation, he keeps saying, "It's scientific! It's scientific!" It sounds silly. I'd like to see some evidence if it's honestly scientific.

While in the orientation room, I meet a man from Chicago named Greg. When I run into him later, he asks me to take a walk with him to Osho Teerth Park. I had checked this place out on the Internet before I arrived. It used to be a sewer or toxic waste dump, and the ashram restored it into a beautiful park. I see a flycatcher that is the most beautiful iridescent blue that I've ever seen on a bird. There are many other birds I can't identify, and beautiful foliage all around.

The best part is a sign at the entrance with rules on it. The rules include "Stay on the trails" and "Beware of snakes!" I might get my wish to see a cobra in the wild.

The sign also says no photography. I knew there was no photography in the ashram itself and I understand that. But, why can't you take pictures in this beautiful park? Because I don't understand it, it gets my rebel streak going.

Greg and I sit on a bench and talk. He touches my hair softly and says how pretty it is. There is a light in his eyes. I smile and say, "Thank you," but don't realize until later that it could have been a come-on. I'm not interested.

The atmosphere at the ashram is not what I expected. People here are not friendly. Also, it's a little weird with everyone wearing maroon. Although I do it without reservation because it's part of the program, I still find it weird.

This morning at orientation, Anugyan said not to look at it like rules that you might want to disobey. He said to look at it differently, as if it serves a purpose. That's convenient.

The people here are so into all of this. I wonder if I'm missing something. Because I don't know much about Osho and his whole philosophy, I feel like I'm in a place where everyone is in the same club except me. Always an outsider. I have felt that way most of my life. Will it ever go away? Should it? Is it serving me somehow? Do I deliberately put myself into positions like this?

Tomorrow I find out my work assignment and my schedule. I have no idea what job they will give me. Embrace uncertainty! I'm not sorry that I came. I'm eager to catch up on my sleep, so I can feel whole again.

In many ways I feel scared, overwhelmed, and intimidated. However, at the heart of it, I still feel a quiet contentment. I know this is the right path for me. Although I'm trying to embrace uncertainty, I'm still feeling some apprehension right now. However, the days of feeling horrible with work issues and feeling bad with Sam issues are behind me now.

Most of the time, Sam was fine. That's why I could stay with him for so long. When he was uptight, angry, and not accepting the "is," I couldn't stand being around him. Tomorrow, I should receive an email from him. I wonder what it will say and how I will feel about it. I'm hoping it will be neutral, so I don't have to deal with it.

Tonight there is a talent show in the plaza, and so far, it's not too loud. A train goes by the ashram, which I hear mostly in the evening. I like it in a country-song way and feel my Mom's presence in its whistle. It may sound silly, but it works for me.

Day Three – Meditation Exhaustive

This morning I receive my work schedule from Nimisha. For the next three days including today, I will experience all the different meditations the ashram offers. They call it a meditation intensive.

"Do I have to attend the meditations that I already know I don't like?" I ask Nimisha.

"Yes," she says. "Something unexpected may come up that you need to process."

"The jet lag and lack of sleep have exhausted my body. I'm concerned about doing fifteen minutes of strenuous exercise while I'm so tired," I tell her.

"You know, it's amazing how much the body can take," she replies matter-of-factly.

My silent reply is: why would I want it to? It strikes me like someone trying to talk me into having another drink, or trying heroin - - it's amazing how much the body can take.

They hold all the meditations at the Osho Auditorium. The auditorium is a giant pyramid-shaped building. I cross a small bridge to get inside the building. Osho said the bridge was to remind you to leave your mind behind. Just inside the main doors, walls lined with shoe racks accommodate everyone's shoes. You must remove your shoes before entering the auditorium. It is the size of two large gymnasiums, has beautiful marble floors, and holds more than eight hundred people.

My first Osho meditation experience is called No Dimensions Meditation. An older gentleman with a white beard, smiling eyes, and a Sufi hat is the facilitator. He is funny, gives a great demonstration, and encourages us to smile and have a good time.

This meditation consists of three parts. The first part is hand and arm movements as you say the Sufi sound, "shoo." Then you move your right hand forward from the hara (the spot beneath your belly button), then left hand forward, then right hand to the right, left hand to the left, right hand to the rear (turn your hips) and left hand to the rear. Then, do it all again. It feels pleasant but also feels like it goes on forever. Sometime in the middle, I think, "All right, already!" It still goes on and on for thirty minutes.

Fifteen minutes of Sufi Whirling is the second part of this meditation. I go slowly, walking in a tight circle, because I don't want to feel dizzy. As I look around, some people whirl rapidly. Although I expect them to fall over any minute, they don't.

9

This meditation ends with fifteen minutes of lying on your stomach. If you don't have a mat, which I don't, the marble floor feels almost unbearably cold.

The ashram calls the next meditation that I attend Nadabrahma Meditation. This one also has three parts. I sit and hum for the first part of it. Since I'm not into it, I hum Christmas music until I can't remember any more lyrics. Then I switch to old camp songs, like Michael Row the Boat Ashore and Frere Jacque. After a while, though, it feels sacrilegious, so I stop. If I listen, I feel like I'm in a beehive. After the humming comes simple hand movements and then lying down.

As I walk across the bridge that leads away from the auditorium, I stop by the water to watch a dragonfly. It is solid black, with a dull orange fringe where its tail meets its body. It has translucent wings with black wing tips. The dragonflies and butterflies fly much faster here than at home.

They call my next meditation Kundalini Meditation. It has four parts. The first part consists of shaking your body for fifteen minutes. All the blood rushes to my fingers, and they hurt. Then we dance for fifteen minutes. Next, we can sit or stand while soft music plays in the background. Lastly, everyone lies on the floor for fifteen minutes.

Later, back at my room, when I try to put on my white robe, it feels too small. Therefore, I have to skip Evening Meeting Meditation. My breasts are busting out all over. When I bought the white robe, the salesgirl said since I had a maroon one already, then I can get the same size. However, the white one has a different fit. I need to exchange it. I also bought a large "back-jack" at her recommendation. It is excessively large and heavy to be carting around, so I left it in its wrapper. I'm hoping they will exchange that one as well. Back-jacks are mini-chairs that allow you to sit on the floor comfortably.

The last meditation of the night is late at 9:30. The ashram calls this one Mahamudra Meditation. I expected it to involve hand movements because that's normally what mudras are. First, we have to stand and let our body do what it will do. That lasts twenty minutes. Next, we kneel and lift our hands to the sky. Then we do the yoga child's pose. I believe the instructions are to do them seven times to cover all the chakras. Most everyone, including me, keeps doing them for the entire twenty minutes. For the last part, we lie down. I have had enough so called meditations for the day. Instead of closing my eyes, I gaze up at the stucco ceiling searching for interesting shapes and patterns.

When I leave the auditorium, I look up and see stars! It thrills me to see my favorite constellation. There aren't many stars here because of the city lights, but I do manage to find Orion! I walk back to my room smiling.

As often as possible, I try to smile. Before I arrived, I read on the Internet about all the smiling faces here. So far, I haven't found them. Most people don't smile and don't even make eye contact. There are not friendly people here like I expected. About the only people who smile back at me are the Indian nationals who work for Sudexo.

Back home, when I hiked and ran into people on the trail, I could always tell city people. They wouldn't make eye contact. That's how it is here. People walk around with an intent look on their face, but not looking at who is around them.

It reminds me of something that happened to me many years ago. I had just had a major emotional upheaval in my life, and I was in a bad state mentally. There was this group going around the country offering to take people to another planet. I wanted to go! What an opportunity to get out of the emotional mess that I found myself in. My brother was kind enough to go with me to the orientation meeting.

Even in my fervor to go and to believe, I couldn't help noticing how much like little automatons all the people were. None of them smiled. When they spoke to you, it was in a monotone like they were on drugs of some sort. That's what it feels like here. Maybe everyone is just too tired to look around because of all the active meditations!

The facilitators that lead the meditations dress in black robes with white belts. All my facilitators today except the first one are not good teachers. They announce how to do the meditations in a lifeless, monotone voice and do not even demonstrate the moves. I have to watch other people to discover what I should do. They have no personality, and as my mother would say, no pzazz.

I hate to be judgmental when I am trying so hard at practicing non-judgment, but I find it difficult not to judge them. Perhaps that is my lesson here. It is difficult to practice non-judgment if a place is perfect and there is nothing to judge.

While I eat lunch outside, I see two peacocks. Although they don't have their tails displayed, they are beautiful. They walk around hoping for a handout.

I checked with my sister-in-law's friend on how to give more money to the driver. She said that giving him two hundred rupees was fine. There was no need for all that anxiety. Learning to let go is another lesson I need to learn.

I want to make something of this journal. That thought popped into my head during the last Mahamudra meditation. I don't know if I will continue to have so much to say. There is only one way to know - - wait it out! Meanwhile, I will write what I know.

Tomorrow I may skip some meditations. I wonder what happens if they catch me?

Day Four – Evening Meeting

Early this morning at six o'clock, I go to Dynamic Meditation. First, we do chaotic breathing, a modified version of a yoga breathing technique that I learned. For this one, I begin by breathing chaotically through my nose with a forceful exhale.

They call the second part of the meditation "going crazy." I scream, I howl, and I move my body all around. For a couple minutes, all the craziness feels good.

Then, I tire of it all and want to sit and rest. No resting here. Next, I hold my arms above my head and shout, "Hoo! Hoo! Hoo!" At the end of this part the music stops and I have to freeze in whatever position I am in - - with my arms still in the air. These last two parts bother my sore shoulder. The last step is dancing, but when the dancing part begins, everyone feels too exhausted to do much besides sway.

I don't remember the last time I sweated this much. I guess it's good for eliminating toxins. Nothing came up, as Nimisha suggested, except when I say an expletive wanting it to end already.

As I leave the auditorium after this meditation, I do feel a quietness similar to my personal meditation. Although, I don't like the vehicle that got me to this quietness. I can find the stillness sitting pleasantly by myself. Or, I can find the stillness with fifty of my "closest friends," sweating profusely, hurting my muscles, and eager for it to end. Guess which I prefer?

Back at the auditorium again, the ashram calls the next meditation Vipassana. We sit quietly for most of this one. The last fifteen minutes I can either walk around slowly and deliberately, or I can stay seated. I open my eyes, and the few who are walking around remind me of zombies. They put one foot in front of the other slowly, slowly, slowly, with vacant looks on their faces. As they walk by, I hear their toes or feet cracking! I close my eyes and go back to my mantra.

Hara Stop meditation is next. It starts with arm movements and one of my hands on my hara, the place beneath my belly button. Then, the music changes and I walk around the room. Periodically, the music stops and I freeze, but not for long. Then, each time the music begins again we walk faster. After several stops and starts, most everyone runs around the room, some with one hand on their hara. I keep both hands on my hara, but never do more than a fast walk. It is an interesting meditation, and I don't mind it too much.

The facilitators today are better than yesterday. I think their instructions had been to speak slowly and enunciate each word, but they somehow lost their personality in the process. Today, though, they don't always demonstrate how the arms should move. It is difficult trying to figure that out.

I only skip one meditation today, the Kundalini Meditation. I'm not counting the Whirling Meditation that goes with an Osho talk. Tomorrow I will skip both of those again and the morning's Dynamic Meditation, also. I'll do the rest of them.

One meditation that I attended today had a different facilitator than yesterday. This is a peaceful meditation where we sit quietly for forty-five minutes, and then either continue sitting or walk for fifteen minutes. The facilitator carries a long stick. He says if he taps you on the head with it, it isn't because you are doing something wrong. The tap reminds you to be present. I sit and hope he taps me because I want to experience it. I continue hearing loud whacking sounds. If that's one of his taps, it sounds like it hurts! After a while, when he doesn't come around I forget him. Then, when I am in the middle of a thought, suddenly I feel a tap on my head! It does not hurt, but brings me quickly back to the present! I am grateful for the experience.

It's difficult to imagine, but I can't drink the water from the faucet, or use it to clean anything like bowls or spoons. What I don't understand is washing your hands with soap in water that is not clean. What's the point? I've always been an obsessive hand washer, but I'm about to get over it.

Since the drinking water faucets are downstairs from me, it's not that bad. Every time I want to fill my water bottles, I do have to walk up and down the eighteen steep steps. Also, I can't fill more than two, because I don't want to put them down anywhere. The whole concept of what's clean here and what's not still eludes me.

I am standing at the drinking water station washing my toothbrush under a stream of water. You know how when you finish brushing your teeth, some toothpaste sticks to the bottom of the toothbrush and you have to hold it under a hard stream of water from the faucet to get it out? Since there are no faucets with clean water here, I think the drinking water place is perfect for cleaning the toothpaste off. It is a serious blunder. One of my peers reprimands me and tells me I'm not allowed to do that. I feel bad about it. When I mention it to Chandra, she agrees that I can't do that.

Evening Meeting tonight starts with everyone lined up outside. When they turn on the lights in the auditorium, it means you can enter. Then, everyone walks across the wide cement bridge to cross the water.

Osho said that crossing the bridge will remind people to leave their mind behind. Everyone must wear white robes. It's bizarre seeing so many people in one place dressed in white.

After placing our shoes in the racks that line the walls, some of us need to see the person with the checklist so we can have our name checked off. Everyone in the residential program is under orders to appear at Evening Meeting.

At the beginning, as I wait for everyone to enter the auditorium, I hear a short announcement that says there must be "pin drop silence" in the room. It also says that if you cough or sneeze you have to leave immediately and go to another place. Although, the other place is not an alternate place, because everyone there coughs and sneezes!

Then the music begins. The first fifteen or twenty minutes consists of optional dancing. Almost everyone joins in. Some people sit and eventually sway to the music, and then stand and start dancing. The music gains in intensity as it goes along. As each song ends, everyone throws their arms into the air and shouts, "Osho!" After the last song, it's shouted three times in a row. I do not join in the dancing, and probably won't. Fifteen minutes of straight dancing is not my idea of a good time.

After three or four songs, everyone sits on the floor. Several minutes of silence ensues. You will not find a more enraptured audience. The absolute silence impresses me. You cannot hear one whisper, one cough, or any movement.

A few minutes of Indian music follows the silence and then abruptly ends. This sequence repeats three times. Why? What does it mean? What is the purpose of the silence/music/silence/music segment? It feels like manipulation.

For such a huge auditorium, there is a tiny little screen. After the music and silence, the screen lights up. A white robed figure comes out from backstage and pounds three times on a loud drum. The person then returns to the back and announces which talk Osho will give tonight. When the video starts and Osho appears onscreen, everyone listens with rapt attention.

This is the first time I have seen him, except a short clip on the Internet where he talked about the virtues of a certain four-letter expletive. The ashram calls these Osho videos, "discourses." Osho always sprinkles his discourses with humor. He is attractive and charismatic. Osho died or as they say here, "left the body," more than fifteen years ago. His teaching lives on. With his heavy Indian accent, I can't always understand what he says.

When the video ends, I hear a loud drumming sound, and then an Osho audio plays. This part of the audio is mostly jokes. Shortly after that, Osho says something and everyone in the audience makes noises. Well, not exactly noises. I finally understand when the woman next to me is talking loudly, to no one. They call it "gibberish." You can "speak" any language that you don't know. It doesn't make sense, but Osho didn't design gibberish to make sense.

Then, a loud drum sounds and Osho says, "Silence," and everyone stops. Osho says something else, and bam! Everyone falls to the floor in unison like well-behaved dogs. The instructions are to fall to the floor - - not to adjust your pillow so you will be comfortable - - just fall. But, it's a marble floor! If people truly fall to the floor, there is going to be some blood spilled or concussions. The whole happening is irksome. Almost everyone lies on the floor. Only a small handful of people, including me, don't hit the floor.

Osho continues talking for a few minutes, and then he says something and everyone sits up. After a few more minutes of talking, Osho says something else, the drum sounds, and it's over. People stand up to leave. This part feels weird, too. No fanfare, nothing, everyone just gets up and leaves.

Evening Meeting tonight is nothing like I expected. I've heard that once you experience it, you understand why it's done that way. Now that I see it's mostly watching a video, it makes even less sense. I must be a hard case, because I don't get it.

The event feels too benign for the white "costumes" to look like the Ku Klux Klan. An assembly of choirboys and choirgirls or angel-wannabes might fit.

After crossing the street, everyone piles into the main part of the ashram. This is the only time they don't check your pass at the gate.

Day Five – Sounds, Sights, and Perceptions

I skip Dynamic Meditation this morning and manage to sleep until 7:30. I woke up during the night, but convinced myself to go back to sleep. My feet are cold when I go to bed. That makes the rest of my body cold and keeps me awake. Tonight I will use the hot water bottle that I brought to keep me warm.

Every morning when I awaken, I hear many different birdsongs. One sounds like an elephant, one sounds like a seal, and I can hear crows cawing. A confused rooster crows late in the morning and a couple more times in the afternoon.

While I wait for my meditation at the Osho auditorium, I look up at the sky and see birds that look like birds of prey. They glide along and ride the wind currents. Then I look farther over in the sky and see more of them flying at a different altitude. I need to find out what they are.

They call the noon meditation Heart Dance. I come into the meditation hall, and it delights me to find a live band in the middle of the room. We sing lyrics - - most foreign, some English - - to other people in the room, as we hold their hands and gaze into their eyes. Sam made me feel so bad about my singing that I couldn't enjoy it for years. This feels good.

It feels hot today so I turn on the ceiling fan. Not only does it cool me off, it makes me feel like writing a novel! After a few minutes, it starts going fast and swaying and making creaking noises, so I turn it off. This building is old, and I fear the fan might come flying off the ceiling.

This afternoon as I walk through a garden area, I see a cat! When I walk close and look, it meows at me. Then it rolls onto its back. It won't rub against me, though. I am suffering from pet deprivation.

After my last afternoon meditation, I come back to my room, put on my jeans, and venture forth into the Indian city. What could possibly have given me the courage to do this by myself? Cobras, of course! My sister-in-law wrote that there were men with cobras in bags on the main street. She sent directions on how to get there, but I must have fouled it up somehow, or didn't read it correctly. On the way to the end of the street, I walk past an eye specialty hospital and a cancer hospital. I pass two dogs that don't appear mean. Following my cousin Dan's advice, I don't offer to pet them. I return to the ashram discouraged that I went the wrong way.

The foliage here is beautiful, and I wish I could identify it. There are several different ferns including one that is big and round like the sun. The bamboo trees are huge. Besides the birds I have seen and heard, I haven't seen much wildlife here, and I'd like to.

It's fascinating how perception and choice color our life. For instance, take the train whistle I hear at night. I choose to like and embrace the sound. I allow it to remind me of my mother. If I choose to look at it as a sleep disturbing sound, then every time I hear it, it will annoy me and create anxiety that I am powerless to stop. It would make my nights hell every time I heard the sound. Then I would probably anticipate the sound and that would make it worse. When I hear it now, I feel like it is a comforting sound and it soothes me.

It reminds me of a situation that happened many years ago with my ex-boyfriend, Frank. We started living together as roommates, and it developed into a romantic relationship. We had fooled around a little, but he hadn't pressed me into "going all the way." I appreciated that and thought of him as a gentleman.

Then I had lunch with my adult niece. I told her about the situation and she said, "Oh, go for it!" That convinced me that's what I should do. The next time we fooled around, I pressed for more. He refused! He was in the midst of a divorce and didn't feel comfortable going any further than we already had. I was angry! What did he mean saying no to me?

Suddenly, my perception had changed, and he went from a gentleman to a jerk. It was my choice to try to change our relationship status and my choice to look at him differently when he refused. We are all infinite choice makers, according to Deepak Chopra, and we make choices constantly that we don't even realize are choices.

Day Six – My First Beggar

Last night, mosquitoes besieged me starting at 3:30 in the morning. After taking care of one, I heard another one off in the distance gathering for attack. There is no way to sleep with an imminent attack like that. Sleep was unattainable until I got rid of the last one. I'm not sure why I had so many in my room. This was torture.

I don't get my job today. My coordinator (ashram euphemism for boss) is involved in something else, so I start tomorrow. Ironically, my coordinator is the one man here who I find attractive. He is skinny, of medium height, and has a long ponytail. I meet him briefly, and he speaks with an accent I don't recognize. I'll see what tomorrow brings.

I had my first taste of the real India today. Someone I met before I came here had just returned from India and the Osho International Ashram. She told me, "You know that isn't the REAL India." Her comment made me want to see the real India. And I found it!

Dilasa is a guy I met on my first day here. He helped me find someone to carry my overweight luggage up the eighteen steps to my room. Today, he tells me how to get to German bakery. I leave the ashram and go looking for the guys with the flutes and the cobras. On my way up the street, I find a someone on the side of the road selling maroon robes, shoes, shawls, and other items. He has a dog that I can pet. It looks like part golden retriever.

I venture farther up the street and there are more street vendors hawking their goods. After I turn the corner, I come to a woman with items for sale. Her name is Gowri, and she allows me to take her picture. She tries to sell me a beautiful shawl with little mirrors on it.

After I pass her roadside stand, I look around at the cars, motorcycles, and auto rickshaws going crazy in the street, the run down condition of everything, and the "foreign-ness" of it all. I feel this welling up in my solar plexus, which rises into my chest and I feel like I'm going to explode - - in a good way. I am in INDIA! This is the REAL INDIA!

Then I take out my camera to capture the real India. That is a mistake. Immediately, out of nowhere, a woman appears with a baby wrapped in a shawl. She shows me her sleeping baby who has long, beautiful lashes. Then, she tells me the baby is blind and she holds out her hand. She is my first beggar.

I know that some people here make a profession out of begging. Perhaps she is one of those, although there's no way to know. She wears decent clothes, not rags. I keep saying I'm sorry and try to get away, but

19

she follows me.

Then I notice that German Bakery is across the street. With no crosswalk, no lights, and cars and motorcycles racing by, I don't have much hope to get across. She offers to take me across. I keep saying no and try to do it myself, but to no avail. Finally, other people cross in the same spot, and I cross with them. The beggar woman leaves after that.

Behind German Bakery, I change dollars for rupees and get a better rate than at the ashram. At a small shop, I buy the Indian deity, Ganesh, for my room. He is a big fat guy with an elephant head who stands for removal of obstacles.

Inside German Bakery, I see a man who I think I recognize from the ashram. I speak to him, and he tells me that he has a famous face but he's not from the ashram. He sounds Indian. I ask him where the cobras are, but he doesn't know.

Nobody knows. Looking up and down the street, I manage to cross again by following some locals, but I still can't find any cobras. One woman tells me she thought they'd be here in the afternoon.

On my way back to the ashram, I stop to visit Gowri again. I sit beside her on the curb. We talk as best we can for fifteen minutes. She doesn't know where to find any cobras. Then she tells me about her husband who has a heart condition, and about her son, and her grandchildren. The conversation is difficult because she speaks limited English, and I speak no Hindi. I feel a true connection with her and I think she feels it, too. She doesn't try to sell me anything until I am ready to leave.

While I sit with her, the cars, motorcycles, and auto rickshaws speed by us. I look up and suddenly in the middle of the street is a man with an ox-drawn cart. I take a picture. When I look up, he has stopped the cart and is smiling at me. The people here are so friendly and kind.

Then a family of beggars with the cutest little eight-year-old boy stops and tries to harass me. Gowri yells at them and chases them away. My hero. I will go see her again.

After returning to the ashram, I eat a wonderful lunch of green salad and noodles. Then, I find the cat again. It allows me to stroke its head for thirty seconds before it wanders off. Later, I run into a peacock. While exploring, I discover the swan in a back area of the ashram. It's private and I can't approach her. While watching her, I discover her vocalization sounds like an elephant.

Then I go out the back gate to walk over to Osho Teerth Park again to look for some wild cobras. A young Indian man approaches me and asks, "Where are you from?"

"America," I tell him.

He shakes my hand and says, "My father has been to America."

I say, "Oh, wow. Where?"

"I don't know," he says. "Let me show you a magic trick! Blow on this leaf, and it will turn into a bird!"

He reaches out to hand me the leaf, but I say no and won't take it. A canvas bag hangs over his shoulder. I think it might be a snake.

"Do you have a cobra in your bag?"

"Sit on this rock," he says and starts undoing the canvas bag. I keep backing up.

"No, no," he says, "The snake is not in here." When he gets to the bottom of the bag, there is no snake.

All this time, another young boy about twelve years old with a baby on his back waits in the background. When I walk away from the magic trick guy, the younger boy starts following me to the park. I realize then that I can't go there today with these interferences, so I return to the ashram.

It's interesting that I am in this ashram where everyone dresses exactly alike, and I consider myself a nonconformist. It doesn't bother me because I knew that was part of the program before I signed on. Although, I do feel like a lemming.

Today I read what Osho had to say about the maroon and white robes. I don't accept his explanation. At Evening Meeting tonight, I don't always agree or believe everything he says in his discourses, either. Do I have to believe in everything he says?

Day Seven - Snake Charmer Salesman and Weird "Birds"

Thoughts about my adventures yesterday in the "real India" still thrill me. It's like cousin Dan told me: how intoxicating India can be. I am living in a safe environment, well cared for, well fed, and outside my door is a veritable treasure chest of adventure for me to discover.

As far as wearing the maroon and white robes, it is like being in a play. If you had committed to playing a character in a play, you would naturally wear the clothes of that character. You wouldn't insist on wearing your own clothes. That would be stupid. In this place, I look at it like I'm playing a character. This character dresses in maroon and white robes. It does not change me as a person, or make me less my own self. I am still me under the robes. Just as I am still me when I am in my "chosen costume" of jeans and a sweatshirt.

Today I receive my job - - sitting in front of a computer and sorting photographs. Why is this not a surprise? They are engaging ashram photos, so I am enjoying it.

The only problem is the last person, Cathy, left the job because it was so unclear. Unfortunately, Cathy explains it to me. When she shows me what to do, she still isn't sure. Tomorrow, I'll get more answers. Although it confuses me, I do a small part that I'm sure about. I hope it will come together later. Since there isn't much else I can do, Cathy told me it is all right to check my personal email.

When I check my email, I see one from a friend of my sister-in-law who wants to have lunch today. Her name is Devika and her husband is the Indian guy who I have talked with in the cyber cafe. It is difficult conversing with her because she is shy. We will probably get together again, though. It feels good talking to another American. There are so few of us here.

I tell her how scary it is for me crossing the streets here. She says I only have to remember the cars have a brake. That sounds crazy to me. It reminds me of something my mother said when I was sixteen years old and learning to drive. We would come to an intersection where the cross traffic had the stop sign, and she would want me to slow down.

I said, "They have the stop sign. Why should I slow down?"

Her comment was, and I have remembered it to this day, "You are right, but don't be dead right." I've thought about that comment in many situations in my life that don't even involve driving. No, I will not depend on crazy drivers to brake for me.

In the office, the woman sitting across from me, Prana, is another good friend of my brother and his wife. Prana can't stop talking about my brother and how wonderful he is. Perhaps he's more pleasant to everyone else than to his family. She's known him twenty or thirty years. She is friendly and supportive.

After work, I start walking to Osho Teerth Park, the beautiful park I walked to a few days ago. I take only a few steps down the road when someone calls out to me asking if I want to see a cobra. The young man that I spoke to yesterday must have told this man about me. He gives me information that doesn't sound true.

"We've cut off the cobra's teeth with a scissors, so it is harmless," he tells me with a con man's slick smile. "The cobra lives in the house with my family," he adds. "It will only cost you two thousand rupees!"

"That is too much," I tell him. "I love snakes, and since I'll be here three months, I want to see them often."

"Okay then, twelve hundred rupees the first time and six hundred rupees every time after that."

"It still sounds too expensive," I say.

"Name your price then," he answers.

"I have to find out what is a fair price," I say. We leave it at that. The whole conversation takes fifteen minutes, as he tries to sell me on this. It feels so awkward, that it wouldn't surprise me if there weren't any real snake at all.

Now, I'll have to find out the "going price" on snake charmers. If I can't find anyone around here that would know, I'll ask my new friend, Gowri.

I arrive at Evening Meeting early tonight, so I can get a chair. The auditorium isn't open yet, so I stand in front, waiting. The sky draws my attention as it often does and I see many birds flying around. Since it is almost dark, I find that unusual. As I watch the birds, I notice their body shape and wing shape and the way they're flying. Suddenly, it occurs to me they are not birds at all! They are big bats, the size of crows!

A hundred of them fly by. They just keep coming. It isn't a hundred all at once like a horror movie - - descending on the crowd of white robed Osho ites, biting, tearing flesh, screaming - - no, nothing like that. It is more like five or ten at a time flying by on silent wings, looking for mosquitoes or whatever it is that these bats eat. With bodies that size, it would take many mosquitoes to keep them going. I should find out what they eat. These bats are beautiful, and one of my favorite sights I have seen since I arrived in India.

I've been here almost a week, and they haven't brainwashed me yet. There must not be anything in the food, because I still have my rebellious attitude. In exchange for the privilege of allowing this place to be the perfect transition away from my marriage and my job, I will do what I have to do. That includes attending Evening Meetings.

Day Eight – Local Connections

Today, Saturday, is room cleaning day. Two local Indian guys from Sudexo come in, make up the bed, and clean the room. I wake up early so I can prepare. First, I strip the bed of sheets and blankets. Then I bring out the clean set and put them on the foot of the bed.

The laundry should open at 8:15, so I walk down and they aren't open yet. They, like almost everyone else around here, are on "Indian" time.

Later, I walk back down. When I arrived, I was assigned a laundry number. Now I write that number on several small fabric "tags." Then, I bring them and a handful of safety pins upstairs to my room.

I attach each piece of numbered fabric to each sheet, each pillowcase, each towel, and each sock with two or three safety pins. Chandra, my bathroom roommate, told me the laundry lost some of her belongings. Consequently, I put two safety pins on regular items and three safety pins on my important items, like my feet pajamas!

When I start collecting everything to get ready for the laundry, I go into the shared bathroom to get my towel. It isn't there. I knock on Chandra's door and ask, "Did you take my towel?"

She says, "No, what would I do with your towel?" Although I accused her, she reacted well - - probably better than I would have in the same position. I go into my laundry bag to get everything ready, and there is the towel. It was already in the bag. I knock on Chandra's door again and tell her that I found it.

A lesson I need to learn here is not making hasty judgments about someone or something. This isn't a good beginning! Awareness of something is the first step to fixing it, so maybe I've taken a forward step.

After I mark everything and put it in the bag, I leave it at the laundry and pick up the bag that I had dropped off before. It takes three days to have your laundry done. Then I lock my valuables into a locking closet in my room and go to work.

I arrive at work at two minutes of nine this morning. Only a couple people arrived before me, so I have to unlock the front door when I come in. Most everyone else walks in five, ten, or fifteen minutes later. That's Indian time!

When I signed up for this, I knew I would be working seven days a week. But, I thought it was because I was a novitiate or a plebe. I had no idea that everyone who works here works seven days a week. I speak to Prana about it today. She says that is Osho's vision - - no distinguishing between work and recreation. What a crock! It sounds more like slaves to me! And willing slaves - - the ones who buy into this crap.

Prana says that they have always worked seven days a week. She says that once there was a rumor that they would get a day off. Everyone said, "Oh goodness, what will we do?" That strikes me as so sick. But, maybe they're right and I'm wrong. Who's to know?

It's intriguing with Osho - - he is obviously spiritual, enlightened, and a mystic. He makes many enlightened comments. Then ideas like this make me doubt him altogether. This must be one of those lessons in disregarding everything when only one part is bad. What is that old cliché: don't throw the baby out with the bathwater? Just because I don't like this part of his philosophy, doesn't mean that I should disregard everything he says. Except that I don't agree with the whole robe charade, either.

I feel almost like a traitor or a spy and that makes me feel paranoid. I'm afraid to even write that down - - although I have no reason to feel paranoid - - I don't think.

Today, I have a two o'clock meeting with my coach, so I look all over for him. He is out of town. The ashram reassigns me to the one guy who I don't want. His name is Andre, and he is the guy I spoke of earlier as looking at women as a wolf looks at sheep. There must be a lesson in here for me.

The coaching itself is nothing like I expected. There are four of us here, but maybe it is only four for the first meeting. I thought it was a counseling session for support for the whole ashram experience. With four people, it would be difficult to do that. There is a woman here with Andre today. She is the same woman who gave me my room when I arrived. Her name is Dulari, and I like her. The other person has also just arrived, like me, and his name is Felipe.

Dulari talks about not looking at the program like we are doing something for the ashram, but looking at it that we are doing something for ourselves. She talks about the way we look at our experiences.

Sakra, my boss, calls me in today to talk to him. He wants to know how it is going and if I have enough to do. He asks, "Do you feel comfortable?"

I say, "pretty comfortable," and he squeezes my hand. Because of his heavy accent, I find him difficult to understand.

Often I have trouble understanding Osho during his nightly talks. I usually miss the punch lines of the jokes he tells. I notice something else about him. You can see the whites at the bottom of his eyeballs. The

26

book *Your Body Doesn't Lie* by John Diamond calls them Sanpaku eyes. When you look at them, they cause your body to go weak. Every time he looks toward me while I'm watching the video, I thump my thymus, which equalizes the negative effect. Like many before him, Osho let power affect him.

My roommate, Chandra, spoke to Prana today about taking tomorrow afternoon off because she's not feeling well. Prana said, "Being enlightened is taking care of yourself."

After work, I dress in my civilian clothes and go outside the gates back to my beloved real India. I love the feeling - - the exoticness - - the danger - - the people. It is later in the day than the first time I went out, and many more vendors line the streets.

I find Gowri sleeping when I arrive. She says she doesn't feel good. There is something wrong with her eyes, and to fix them will cost forty thousand rupees. I give her some Reiki, and afterward she says, "No change!" She is so cool. Although she has eye problems, she is still happy and laughing with a great attitude. We talk for a short time and then I wander down the street.

Farther on past Gowri is a young guy with some crystals. I choose a quartz heart and ask how much it is. He says forty rupees. Before I came here, I had read to have small change ready, because no one will give you change. I hand him a fifty-rupee bill and he gives me change! That tells me he is an honest man.

After I buy the heart, I walk down the street to look around. Eventually I come to a gas station. It is as hectic and frenzied as the traffic in the streets. It's an interesting contrast - - the traffic moves so fast and yet the people move at a slow, easy pace.

On my return trip, I stop at the crystal guy again. All his stuff is so inexpensive. I am a total sucker for crystals and can't help buying a few more. He offers to show me more crystals at his shop across and down the street. He wants to take me on his motorcycle, but I decline! While we walk across the street, we get stuck in the middle with traffic racing by on both sides and no island to stand on. He says that it is easy for him, but hard for me. It scares me, but we make it across safely!

We walk down a narrow street to the side of German Bakery. There are a few vendors on the side of the road. Then I see the saddest, most heartbreaking sight since I've been in India. I see a woman who looks blind. She sits on the side of the road and holds out her fingerless hands to me as I walk by.

We arrive at the shop and he introduces me to his father. The place is clean and orderly, and displays beautiful crystals of all shapes, colors, and varieties. I buy two crystals for the equivalent of a couple dollars. One is for a chandelier: it is round and has facets all over it. I've never seen an amethyst like this.

After my meager purchase, the father and son show me some incredible crystals. I get the feeling they aren't trying to sell me on them, but they want to share something special with me. At one point, the father is showing me something and the son has disappeared. I start toward the door and say, "He won't leave me here, will he?"

The father says, "No, he won't leave you. Don't worry." Then the son comes back in, and we start walking up the narrow street.

He tells me his name is Manik. As we walk back, he holds out his hand and says, "I have a present for you." He holds out a beautiful piece of amethyst. It is unique and looks like a slice of a geode. I ask him how to say thank you in Hindi and it is "shukriya." This kid is kind and generous, and I feel a connection with him.

It's curious that I am finding more connections among the Indian nationals instead of the people at the ashram. Maybe I'm not giving the Osho-ites a chance. Prana is pleasant, but still these ashram people are so different from me. I can understand the Indian nationals better. Ironically enough, they are more my kind of people.

Both Manik's father and my friend, Gowri, offered me Chai tea today. They don't use filtered water, so I couldn't accept. Between Manik and his father and Gowri - - I love these Indian people.

Both Gowri and Manik thought the cobra show should be more like one hundred fifty rupees not two thousand! Tomorrow I will offer the guy two hundred rupees for the first time, one hundred fifty for the second time, and one hundred after that. I'm sure I will want to see it many times. Except the cobra guy felt so dishonest that I'm not sure if it's even a real cobra.

Evening Meeting tonight is great - - complete with those lovely flying bats overhead. They are so cool! They make the whole trip over there worthwhile! Don't tell that to the Osho-ites, though! At the end of Evening Meeting, I step out of the auditorium and from the hotel next door, I hear an American cowboy voice singing, "These Boots Are Made For Walking." It is both incongruent and ironic. I love irony.

Day Nine – Attractive Again

I get up early today so I can eat breakfast "out." Normally, I have oatmeal and some fruit in my room, but I am ready for something different today. I have fried eggs, toast, and juice in an ashram restaurant. Although no one asks how I want the eggs, they turn out exactly how I like them. This whole breakfast costs only a couple dollars.

Today at work is office-cleaning day. For the first hour of work, everyone cleans around their personal area. I dust and then start to sweep the floor. The woman next to me says she has already done that. Some people mop the floor of their area, also. Why can't they get the Indian nationals who do the other "dirty work" to do this? More manipulation?

The brooms here are cool. Imagine a giant paintbrush, except the bristle part and the handle part are equal lengths. They are neat - - as brooms go, that is. There are also other brooms with longer handles, so you don't have to bend down to use them.

Chandra was going to give me a different project today, but she didn't come in this afternoon. She is sick. This morning, I heard Prana tell her that it is easier asking for forgiveness than asking for permission.

After work, I go looking for the cobra guy and find his two brothers. They are by the vegetable cart right down the street. When I tell them about the two hundred rupees, they aren't happy. They keep insisting on twelve hundred rupees. I tell them to tell their brother and see what he says. It doesn't sound like it's going to happen. I'll see what comes of it.

Then I go to Osho Teerth Park and walk around. There are couples all over the place. Boys and girls together, strolling through the park, arm in arm, and talking. With everyone walking around, the park feels crowded. I walk across the street and wander through the other side of the park. Then I can't find my way back until I go under a tunnel. Unfortunately, the tunnel is muddy, and I get mud all over my clean shoes.

I come back to the ashram and walk around looking for someone washing down a walkway. While I am walking, a man starts talking to me. He is a Pune businessman. An article on the Internet told how businessmen come in to the ashram thinking they'll get lucky with the Osho-ites. This guy hugs me - - a long, tight hug, and then says I have good energy. We find a bench to sit on in the foliage.

We are close to the plaza, where music plays quietly. When he says it is a romantic spot, I don't respond. We have an entertaining conversation, though. I tell him I am forty-eight, and he says he thought I was forty. As his hand rests gently on my back, he says that my body is that of a thirty or thirty-five year old. That cracks me up. He is forty-five years old and married with a seven-year-old son. Through my questions, I find out that he travels a lot and is not faithful to his wife. He is exactly what the Internet was talking about! But, he serves his purpose. He makes me feel attractive and desirable again. It is a positive experience.

During our conversation I ask him about arranged marriages. He tells me that in his own marriage, he had dated his wife a few times to see if they liked each other before it was officially arranged. I say, "You date?"

He says, "Of course!" That isn't the most interesting part. His nephew had met a girl on the Internet. The families were ready to arrange the marriage, but the girl backed out at the last minute. That sounds incredible to me. Arranged marriages from the Internet! Meet the new India of the twenty-first century!

Tonight I see the bats again before Evening Meeting. Besides the big ones, there are much smaller bats flying around the water catching mosquitoes. They are so beautiful.

Osho's talk during Evening Meeting tonight gets to me. Here is the line I remember: "If you don't live dangerously, then you are not living. Don't live a lukewarm life." There was a lot more, and I enjoyed it. I need to get a copy of this one.

Day Ten – Bad Meeting

Something remarkable happened today. I asked someone if there was a book with the Rebel in it, from Osho's speech last night. He told me there wasn't. Then today, my new job on the computer included that speech, so I could read it again! It's almost like it's meant to be.

Still, I feel paranoid about all of this. I'm even typing with my computer screen halfway down.

My job bores me, but as I work, I read some of Osho's works, which makes it more stimulating. I'll see what tomorrow brings.

Today, many new people and I have a meeting with Dwami. Chandra told me to arrive early at the meeting, because Dwami doesn't like when people come late. A couple people did come late, and Dwami didn't want them to stay, but then reluctantly allowed it.

The speech goes on for an hour and has the same tone as all the other rhetoric around here. The word scientific bantered about. He does say something interesting, though. He talks about the outer world in "horizontal" mode, meaning that we do everything for barter. Your job pays you for your work, or I do this for you and you do that for me. Inside here, it is "vertical" mode, which means you do it for the sake of doing it. I'm not sure what to make of that.

The whole speech and its delivery make me feel scolded. With a condescending tone and riddled with four letter words, the speech drags on and the minutes roll by. No one says a word. We only listen. His words carry an underlying hint of anger.

Normally, four letter words don't offend me, but this was offensive and distracting. I used to want to use one such word for emphasis, and my ex-husband always told me not to because it took away from the message. Thank you! I finally get it! The use of them today makes me focus more on them than on the message. Not only does it distract me, but it also makes me question the validity of the person delivering the message. I hate being here and I hate listening to him. It is a distasteful experience.

Dwami talks a lot about Evening Meeting. He says the dancing is to tire your body, so no one fidgets during Osho's talk. He says the part at the end of each song when you raise your arms and shout, "Osho," isn't as a celebration - - like a soccer coach might do, but the sound should draw you inward - - or some garbage like that.

I ask about the silence/music part of Evening Meeting. Dwami says it is how Osho set it up, so there must be a reason for it. Then he says, "This is not the place for asking why." Okay, then.

During the day, I wear my maroon pants underneath my maroon robe. Tonight at Evening Meeting, I had forgotten to take off the maroon pants. The person at the door pulls me aside as I start to walk into the auditorium. "You can't wear maroon in the auditorium," she says.

"Can I hold them on my lap?" I ask.

"No, they have to be outside the auditorium."

After removing them, I put them with my shoes. You have to dress completely in white for Evening Meeting. There is no maroon allowed.

My lovely little Spartan room is within fifty feet of Osho Plaza, the main party place at the ashram. Loud music plays most every night. It starts at 9:30 and ends after 11:30. When I'm ready for bed, I put on my noise cancellation headphones and listen to Christmas music or something soft and easy. Usually, I can still hear the hard beat of the Plaza music, but I do my best to blank it out of my thoughts and concentrate on my music.

I have always been so sensitive to noise pollution - - that is, other people's music - - and here I just accept it. It wouldn't do me any good to get upset about it. I love my room and its location, so I do what I can and not let it get to me. Part of my journey here is to learn certain lessons, and flexibility is one of them. Also, I need to learn about accepting the is. I am learning!

Day Eleven - Gifts

Work is fine today. I read many of Osho's answers and enjoy the reading. When I mention it to Chandra at the front desk, she encourages that and tells me to take my time.

There is one word for today: smog. I noticed it for the first time yesterday. Pune is a city of nine million people and has abundant smog. It hurts my eyes and my lungs. I remember this feeling from when I grew up in a large city. Yucky. I don't like it. This reaffirms my life choice of not wanting to live in a city. They all have smog; it's a matter of how much and how often.

After work, Prana and I ride in a rickshaw to her flat, so I can pick up a package that my sister-in-law left for me. The ride scares me when the driver turns right into traffic. We're in an open little cart, like a big golf cart, and cars race toward us. I'll have to learn to ride in them if I'm going to venture farther than where I can walk.

At Prana's flat, I ask her if it is all right to eat the food at German Bakery, and she says it is. Then I ask, "I won't get sick, then?"

She says, "I can't tell you that you won't get sick."

I ask, "How long have you lived here?"

She says, "Thirty years."

I say, "Your system has probably already adjusted to the food here." That might have offended her. I'll find out tomorrow.

Since I decide to walk back instead of taking the rickshaw, I can't venture far because the packages are so heavy. On the way home, I stop at a shop that has Indian deities displayed in the front. The owner invites me in. He is a wonderful man named Omar who fixes me some tea, but again, I can't drink it. He has beautiful items inside: sequined wall hangings, deities, crystals, and all kinds of Indian souvenirs. Although he is from the Himalayas, he now lives in Pune.

I don't buy anything, because I want to check prices. After I do that, I will probably come back tomorrow. Omar offers to let me take the stuff home with me and decide. He says, "I trust you." How often would that happen with a stranger in the United States? I love this place.

When I leave his shop, I have to cross the street to get back to the ashram. I still don't have the hang of it. After trying for several minutes, I give up. Returning to the shop, I ask Omar if his associate would help me cross the street. The other man goes outside with me, takes my hand, and we run across the street together. It's easy when he does it! But, oh, it's not easy at all. Cars coming from all directions, no crosswalk, no light, barely any lanes - - too much for me!

Back home at the ashram, I open the package I received. What a gift it is! She left me a white robe, white leggings, maroon t-shirts, and all kinds of items including a towel. I am so happy to see a towel. The simple details are what matter here. I brought one big bath towel, one hand towel, and a washcloth. Somehow, I forgot about laundering my belongings. I received two towels with the room, but they are not enough. An extra towel now is wonderful.

Day Twelve – Tough Beggar, Yoga, and Flickering Lights

Prana is a little weird. Today she talked about a virus on her foot. When she told someone else in the office, she mentioned herpes. I ask if it is related to herpes, like cold sores. She says, "No, I have herpes on my cunt - - from sex." It is so weird how she said it. She's another casualty from the free sex in the early years here. What would Osho say about that?

I go to the events office today to speak to Anugyan about teaching yoga. My yoga teaching instructor told me to offer, which I did. Anugyan takes me to Nimisha, and she says I can probably teach two days a week. I ask about teaching in the afternoon. Anugyan says, "No, that's when they have Kundalini Meditation."

"Can't there be yoga, too?" I ask.

He says, "No, nothing can interfere. The Dynamic Meditation in the morning, Kundalini in the afternoon, and Evening Meetings are the spine of the program."

Nimisha suggests I come to yoga tomorrow morning at 7:15. I ask if I can teach one hour instead of an hour fifteen, and she says, "No, it would mix people up."

I say, "I can give them longer Shavasana." That is the lying down part at the end of a yoga class.

She says, "Then you'd have to have towels to cover them. It's cold out there."

I also speak to Anugyan about Reiki. He says to come talk to him tomorrow. I will have to do a session and have feedback. That's fine. Although I haven't done it for a couple months, I know I'm good at Reiki.

My sister-in-law recommended talking to Kanti about shopping matters. So I tell her the price of the wall hangings I looked at yesterday. She says, "You should always offer half of the price they ask, because they like to bargain. Remember they are merchants; they are not your friends. Don't misunderstand the dynamic."

That sounds like a negative view of Indian people, although she married an Indian. I still find the Indian people friendly, kind, and generous. The locals I've met outside the ashram are my best friends so far.

Kanti's suggestion for crossing streets is to watch how women cross. She said not to watch men, because they cross differently. Most of the women here wear saris, so maybe it would be better to watch the men, since I'm always in jeans when I cross streets.

After work, I walk over to see Gowri and Manik, and they aren't there. They said that Gowri didn't come today. She told me she works everyday, but last time I saw her she said she was having trouble with her eyes. That worries me.

I pass one street vendor and he offers to sell me a large sari for one thousand rupees, then seven hundred fifty, then five hundred, and eventually three hundred! It surprises me how they adjust their prices.

I cross the street by hanging with some locals while they cross. They laugh when they see what I'm doing. Then I walk down the opposite side of the street for a long time.

After I've gone a short way, I have a disturbing encounter with a beggar. She says to me as I pass her, "Mon - ey." When I say, "I'm sorry," and keep walking, she screams at me, "MON - ey!" It is disconcerting. I hurry away, and she goes the other direction.

I stop by some shops looking for Indian deities. I think of purchasing a singing bowl at one place, but the proprietor pushes me hard to buy it. That makes me back off, so I go back to Omar's shop from yesterday. His prices are higher, but he has a more pleasant manner. He is busy with someone else. Since I want to bargain, I leave and tell him I'll return.

When I leave his shop, I watch traffic and can't cross. Continuing up the street, I search for someone crossing, but there is no one. Finally, a break in traffic! I dash across safely! My first street crossing alone!

As I am about to turn onto the street where the ashram is, I find a beautiful, carved wooden cobra. Sitting on a table among some purses and other knick-knacks, stands the cobra tall and proud with its hood up. I bargain the person down and finally have my cobra. If I can't get the real snake - - I'll take what I can get!

When I ask the man about real cobras, he says sometimes people will walk up and down the street doing a "magic show." He also says it takes forty minutes to get to the snake park - - too far in a rickshaw! I'll find a cobra when I'm meant to find one. For now, I can look at my beautiful, wooden cobra.

Then, at a shop close to the ashram, I bargain the woman down for a maroon purse. This one, I don't have to unzip every time I go by a gate. It has a plastic holder on the front of it for my identification pass. Whenever you go inside the ashram, you have to show your pass.

I'm reading a novel about dolphins, and last night at the end of the chapter, it got to me. It was about a woman who went somewhere - - not sure if she should, and suddenly she got the feeling, "Yes, this is exactly where I should be." It gave me a weird feeling when I read it, because it feels like it applies to me.

This evening, after Evening Meeting, I almost start crying for no particular reason. It is interesting that I feel a little sad, and I don't know why. Is the newness of my situation wearing off and now the loneliness begins? I don't know.

This is the first time in my life that I've been single and not actively looking for a man. It's too weird here. These are not my people. Any man who would be here doesn't interest me. I think it's good for me to be "out there" without the desperate need or want of a man. Someday I want a special relationship with a man who is warm and wonderful. Right now, I'm fine the way I am.

After charging my computer, I try to pull the surge protector out of the socket. The electrical panel with light switches on it comes loose from the wall. My lights start flickering, and the panel makes little noises. When I try to push in the loose screw, it makes more noises and creates more flickering.

I walk to the front gate to report it. The guy on duty tells me to turn out the lights and tell them in the morning. I feel the wall around the panel to make sure it isn't hot - - like a fire burning from the inside. This building is old. Since there is nothing else I can do, I take a shower and go to sleep.

Day Thirteen – Ashram Conversations

This morning before work, I go to the yoga class. It is an advanced class where they twist like pretzels. That doesn't work for me and my doughnut abilities. Also, it is not easy doing yoga in a robe, when you normally wear flexible yoga pants. I spend most of the class in child's pose.

After the class, I tell Nimisha that I teach beginning or gentle yoga. She says someone already teaches that. That's not what she said yesterday. After lunch, I go see her again.

I say, "I hope you're not judging me from that class. I don't do those poses and don't teach them."

She says, "No, no, it's the program."

I tell her that I could give her a private lesson to see how I teach. But, we leave it at the program. I don't feel like fighting it.

For lunch today, I meet Devika again. Early tomorrow morning, she will take me to the burning ghats like my sister-in-law suggested. It's only a ten-minute walk, and I heard it's neat over there.

Today I say, "Bless you," when Prana sneezes.

She says, "It is strange hearing someone say that. I haven't heard that in so long. I don't know what to say. Do I say thank you?" Then she tells me that she likes sneezing because they give her orgasms! I'm living in a nut house!

Tomorrow I am going to do a Reiki session with a guy, and the next day a session with a woman. Then I'll have another in a couple days. Anugyan called them feedback sessions. If I get a good report, then maybe I can start doing Reiki. Whatever is meant to happen.

Today, I realize I am walking around with my robe caught up in my pants. Underneath the maroon robe, I wear pants for warmth. When I used the restroom earlier, the robe had caught partway in my pants. At least I didn't have toilet paper trailing behind me!

Earlier this week, I was going to the bathroom and wearing my sister-in-law's old maroon robe that she gave me. Suddenly, I realized that part of it was in the toilet. These toilets are a little different. There is only water in the bottom of them, so the robe wasn't wet. Although, the idea that it had been in there, and I still wore it bothered me. Since my other robe was in the laundry, I was stuck with it. Gross!

Something Chandra told me upset me. Soon they will assign me three more hours a week doing something else. I don't have any free time as it is. I freaked out - - inside - - when I heard that. There is nothing I can do about it now.

Barbara Ehrenreich, the woman who wrote the book called *Nickel and Dimed,* worked menial jobs - - more than one - - for a year to see what it was like to live like that. She had a cheap apartment, which she paid for only with the money she earned. She ate only what she could "afford." If she can do it for a year, I can do this for three months.

Today, I "heard" my mom. As I walk toward a restaurant to look for some sweets, I glance at the smoking section and say to myself, "Maybe I'll start smoking." Mom says, "Stop that crazy-talk!" "Crazy-talk!" I haven't heard that expression since the last time she said it to me when she was alive and whole. And, I haven't thought of it since then, either. It was so "her," I know that it came from her. I know she is here with me.

I get some great news today. I've been here almost two weeks already, and I thought it was only a week. That means "only" two and a half months to go! Whoopee! Yeah! I'm almost there!

I feel like crying again tonight after Evening Meeting. I'm not sure if it has to do with the dolphin book I'm reading, or loneliness sneaking in. Loneliness is not something I expected, and I don't think that's it. I'm alone here because I have no real friends. Despite that, I don't consciously feel lonely. I have my email connections, my computer, my writing, and my books. Having a man doesn't interest me right now. So, could it be loneliness? It's not so much that I don't want a man right now, as I don't want an Osho-ite man.

The ashram has three sections to it, separated by two streets. The main part is where I live. It also has several business offices, the Zorba the Buddha restaurant, the Plaza party area, a snack stand with coffee and snacks, the cyber cafe, the laundry, some housing, the bookstore, and Osho's old residence where they hold some meditations. The main part is also where you get your identification pass when you arrive.

Across the street from the main gate is another gate that leads to the bank, the galleria where you can buy robes and other accessories for the ashram, the safety deposit area, the pyramid shaped Osho Auditorium where they hold Evening Meetings, the Meera restaurant where I usually eat, the hotel called Osho Guesthouse, and some housing.

Out the back gate of the ashram and across the street is the third area. It has several smaller pyramids used for housing and for multiversity events. It also has some business offices including where I work. There are stations with filtered water in each section. Whenever you leave one section to go to another, you have to show your identification pass.

39

There is a regular hired police-type guard by the front gate. I thought that was weird until I walked down the street and found them in front of several businesses and residences. The street by the front gate is also busy. You have to be careful when you cross because motorcycles and auto rickshaws constantly speed by. There are also auto rickshaws lined up and ready to take people wherever they want to go.

Day Fourteen – Outside the Gates

The semi-crying I experienced the last couple of days is not loneliness. I've decided that, for sure. I am not feeling lonely. However, I have been craving sugar lately. That might be from the comfort food side of it.

Also, today I checked my email and no one had written to me. In some ways, I feel abandoned. It makes me feel bad - - not lonely, just bad.

This morning, Devika shows me the burning ghats. This is where they burn people after they die. It is where they burned Osho after he "left the body." The burning ghats are rectangular holes in the ground where they put the body and fuel to start the fire. They are by the river and parts of the ashes go into the river. It has something to do with the water running eternally.

We walk alongside the river and come to some buffalo. A dog barks viciously at them. Devika points out that it is a female protecting her pups because the buffalo were getting too close. I look carefully and see several puppies playing all around.

Devika tells me if you mix cow pies with some water, you can make satisfactory flooring. Also, you can use dried cow pies for cooking fuel. It doesn't sound appetizing, but she tells me it gives off a pleasant aroma!

We pass a pile of garbage on the side of the road. Devika says there must have been a celebration there. Although it looks like a bunch of garbage to me, she points out several leaves in a circular pattern. The locals use them as plates.

Then we walk to a beautiful, new Muslim Temple, but it is not a mosque. Devika shows me an eight-pointed star in the gate grating and then says the lotus on the building also has eight leaves. I don't know what that signifies, though.

After leaving the burning ghats area, we run into her husband who is going to work at the ashram. I walk back with him.

The guy scheduled for my Reiki session today called to cancel. He said his body wasn't up to it. Then I saw him at Evening Meeting. I had talked about my sessions to that woman in my office who is also a Reiki person. Now I wonder if she sabotaged me. I'm writing all these secret and derogatory comments about life and the people here, and I'm starting to get paranoid about it! I'll see if he reschedules.

After work today, although it is smoggy and I feel tired from the morning trip to the ghats, I decide to go outside the gates again. That's where the excitement is, the people I resonate with, and my heart. So, I dress in my street clothes and leave the ashram.

Normally when I go out, I turn right at the main gate. That's the way to the street vendors, the shops, and German Bakery. Instead, today I turn left to see what I can see. Shortly, I come to a T-intersection and walk a couple blocks, but there isn't much there. I turn back, go the other way, and walk farther down the street. I come to some children playing. Across the street from them, several men carry shovelfuls of dirt.

As I walk back to the ashram, I suddenly realize that I'm in India! I've been here a couple weeks now, and life has already become familiar and comfortable. It is my life. The thought that I am living in a foreign country escaped me. It has lost its "foreign-ness" and become my new reality. I am walking down a street like any street in America.

Day Fifteen – First Reiki Session

I can't believe that two weeks have already gone by. What they say might be true. If you have no weekend to look forward to, you are more in the moment. It bothers me, though, that soon I will lose three more hours of my free time. Since there is nothing I can do about it, it's silly to fret over it. I'll deal with it, like I deal with everything else.

Before coming to India, I told a friend about my trip and called it penance. In many ways, that's exactly what it is. Although, penance for what, I'm not sure. But, I do see the value of being here in teaching me some important lessons that I need to learn. This ashram can become a growing experience, if I don't become too entangled in the absurdities of the place.

Today, I ask Prana about working seven days a week again, so I can look it up. She gives me a "darshan" - - from one or several of her meetings with Osho. In one that I read, he told her not to have sex! What a shocker!

She also gives me an autobiographical piece of how her path led her here. In it, she had been traveling all over. I felt resentment over her evident financial freedom to do that. When I felt the resentment, I immediately felt bad about feeling it.

Years ago, my niece, Elsa, and her boyfriend came to visit. We took a hike up to a lake in the mountains. At the top, Elsa and her boyfriend hugged. A few minutes later, she sat beside me on a log and asked if it bothered me to see that. I said, no, I want that. Soon afterward, I met Sam.

You can't achieve something that you resent. Financial freedom should be a goal without feeling resentful toward it.

I have my first Reiki feedback session today, so any thoughts of sabotage were only paranoia. This is a test to see if I can work with the public as a Reiki practitioner. It's called Osho Reiki here. I have no idea how different it is, or if they will want to train me differently. My session goes well. The woman's name is Tanha and she liked it. Tanha is a Reiki master, and she said that she would book an appointment with me anytime. Success! Finally! It feels good. I have two more to go, so I can't get too cocky yet.

When I return from lunch this afternoon, I have chest pains. I just witness them. They don't scare me or thrill me. They probably aren't indicative of a heart attack because the symptoms are different for women. So I just witness, and they eventually go away without notice.

Day Sixteen – Too Much Food

Today, Sunday, is office-cleaning day again. To me, the whole cleaning arrangement is such garbage - - more manipulation. I see my boss, Sakra, collecting cleaning supplies to clean his area. Why can't the ashram have some locals clean the office? Why force the workers to do it? Although, the workers do it with no questions asked like little lemmings. The problem here is that no one questions what goes on. Osho talks about robots, and that is what many of these people have become. What would Osho say if he saw this today?

I have my second Reiki feedback session today with Gati. He says he likes it. I'll find out soon. Tomorrow is my third one, and I will be happy to get that behind me. I am eager to return to the India outside the gates, which I love.

While I give Gati Reiki, I look in the mirror and smile at myself. As I look at my smile that is similar to the one I wear on my face as I walk around, it looks full of pain. It doesn't look like a smile at all. It almost looks like I am getting ready for the doctor to give me a shot - - an almost wincing look. The unsmiling smile surprises me.

It reminds me of a recent conversation I had with Dilasa. I complained to him that people didn't smile back at me. I can't remember exactly what he said, but it gave me pause for thought. After that talk with him, I tried to have more feeling behind my smile. Now, I'll try to make it a bigger smile, so it doesn't look so painful.

The smog is bad again today. It affects me too much to consider living here full time.

In Evening Meeting during the dancing part, I chuckle as I look around at everybody and see how much they look like they are jumping around wearing only their white nightgowns. What a hoot that is.

As I walk back from Evening Meeting, I see the full moon and it makes me sad about Sam. For so many years, the full moon entered the window behind our bed and shone on us through the night. I will miss that full moon, because I looked forward to it every month - - shining on me like that. It is one of our shared experiences that is gone for good. When I return to America to collect my belongings, I will sleep in the spare room - - exactly where I should be.

I have gained weight! How does someone go to India and gain weight? Although there is no scale here, the jeans that I wear when I leave the ashram have become suspiciously tight. When I arrived, they were loose. Oops.

I know how it happened. I had a minor sugar binge lasting several days. Since there is not much chocolate here, I had to accept anything they had. They had a lot, including Baskin Robbins ice cream (but no chocolate)! I had cakes, cookies, and all kinds of treats that I normally don't eat. Maybe I was searching for some comfort food. That is not like me, but I'm in India now and it's a new me!

Also, I have been eating great quantities of nuts. I brought a one-pound container of mixed nuts with me. That's what I eat when I get off work. I can't stop eating them! Nuts are high in fat and there you have it. Sugar and nuts. Nuts and sugar. Sounds like Christmas cookies, which you will not find here!

There is another reason to eat the nuts. I am not taking any anti-malarial pharmaceutical. The side effects scare me more than the chance of malaria. From what I read, the amino acid arginine is a natural way to cure malaria. So, I figured if it can cure malaria, it could probably prevent it. This thinking may not be valid, but it works for me! Nuts are the best dietary source for arginine.

My other self-treatment for malaria is an Indian herb called Ashwaganda, which has anti-malarial properties. I recently learned about that at an Ayurveda seminar in Colorado.

Since I'm talking about my weight, let me talk about the food here. It is wonderful. Lunch is the time I look forward to everyday. I eat like a queen. It costs me five or six dollars a day, which leaves me stuffed at the end of my meal. (This is not Ayurvedic. According to Ayurveda, you should always leave your stomach one-third to one-quarter empty. Oh, well.) This morning, I decided to splurge and eat out for breakfast, too. Today, I ate two eggs, toast, and juice for only a couple dollars. You can't beat that.

Not all the food is cheap, though. Fresh fruit and vegetables can be expensive. Apples and pears cost about one dollar and twenty-five cents each, and a small salad is about three dollars. I try to eat some fruit and vegetables every day.

Now I have to concentrate on losing the weight I've gained. Without a scale, I can't monitor my progress. I'm not going out for a few days, so no jeans, either. I walk a lot, though. The restaurant where I eat lunch is "two blocks" one way and Evening Meeting at night is at the same location. From my room to my job is "one block." When I go outside the gates, I walk even farther. So, I should make some progress. Of course, in these loose robes that I wear, who is going to notice, anyway!

45

My life feels unreal sometimes, as if I am living a dream. Tonight, as I get ready to go to an evening meditation, the unreal feeling comes on me. Often I feel as if I am witnessing my own actions, and that is good. If I can witness the mistakes I make, then it is easier to correct them.

Tonight, I attend the Chakra Sounds Meditation in the main auditorium. Since I learned something similar in yoga and liked it, I thought I might try it here. But, they don't do the yoga chakra sounds like I expect. Instead, they play loud music that hurts my ears. I stay for one round of chakras and then I leave.

Day Seventeen – Howling at the Moon

Early this morning when I mention last night's chakra meditation to Chandra, I say, "It wasn't like what I learned in yoga."

Chandra says emphatically, "Forget yoga!"

I say, "I can't forget it because yoga is my life." Hah, I haven't done any since that ill attempt at advanced last week. Before that, I hadn't done any for weeks.

I had also considered going to an evening event last night called Breathe in the Full Moon. Then Chandra told me that it cost nine hundred rupees - - twenty-five dollars - - so I decided against it.

Thank goodness! This morning, Chandra mentioned mattresses. Confused, I say, "It was inside?"

She says, "Of course!"

I say, "But the moon is outside."

She says, "It is the moon's energy that is important. It was very intense, and there was screaming involved." I am so glad that I didn't go. I'd rather howl at the moon and enjoy the view. Some of this stuff is so weird.

Later, I run into the woman who led the chakra meditation. She asks, "Didn't you like the chakra meditation last night? I noticed that you left early."

I say, "The music bothered me."

She says, "Years ago, they specially designed the music to resonate with each chakra."

Then I say, "During the instructions, you said, 'sing.' Since I can't sing, I felt like I couldn't participate."

She says, "I have to choose my words carefully so everyone can understand."

Then I try to soften my rejection of her meditation by saying, "I can understand that. It just wasn't right for me."

I had my final Reiki feedback session today. I have no idea what the last two people will report. Although I worried the most about Tanha, she turned out to be the one with the most glowing reviews! Think before you swat that fly!

I am referring to a story a friend told me about a musician we both like. He always warns the fly before swatting it. After swatting at a mosquito the other morning without remembering to warn it first, I thought it would be a good metaphor for my "jumping to conclusions" before giving events a chance to play out.

Everyone around here talks about their sannyas birthday - - the day they "took" sannyas. It apparently means when they made a commitment either to Osho or to meditation. They treat it like it's a huge deal, which I don't understand. I made a commitment to myself to do my meditation every day. I don't need to call it anything or announce to the world that I'm going to do it - - I just do it.

Day Eighteen - Weird Workshop

Is today Christmas? There is no sign of it here: no Christmas trees, no Christmas lights, no Christmas songs, no Rudolf, no snow, no Santa Claus. It's sad for me. I've always loved Christmas. At home, we have Christmas lights strung up in the living room, which I used to turn on throughout the year.

I read where Osho doesn't believe in Christmas because Jesus was born on January 6. There is so much more to Christmas than the religious part or the commercial part, though. There is the spirit of giving, and all that goes with it. I miss that Christmas feeling; I miss the trees, the lights, and the songs. I miss Christmas.

My favorite movie in the whole world is a Christmas movie called *Miracle on 34th Street*. It is about the real Santa Claus. My favorite quotation from the movie is, "Faith is believing in something when common sense tells you not to." Every year, except this one, I watch this movie.

I think Osho's decision not to have Christmas in the ashram is about something else. It has more to do with the adverse effect Christmas can have on lonely people. Eliminate weekends, eliminate holidays, eliminate everything that could possibly make people feel bad. Institute loud music, dancing, and free sex. Osho found the recipe for success!

This morning, Chandra tells me that because her mother is alone, she called her for Christmas. It sounds like a concession. I wish Chandra Merry Christmas, and she does the same. She probably wouldn't have said anything at all if circumstances were different.

Today, I attend a workshop called "Fast Track to Yourself." It is experiential rather than a lecture - - doing rather than listening. There are many different pieces to the day, and for me each piece feels too long. Interspersed throughout the day, and not just for dancing, is music that is too loud, often ear-shattering loud. I hate that.

The workshop starts with dancing to the music. Dancing and loud music must be the themes of this place. Next, we sit in a circle and go around the room saying our name and the name of each person who came before us. There are sixteen of us. Since I am midway, I don't have to remember everyone. When my turn comes, I have to say, "Hello Svatma, hello Derek, hello Gamel, hello Felipe" - - until I get to me. If we can't remember someone's name, then we have to say, "blob." The leader, Svatma, periodically asks, "How does it feel to have to say, 'blob'? How does it feel when someone calls you 'blob'?"

When we get to the end, Svatma says, "What if I say we will go around again?"

Everyone moans, and I say, "How about if you do it?" She says she can't, and we move on to something else. I wonder if we would have had to go around again if I hadn't said that.

Svatma beats a drum for the next part, and we are to take one step for each drumbeat. She slows down, speeds up, stops abruptly, and we have to freeze in position. Then we do it again with a partner. Next, we have to join with a second group, so we are now four people doing it. A guy from the new pair leads the way, and it is a little difficult.

Svatma asks how it feels being a leader or a follower. Although I don't like following, I also would not like leading. I want to make my own path; I don't want to follow or lead.

Then we line up in two rows facing one another, and the person opposite is your partner. My partner is Sajeev, an Indian guy from Bangalore. We have to stare into each other's eyes the entire time, while doing other movements with our arms, then legs, and then hips. All the while, our eyes are never to leave the other person's eyes.

Sajeev, at some point, has tears sliding down his face. It amazes me and his sensitivity touches me. When it ends, I give him a big hug. The lights had gone out a couple times during the exercise. I tell him that I could see his eyes shining even in the dark. He tells me that he could see my aura in the dark, and that it was very beautiful.

Next, we do the statue game. We have another partner, and one of us is the sculptor and one of us is the clay. The sculptor can move the clay into any position and the clay has to stay in that position. I am the clay first. My partner moves me around for five minutes in different positions. At the end, she has me sit on the floor, with my right hand behind me, my left hand held out, my knees bent, and the soles of my feet together. It feels uncomfortable sitting here like this.

Then Svatma calls time. She leads the sculptors around the room, where they critique the sculptures and move them around to "better" poses. When they come to me, someone pulls off one of my socks and places it in my outstretched left hand. Svatma pulls off my other sock and says, "How about a sock eater?" Then she pushes the leg-end of the sock between my lips. I hope that I would have had the nerve to refuse if she would have put the toe end in my mouth. Regardless, I let it go. Then someone else places a heavy bottle of water in my outstretched left hand. Svatma says, "That's mean," but she leaves it and the sock in place. Luckily, some kindhearted woman takes the bottle away, and although I

50

am a statue, I say, "Thank you."

Just when I think that Svatma stuck the sock in my mouth to retaliate for what I had said earlier, the group moves to another seated statue woman. Some people make a small change to her. Then Svatma says, "Let's give her bigger boobs." She stuffs a shawl down the front of her maroon robe! This surprises and appalls me!

After that, we get into groups of four or five and discuss how everything felt. None of us are big talkers, and I don't say much. I am still uncomfortable talking. I've noticed there aren't many big talkers in the ashram. I haven't met anyone who talks and talks and never shuts up. That's a pleasant change.

Next, we stop for a cappuccino break. Svatma tells us to be aware the whole time. After the break, I arrive back on time and am the only one there for several minutes. I'm too punctual to adjust to this Indian time.

After most people return, we dance while waiting for everyone to arrive. Then we start on the emotion phase of the workshop. First, Svatma tells us to feel anger. She raises the music to an ear-splitting level. That makes me angry. Luckily, I have pieces of tissue to stick in my ears.

I try thinking about a couple incidents that happened shortly before I left for India, but I can't feel riled up about them. Not only are they over and done, but they are ten thousand miles away. I am too much at peace here to let it affect me.

I walk around swinging my arms and doing what I think might look like anger. While waving my arms and shaking my fists, I yell some expletives for effect. Other people in the room yell and scream and whack pillows on the floor and on the walls. I can't get into it.

Next comes sadness, which I thought would be easy for me. Again, I can't get into it. There is something about someone saying to me, "Feel sad," that makes me unable to do it. I'm not sure if I'm not open to the whole idea because I feel cynical about it, or if it's the rebel in me coming out. Don't tell me what to feel! You're not the boss of me! Most of the people in the room are into this. I hear crying and heavy sobbing all around me. I know it's real, because I can feel their sadness.

Svatma tells us to feel romantic love next. That one makes me sad. The beginning with Sam comes to mind, and how happy I was, and then the bad parts start coming in. I remember everything leading to the sadness at the end. Then, I think about my fantasy love, and how sad that was.

After that is fear, and I lie down on a mat in fetal position and stay there. Happiness is next and everyone dances around. Waving my arms in the air, I do the touchdown movement a few times, and then dance around with everyone else.

Then Svatma says, "Now feel angry again." It feels so stupid. Everybody starts yelling and whacking pillows again, and then Svatma says, "Freeze! See how easy it is to go from one emotion to the other?" Well, maybe for them. I have had enough by this time and I'm starved since we are late for lunch.

I deliberately come back a few minutes late from lunch and I'm not the last one there. After lunch, we talk about how aware we are at lunch. I talk about how I became aware my elbow was on the table, and how embarrassed I was but didn't move it. Two guys talk about how no one here smiles. Svatma's answer to that is, "Well, it is a meditative place." Usually, I smile when I'm meditating. My meditation instructor always used to say, "Enjoy," when she started us off in meditation.

After our talk is a body exercise. We have to move our arms a certain way and then talk to someone while we do it. Then comes a stepping exercise where we have to move our feet a certain way.

After that, we do another awareness game. Most people have a different partner, although I have my same sculptor/clay partner again. We have to face each other and look into each other's eyes and say, "Right now, I am aware . . ." and then say something we're aware of, like "my breathing" or "the sound of the air conditioner" or "I'm feeling self-conscious." It is an interesting exercise, but it goes on and on. We were only to do it twice each. Unfortunately, Svatma loses count and some of us, me included, have to do it three times. It feels awful.

Then we go through the senses, but we only have time for touch and hearing. We could have a partner or be alone for touch, and I am thankfully alone. Hearing is listening to some music and sounds, and then listening to Osho talk about senses. It is a good dialogue of his, and I'll look it up tomorrow. I believe it is no accident that my job gives me access to read and listen to many Osho discourses.

They designed this workshop so we can learn to live in the moment and be aware of what we are experiencing while we experience it. We have to meet with Svatma again tomorrow to see if we have learned to be present and be aware while doing our normal jobs.

Four o'clock can't come soon enough for me. Not only because I want to get the stupid workshop finished, but because of what waits outside - - the real India! Finally! Those three days of Reiki nearly killed me with longing for the real India.

What an incredible Christmas gift I am given! As I approach the corner, I see two camels. I pull out my camera and feel so excited to take their picture. One guy asks if I want a ride. He said it costs two hundred rupees. I say, "Too much." Then he offers one hundred rupees - three dollars. Oh, yeah, I climb on and I am riding a camel! It has a big saddle that can hold three or four adults. I sit alone at the front.

We walk down a major boulevard in Pune, as cars, rickshaws, and motorcycles race down the same street, often right toward us. The camel's name is Lucky and he is one calm camel. He walks me down the street and back, and then up the street. We walk past Gowri, and I call her name and wave to her. She asks if I am coming to see her.

A thin, little beggar girl about nine years old follows me the whole time I ride the camel. She asks me for money once and then just follows.

Lucky walks back to the corner and plops down on his knees to let me off. It sounds like it hurts. He has bells attached above the big calluses on his knees. After I get off the camel, the guy offers to take a picture of me and Lucky. I try to reach over to pet Lucky, but he turns his head toward me, makes a grunting noise, and shows me his long teeth. If camels are like horses, then he is an old camel.

I've ridden camels before in amusement parks, but I've never ridden a camel in India. The only way it could have been a better or a more fitting Christmas present would have been if there were three camels. It is such a cool experience.

After my great adventure on the camel, I go visit with Gowri. I love that lady. I tell her that I worried about her and ask where she was the other day. She says the police were getting on them. When I ask about a license to sell on the street, she says she doesn't need one. She also tells me that business has been bad because not too many people from the ashram were coming. I tell her I think it will get busier in January.

While I sit with her, a beggar comes by and starts harassing me. Gowri yells at the beggar to leave me alone, and I keep my head down and don't look up. After the beggar leaves, I ask, "How do you say 'I'm sorry' in Hindi?"

She says, "Sari?" and points to what she wears.

I say, "No, like I apologize, to say to the beggars."

Gowri says, "You say, 'No money. Sorry. Namaste.'"

I ask, "Yeah, how do you say that in Hindi?" She repeats the words again. I'll try it.

Next, I go looking for Manik, but he isn't there. Another guy there sells clothes, and I ask him about Manik. He points toward their store that I went to the other day.

I don't feel like going down there today. By following a couple Indian women, I cross the street easily. Soon, another beggar woman approaches me. I say, "No money. Sorry. Namaste," and she immediately leaves. I can't believe it! It works! Wow. Namaste! I walk to the back of German Bakery and change some money. The rate has gone down since the last time I was there, but still better than the ashram.

I walk all the way down the street to the store with the Indian deities where I had been to last week. Omar wants to give me tea, and I can't take it.

In the store, I buy a Shankara wall hanging, a wooden dancing Shiva, and a pair of hands that when you open them, Ganesh and Lakshmi are inside. While he wraps the items carefully in paper for me, he holds up the wooden Shiva and says, "You take good care of this. It is special." That touches me. He has more than one - - it isn't like it is an original, but his words make an impression on me.

While I'm in Omar's store, I ask him about cobras. He says that sometime he will take me on his motorbike to the train station, and I can find them there. The generosity of these people continues to impress me.

I manage to cross the street toward home by myself. It takes me ten minutes to find a good spot, but I do it. It scares me, though.

As I walk back, I see a woman with a big bundle on her head. It's a cool shot, so I take her picture from far away with the telephoto lens. A few minutes later, she and I are both heading the same direction, and she says, "You want to take my picture?" I take out my camera, snap a close up, and show it to her. Then she says, "Money?"

I start laughing and say, "That wasn't part of the deal." She is a good sport and leaves me alone.

Both camels have disappeared when I arrive back at the corner. If I see them again, I'll ride again. Who can resist riding a camel in India?

I run into Chandra in the bathroom before Evening Meeting. She wants to know how Fast Track was. When I tell her the workshop didn't impress me, she acts disappointed. Chandra is so into everything here, no questions asked, and I'm not. She thinks I should be and she's always curious when I'm not. I tell her how exciting it felt riding the camel. Chandra isn't impressed. She can't understand how I can be so excited about a camel and not excited at all about such a great opportunity as Fast-Track.

Day Nineteen – Not One of the Crowd

When Prana sees me today, she asks enthusiastically how I liked Fast Track. Then she gushes about how much she loved it when she and the whole office went together. These people are in so much of a different place than I am.

At three o'clock, I meet with Svatma and half the group for a Fast Track feedback session. They all express how much they had gotten out of it. They speak about the different parts, and how much they liked all of it.

Maybe I'm not giving it a chance, or maybe I'm too cynical. Perhaps there is something missing in me that I couldn't get or couldn't accept what this workshop had to offer. I can't get past trying to be angry on command. It doesn't resonate with me. Maybe they know more than I do, or maybe I don't belong here.

I realize something else today, thanks to Osho. In a discourse that I read, he talked about being empty and filling that emptiness with food. And how if you feel loved you won't do that. I think maybe I've been eating to fill the emptiness. I've already said how I look forward to my lunch. Thinking about it, I always leave lunch feeling stuffed. I'm eating too much.

It's not only the nuts and sweets that caused me to gain weight, it's the volume of what I ate. Everyday, I go to the cafeteria and have three bowls of food. It would have been easier to judge how much food I ate if the food had been on a plate. Instead, the food was in bowls, and the bowls looked small. Who knew? Also, I always had a piece of fruit and often a small cucumber and a tomato. It was too much food. No wonder my pants are tight. Today, I had two bowls of food and a large slice of watermelon and I still feel stuffed. That might have been because I had a big breakfast today. I'll see how it goes tomorrow.

I feel tired today because I didn't sleep last night. When I'm tired, I find all this crap too hard to take. Today, the crowded restaurant makes me decide that tomorrow I'm going to leave for lunch five minutes early. I've seen other people leaving early, so I might as well try it.

I want to meditate and take a nap before Evening Meeting tonight. In the middle of my meditation, music blares from the Plaza down below. I complete my meditation with fingers in my ears. It's 5:25 now, and the music has stopped. It's too late to take a nap.

A bat flies close over my head as I wait for Evening Meeting. I see his little claws at the leading edge of his wings. These bats have a two-foot wingspan. I still don't know what kind they are, but I get so much pleasure watching them. I'm usually almost the last one to go in to Evening Meeting, so I can stand outside and hope for a glimpse of them overhead.

Day Twenty - Sick

I have felt sick all day. Well, not exactly sick. For the previous two nights, I only slept six hours altogether. This morning, I wake up with a painful headache and shortly after have an upset stomach. At ten o'clock, after working only an hour, I ask if I can go home and try to get some sleep. To my surprise, Chandra, who is the receptionist where I work, says yes. She says she will check on me later.

Just before two o'clock, as I am finally drifting off to sleep, Chandra knocks on my door. She says that Sakra, my boss, wants me to either go to a doctor or go see him. So, I dress in my maroons and walk over to the office. After I explain about not sleeping and the headache, he allows me to return to my room.

Somewhere during the day, I realize that part of the headache may be from dehydration. It is dry here, and everyone drinks large amounts of water. I'm not good at drinking water, and the water here doesn't taste good. I liked our filtered well water back home, and this is nothing like that. It doesn't have a bad taste, just not a good one. After I realize that, I start drinking more water and I think it helps. Today, I have had twice as much water as I normally do.

I sleep some during the afternoon. When I hear Chandra in the bathroom at six o'clock, I go in and ask if I can have the sleeping pill that she offered me earlier. I have never in my life taken a sleeping pill. If I didn't feel so sick and not sleepy, I wouldn't take one now, either. But, I have to listen to my body and I know my body needs sleep. I will take half a pill. Pharmaceuticals scare me, as my body is not accustomed to them. Getting me to take an aspirin is a major event.

Within half an hour, I feel my body begin to tingle, as it reacts to the sleeping pill. I fall asleep soon afterward and sleep four hours straight. Then, I wake up and sleep off and on through the night.

Day Twenty-One – Take it Off!

I did get some sleep last night, thankfully, but my body continues to tingle for almost eighteen hours. And, I don't feel drowsy this morning, a full twelve hours after I have taken the pill. However, I do sense a subtle feeling of fatigue that passes in the early afternoon. The whole experience interests me on a scientific level. I'm hoping I never have to take the second half of the sleeping pill. Since I feel much more rested and more myself, though, the pill was worth it. I get so down, pessimistic, and negative when I don't get enough sleep.

This morning when I arrive at work, I go in to see Sakra to tell him I am doing well and to thank him for letting me go home yesterday. He acts uninterested. Maybe I should ignore his indifference and say that his thoughts were elsewhere. It does strike me as a little rude, though.

Last night, since I did not attend Evening Meeting, Chandra told me to go to the Work as Meditation office and report why I didn't go. Since I have to "check in" every night, there would have been some consequence if I had missed without a reason. Knowing me, I'm sure I'll eventually find out what that consequence is! When I go to the Meditation office, they dutifully write down my name and my absence. You wouldn't think an ashram would be so strict.

Today, I go back to the entrance gate area to get the name changed on my identification card. They had spelled my name incorrectly, and I want it changed. At first, they say it will cost fifty rupees, but I point out that it isn't my mistake. A few days ago, they told me that I have to bring my passport to be certain the spelling is correct. I told her I knew how to spell my own name! Today I get it done. I want them to put my nickname on there, but they say that would cost fifty rupees. There's bureaucracy everywhere these days - - even in India.

Chandra asks me again about my extra job. Tomorrow I need to set up another meeting with my coach, Andre. I'm worried that my new job might be a topic of the meeting. Man, I hope that doesn't happen. I have so little free time now. When I planned this India experience, I expected to have more free time than I did back home. What a mistaken expectation that was!

I've worked this job for a couple weeks now and I've read or heard hundreds of Osho's discourses. Clearly, Osho is anti-marriage. Although Osho talks about women's equality, the paradox is his obvious dislike and lack of respect for women.

He told a joke the other night about a rabbi and a priest with a rapist confessing to his crime. The priest told him to put ten dollars in the charity box and don't do it again.

That feels so degrading to women - - minimizing rape like that. The joke would have had the same impact if the person would have stolen something or even killed somebody. This is only one example of derogatory remarks about women that are common throughout his discourses.

There are other instances with him, too. Osho often talks about nagging wives and hen-pecked husbands, and makes many other similar comments. Although he may have been close to some women in his life, he doesn't like women. There is a ribbon of dislike running through his discourses. It offends me.

In all the discourses that I've read or heard, there is nothing about working every day. I haven't found anywhere that it says Osho said work seven days a week. When I ask Prana about it, she can't find it, either.

I'm beginning to think that Osho never said that. These people wanted to be around him so much that they didn't want a day off. It was never anything demanded of them. It was their own idea so they wouldn't have to come up with something to do on their days off, and so they could be near their so-called master.

Weekends are hard for some people. The people here would be the ones that find weekends hard. Give the crowd what they want. If they can't handle weekends, then don't give them weekends.

I honestly think these people are missing something, and their attraction to Osho fills up their emptiness. He is a wise man, but I've never been much of a guru follower. Although I love Deepak Chopra, or at least his message, I can't see myself following him around. However, if I did work for him, I still wouldn't want to work seven days a week!

I find a spider in the bathroom when I get off work. It is black and dime sized including its legs. Its big pedipalps are far apart and almost crablike. It jumped! I came so prepared, though - - I had the foresight to bring a "spider glass" with me to India. So, I get my spider glass and catch the little bugger. His jumping scares me, but I get him and turn him loose downstairs in the foliage. If anyone asked, I would have told them that I am a Jain. That's an Indian religion that doesn't believe in killing anything, including mosquitoes.

Today, I read what Osho said about communes. It must have been a long time ago, early in his "career" as a guru. He said that if people in the commune have to go on building houses and roads and whatnot, they won't have time to meditate and that wouldn't work. That's almost what's happening with me. I barely have time to meditate. And, I now realize with horror that it's almost Evening Meeting time, and I haven't meditated!

A couple nights ago I read in a book another woman wrote about living in an ashram, that one time when she meditated, she had this blue light and vibration throughout her body. She described it as a Kundalini experience. It made me feel bad that I have been meditating all this time, and nothing like that has ever happened to me. It's all right. What I get out of meditation is good for its own sake. It keeps me centered and it keeps me sane.

After Evening Meeting, I usually go back to my room and read and work on the computer in my white robe until bedtime when I put my pajamas on. Tonight, when I walk into the bathroom at ten o'clock, Chandra is in there and she gasps when she sees me.

She asks, "What are you doing with your white robe on?"

I say, "I'm reading in my room."

She says, "Oh no, oh no, you must take it off right away. Go now and take it off - - it bothers me."

I say, "I just need to use the bathroom and then I'll take it off, I promise." She goes in her room and closes the door.

After I take the white robe off, I knock on her door and call out, "I took it off!" Then she comes into the bathroom with me and reads to me something Osho had written about wearing white robes. It turns out that you can wear white robes when you are doing your own silent meditation. I tell her that I like keeping the robe on after I get home, because I like the "vibe" of it. That's not true, but I knew she would understand that. Besides, it has become such a stupid game that I can't resist.

I ask her when she meditates. She says, "At Evening Meeting." Then she says that she sometimes goes to Silent Sitting at Chang Tzu and sometimes meditates when she can't sleep. The real irony is that Osho said the basis for being a sannyasin is daily meditation.

Although these people make such a big deal about sannyas and being sannyasins, I bet there are a lot more of them besides Chandra who don't meditate anymore. I'm going to start asking and keeping track. The results should be compelling.

I need to take a rickshaw to get to the train station. I know this is the next step for me, but I'm a little afraid. What am I afraid will happen? That I can't get back or something? I'm not sure what my fear is. If I want to see my cobra, I need to do this. Tomorrow, though, I'll walk down to the grocery store that Prana told me about. My pretzels and my nuts are almost gone.

The last couple days before I caught up on my sleep, I felt depressed and wondered if I could manage to stay here for the entire three months. I'm still not sure, but today, I think I can. (I think I can, I think I can, I think I can!) It's only nine more weeks, and what's nine weeks?

However, the noise is starting to get to me and the smog bothers me a lot. I've decided that I will go to the office Wednesday and Saturday nights when they have the Plaza parties. Chandra says she often goes there. That way I could use the computer all I want while getting away from the loud music.

The smog is something else. I have to remember to keep breathing. Smog or no smog, I need to breathe. Seeing the cobra should ensure that I will stay for all three months. Maybe I should go cobra hunting tomorrow!

Day Twenty-two – Cobra!

When I finish my project at work, Chandra tells me to call Nalini for the next batch of DVDs. I call her and she is so brusque. She says she's busy right now, but will bring them down in ten minutes. Since she acts so inconvenienced, I offer to pick them up upstairs. Then she tells me with sarcastic rudeness that she has to come down anyway to get the new ones from the archive. She never considered that maybe I don't know where the archive is. Her continual rudeness surprises me.

While I wait, I surf the Internet because I think she will be here any minute. An hour and a half later, she never shows up and I leave work. I don't feel guilty at all.

After work, I change clothes and find a rickshaw driver to take me to the train station to look for my snake charmer. He will take me there to see the cobra, wait for me, and bring me back. His name is Phani and he is short and round with a red dot on his forehead. I like him.

The ten-minute drive there terrifies me as I expected. I want to take some pictures, but I'm hanging on and don't dare let go. It wouldn't be so bad if it were all rickshaws, motorcycles, and small cars out there. There are also buses and big trucks and all of them together going willy-nilly in every direction.

During the scary ride, there is always that second when you think: I'm in a strange country, and this stranger is taking me to unknown places. Then, the second passes and everything feels all right again.

When we arrive at the train station, it doesn't work out the way I thought it would. Phani drives around and can't find the cobra guy. Then we get out of the rickshaw, and Phani talks to some locals.

Soon, I find myself in an alley surrounded by eight Indian men. Phani tries to arrange everything with the guy who has the cobra. Everyone talks at once, mostly in Hindi, and they tell me five hundred rupees. Finally, I get them down to three hundred rupees. Unfortunately, the snake is at the guy's house.

Where does the guy live? In the village. Where is the village? I have no idea. Two minutes later, two of the Indian guys and I are in the back of the rickshaw racing down the street! I don't know where we are going or how long it will take to get there. Looking at my watch, I wonder if I will get back in time for Evening Meeting. It is too late to think about that now; I am on the way to my destiny. I have no idea what that destiny is, though. I'm hoping it involves a cobra!

We drive and drive, dodging and maneuvering around traffic as we go. Phani and the two guys talk in Hindi all the way there, and I don't know what they're saying. Cars scream by us on the road. We keep turning this way and that, and still aren't there.

I finally ask, "Are we getting close?"

The guy next to me in the rickshaw says, "Almost home." Suddenly, I recognize a playground that I passed on my walk the other day.

Less than five minutes later, after passing the camel guy on the street giving some kids a ride, we come to the end of the pavement. We turn up a rocky dirt road. By the side of the road, I see flames from a burning dump. Then we pull into a big open area. To the left is a large apartment building with some broken windows. Straight ahead is another building that might be a house. Train tracks are to the right, and a train races by while we wait. A few chickens peck in the dirt in a small grassy area. Several birds of prey circle overhead hoping for a chance at the chickens.

Many people mill around outside. While Phani talks to them, I busy myself taking pictures of the birds and trying not to look too out of place. Am I ever out of place. Little children keep walking by to look at me. They're not accustomed to seeing tourists in their home area. I smile and say hello to them, but only one of them smiles back. They're probably afraid of me because I look so different.

I wait anxiously, not knowing what to expect and not knowing if this is fake or not. Finally, a young man comes carrying a cloth sack, like a pillowcase except with a pull cord on the top. He opens the bag and drops out a cobra. Immediately, I see the design on the back of its hood. It's called a spectacled cobra, because the design resembles "spectacles."

The young man does not touch this snake. Its tongue comes in and out of its mouth, and it "stands" there hooded up and looking beautiful. Periodically, the young man or someone else waves something in front of the cobra to get it to turn so I can take pictures.

I can't believe I am in front of a live cobra in India! My dreams have come true. My cobra right there in front of me. I am in heaven!

Then, the young man's father arrives, sits on the ground, and picks up the cloth bag. He opens it, reaches in with his bare hands, and pulls out a second cobra already hooded up! It surprises me as much as if he had reached in and pulled out a genie! Two cobras! Two spectacled cobras standing together, hoods up, and looking more beautiful than ever. What an amazing sight.

The old man is fearless, and at one point the snake's head wipes against his forehead. He handles it like a pet boa constrictor. I don't understand why it isn't trying to strike. It is a small cobra - - three or four feet, but it is beautiful.

Then, the old man puts the snake around his neck! I'm going crazy watching him. I tell Phani to tell the man that I'm jealous. When the old man hears that, he offers to let me hold the cobra. I don't have the nerve. I will never forgive myself for not saying yes. I hope that I can go back there sometime and try it.

But, I do give my camera to Phani, and then carefully creep up behind the old man. He pats the area on the grass next to him, but I want to make sure I am out of striking distance. I ask if I can hold its tail. When I take the tail in my hand, the cobra wraps it tightly around me.

When they start putting the snakes away, Phani says, "Let's go," and gets into the rickshaw.

The young man and his father say, "Did you like it?"

I say, "Yes, thank you!" It feels like they are asking for money. Pointing to the boss man, I keep saying, "He will pay you." It feels like there is a mix-up, and I don't know what to do. I don't want to cheat them, but I don't want them to cheat me, either.

In the rickshaw, I ask the boss man if he will pay the snake guys, and his answer sounds confusing. I keep asking, "You're going to pay them, right?"

Then, the young man stands next to the boss man sitting by me in the rickshaw and says, "This is my brother." I don't know if it is his real brother or only an expression, but it makes me feel better the guy isn't mad at me. The old man's eyes keep haunting me, though. He looks hungry.

When we arrive at the ashram five minutes later, I ask Phani how much I owe him. He says three hundred rupees. Although we had originally agreed on somewhere between one hundred twenty and one hundred fifty, he did so much for me arranging everything, I pay it without trying to bargain.

It doesn't look like he is going to have change for a five hundred-rupee bill, so I say I think I have the three hundred. Going through my pockets, I come up with two hundred eighty rupees. I hold it out and ask if that's enough. Phani has a bad look on his face, so I pull it back, and say all right, then give me the change. He does manage to come up with it.

It cost twenty dollars. Although I shouldn't have paid that much, it is another incredible adventure in the "real India" for me. I wish I would've had the nerve to hold it. If there is a next time, I will hold it. I can't believe I touched a live cobra in India.

After I pay him, I ask if I should have given the snake guys money. Phani is so sweet about it. He scoots over, pats the seat next to him and says, "Sit here." So, I sit crowded next to him in the front seat of the rickshaw while he patiently explains to me that perhaps I should have given the guys a tip. At least that's what I get out of it. Often, he is difficult to understand, and I usually understand only half of any story that he tells me. But, I think that is what he is trying to convey.

It is so hard to know what to do here. The culture and the rules are so different. The right action in America is often the wrong action here and vice versa. At least I'm learning, though, because I know more now than when I came.

I tell Phani I want to return. Since the snake is so close, I ask why we can't go directly there instead of the long trip to the railroad station. Although he explains why we can't do it that way, I don't understand. He gives me his name and number, but I can find him out the back gate.

In retrospect, I think they did something to the second snake so it couldn't open its mouth. Not only did it not strike, but it never even stuck out its tongue. That is not normal. When I think about its eyes, I think it was afraid and confused. It didn't understand. Poor thing.

I can't help myself - - I have to go back and see it again. I am hooked. The guy didn't get the snake just for me. It's his snake, and there is nothing I can do about that. But, I need to see it again and hold it in my hands.

At Evening Meeting, during the dancing part, I am still high from my cobra event. At the end of one song, when everyone raises their arms and yells "Osho," I feel so excited over my adventure that I can't help myself and I raise my arms high in the air and shout, "Cobra!" Osho won't mind.

Since I arrived, the series of Osho talks have been from The Rebel. And, being a rebel myself, I have mostly enjoyed them. Tonight, they changed it to a new series entitled, This, This, A Thousand Times This. They are from after Osho returned from America - - poisoned. He looked pale, sounded weak, and talked slower than normal. I could almost feel his pain. His talk sounded angry, bitter, and difficult to listen to. Of course, who could blame him - - they poisoned him! But, I'm not comfortable with it and I don't want to hear it. I feel such bad vibes from it; I don't want to be here, even more than usual.

After he talked a while, he introduced a meditation technique called Mystic Rose. Now, it is a popular therapy at the ashram. They offer Mystic Rose sessions that last three weeks. This was the beginning of it. He described it, asked someone to bang the drum, and it began. I thought he was only going to talk about it, when suddenly he says, "Let's start laughing now." Everyone in the auditorium, except me, doubles over with laughter. On and on just laugh, laugh, laugh.

Five minutes later, the drum sounds again, and everybody switches immediately to tears - - like the workshop I went to last week. People cry and sob all around me. I know it isn't fake because I am empathic and can feel the sorrow in the room. That's something I don't expect. Mentally, I surround myself with white light so it won't affect me.

When the drum sounds again for silence, I hear sniffles all around me from people trying to contain their tears. One guy abruptly opens the door and before it closes after him, I hear him sobbing loudly outside.

After the silence, the drum beats again, and everyone lies down on the floor for let-go. Shortly after that, it ends, thankfully.

Day Twenty-three – Breaking Rules

Today is another office cleaning day. But, I am smart today. Since I checked my email last night at the office, I don't need to go in early. So I set my alarm for eight o'clock, and after meditating, I don't manage to drag myself out of bed until almost nine. I run into Chandra in the bathroom. That seldom happens in the morning, because I have usually left already when she gets up. When she sees me, she says something about being late and having to clean.

I say, "You're late, too!"

She says, "Yes, but I'm thinking in my head of cleaning."

"So am I," I respond.

I don't arrive at work until nine fifteen. What bliss that is. Immediately on my arrival, I go to the cleaning area to get a dust rag. When I run into Sakra there, I smile and say good morning. He says, "Good morning, Parvati!" If he realizes that I just came in, he doesn't show it. No one says anything. My continued lateness Sunday mornings will follow today's success.

I am slowly finding out which rules I can break. The last three days I have left for lunch five minutes early. It enables me to get to the Meera restaurant before the crowd hits and makes for a much more pleasurable lunchtime for me. I will continue leaving that early. A little here and a little there, and it makes me feel good that I am getting one over on them. Not a big deal, but I still feel like I give more than I get. Losing that other three hours a week still bothers me, too.

I have to admit, reluctantly, but I will admit it - - most of the people here enjoy working seven days a week. However, there are a handful that have such bad attitudes, that I can't help thinking, "These people really need some time off!"

I still have no DVDs to work on this morning. When I see Nalini in the hallway, I put on my best obsequious mask and in my most groveling fashion ask about the DVDs. It must have worked because she smiles at me and brings me the new DVDs. You have to know how to handle these people!

Last Saturday it began, and I see it more today. For the last two Saturdays, Chandra has asked me to help her get the cleaning stuff ready for Sunday. When I do it, I realize I am more comfortable with everything in the office.

It's like when you start a new job. At first, you are so conscious of everything, like walking down a hallway, and hearing your pants brush one leg against the other, or you hear your footsteps on the linoleum, or you're aware of someone saying hello to you. Then, you get used to everything, and all that awareness fades into the comfortableness of familiarity. I'm close to that now.

I may not fit in here, but if you take away the maroon robes, the working seven days a week, and the other fruitcake ideas, I still work in an office like any other office anywhere else in the world.

I'm not as brave as yesterday's cobra event makes me sound. After researching on the Internet today, I realize what had happened. They had sewn the snake's mouth closed to keep it from biting. How sad is that? It breaks my heart, and yet something draws me back there. I must go back, hold that cobra, and put it around my neck. I can't help myself.

Tonight at Evening Meeting, I catch Andre and ask him about the coaching session. He hugs me when he sees me! He's busy until after New Years and doesn't mind waiting. Perhaps my fears of getting the extra three hours at this coaching session are unfounded. I hope so.

Evening Meeting is different again tonight. It used to be after the discourse, they would turn off the video and Osho would continue on audio. Thankfully, there is no Mystic Rose meditation tonight. Instead, after the discourse, Osho tells jokes while still on video. Then he starts us on gibberish. While it is going on, he waves his arms in the air for everybody to continue. He looks like he is conducting an orchestra.

After the gibberish comes the lying down part. At the end of the lying down part, I start putting my back-jack together for my imminent departure. Usually, after he has us sit up, it's time to leave. So I watch, and after a couple other people leave, I get up and leave, too. Inside, I can hear everyone else clapping their hands. They did that yesterday, also. It must not have lasted too much longer, though. I'm not home five minutes when I see other people in the courtyard below.

Day Twenty-four – Indian Amusement Park

The day I have been dreading, arrived - - I received my "floating job" today. I ask her if I have to, and she says that it's part of the program. Since I did sign up for the program, I have to do it. I only have four hours a day free - - and an hour of that is for my personal meditation. Now, I have lost three hours a week of my precious time.

The job is not a bad one. They call it "guest watching." I will be at one of the entrance gates checking the passes of everyone who wants to enter. I'm hoping for the back gate, because I think if I'm back there, I can bring a book and at least feel productive. Although, either of the front gates could be good, because a lot goes on out there that might be engrossing. What I have been dreading has happened, and it's not so bad. I start Thursday. This doesn't prevent me from getting out of other ashram activities as much as I can, though.

When I tell Chandra, she says, "Dress warmly and be sure that you have a shawl to put over your face."

I ask, "A shawl? Why?"

She says, "The pollution is severe at night and in the morning, and you MUST breathe through a shawl!" Oh great, just what I needed to hear.

After work, I leave the ashram for some shopping. As I walk down the street heading toward a grocery store, I see the camel. This one is going my way, so I don't have to walk as far. I talk him down to fifty rupees. That's not much more than a dollar. To ride a camel! In India! Down a main street with cars whizzing by!

The camel has a Hindi name that I don't understand. He has a big plastic sheet advertising something over both sides of his saddle - - a walking billboard. As we walk, the camel guy hands out leaflets to people on the street. Almost everyone takes one. After we walk a while, the camel drops me off and I continue down the street.

Here, it is like living in an amusement park. You never know what ride will turn up on your path next. Today, it is a camel. Who knows what tomorrow will bring? I will never take this for granted.

I'm hoping that I get to the "cobra ride" again soon. That will take some talking, because last time I paid more than I should have, and I don't want to pay that every time. The rickshaw driver will be resistant, but I will try. I need to go back and hold the cobra in my hands.

After I get off the camel, I find the grocery stores that Prana told me about. They are not like I had imagined. They are tiny little places, as big as a medium sized bathroom. Outside, I see a movable rack filled with potato chips and other snack-type items. Inside, I see shelves from floor to ceiling packed with food, toothpaste, shampoo, aspirin, candy, bottled water, and soda pop. I buy two bags of pretzels and a candy bar. The snacks are cheap, but the candy bar costs more than I think it should.

After buying my snacks, I search for the bookstore that Prana told me about. With the help of a merchant that I almost bought something from last week, I find it. These Indian people are so kind and considerate. At the bookstore, I buy a Hindi-English dictionary and a book on birds of Pune.

Prana had told me about a Ganesh Temple on a corner near here, but I see it for the first time today. Right before I get there, as I am about to take a picture, a man kneels on the stairs in front of it and touches his head to the top step. Before he leaves, he gives it a namaste. I should have taken a picture of that, but I am too busy enjoying the moment.

Tired from the long walk, I start back to the ashram. When I pass the corner, I decide to stop for a minute to see Gowri and Manik. Gowri is there as usual, and it is always good to see her. I talk to her for a short time and then continue walking to where Manik usually is.

When I get to his spot, it is his brother, Tanul, and not Manik. Somehow, my new dictionary comes up in conversation. Tanul looks through it and sits there with me for a half hour helping me with pronunciations. He can read English! Hindi is a different alphabet from ours. I am so impressed! I ask how much for an amethyst necklace that I see in his display. He says he has a much better one at the shop. Then he immediately goes back to the Hindi book.

His whole family is so delightful. I love these people. Finally, I have to break away, so I have enough time to do my meditation before Evening Meeting.

On my way back to the ashram, I stop to say good-bye to Gowri. She asks, "When are you coming back?"

"Three or four days," I say.

"I might have my surgery then," she says. Then she starts in on how much it costs. I wonder if she is pushing me with this. I'm not going to bring it up again, but I would like to try Reiki on her.

From my room and throughout most of the ashram, I can hear a constant and pervasive electronic beeping noise. I usually hear it when there are no other sounds. There is music now, and I can't hear it at all. When it's quiet, it's always in the background. I wonder if it's a deliberate attempt to hypnotize me. If I come back from India wearing maroon and spouting some of this nonsense, please hit me in the head so I can come to my senses! Don't take any chances!

Sometimes I wonder if there are microphones or cameras in the rooms. Then, I realize there is no need to watch these people. They are all like little sheep following the leader wherever he goes. They will always do what is asked of them, because that's what they do. I am in the minority here. Although I don't mind, I do get a little paranoid at times! I wouldn't mind having a friend who I could talk to about it.

At midnight, I hear fireworks. Although I hoped I could see them from my room, I can't. I go outside and enjoy the end of them for five or ten minutes. There are some beautiful displays. By Buddha Grove, I run into an Indian man that I know. He wants me to stay there, but I only want to go back to my room. I manage to go to sleep shortly after 12:30 despite some background music that plays. Ah, peaceful slumber.

Day Twenty-five – Choicelessness

This is the New Year and I am in India! Sometimes it doesn't seem possible, but here I am. Although I am on the other side of the world, we are all connected and all under the same sun and the same moon. It is now a new year for all of us.

This morning, I run into Chandra in the bathroom. She has never married. She says that when she meets a guy she likes, she goes with him, and guys don't like that. It's the Osho philosophy. It's not mine. That's one reason I don't fit in here.

On the way to work, I run into a woman from my Fast-Track group. Jiadore was my partner for the statue and awareness activities. She hugs me and wishes me Happy New Year. That is a good beginning to my day.

I arrive at work today at one minute before nine. No one has unlocked the door, and the lights are still off. My boss is in my office (a room with four people in it) talking to the woman across from me. He turns and walks by me without acknowledging me at all. Rules are different here. Common courtesies are often missing. Ignoring someone in the same office as you is not cultural. It's plain weird is what it is. It fits in with the atmosphere of this place, though.

Today when I go to lunch, I see these living "statues." Women painted gold or silver from head to toe, stand like statues until someone comes by. They stay in one position until someone rings the bell or the tingshas (meditation bells) placed in front of the living statues. Then they change positions. I'd take a picture if it weren't forbidden inside the ashram.

Sometimes when I walk among these maroon clad people, I feel so stupid! It all feels so silly I want to break out laughing. This must be an insane asylum or something. These people wearing maroon and doing exactly what they're told. Little lemmings - - or sheep. Here I am, pretending to be one of them.

There are more people at the ashram now. It's getting to be tourist season. Thankfully, many more are smiling. I'm no longer the only one with a pleasant look on my face.

I surf most of the day away, mostly surfing dating sites. Looking at all those men is like being in a candy store. However, I know the reality is most of them are not for me. They either live in cities or want someone much younger. I will join one of these sites soon. Maybe I'll find someone there, maybe I won't. But, I know I'll find someone when I'm meant to find him. And, I can accept that.

When I look at some of my old photos on my computer, they make me feel nostalgic. The feeling makes me wonder if I can leave the island that I have called home for so long now. I do love it there, and there is so much to love about it. Although, the tourists I could do without. Without the forest house to retreat into, the island won't be the same. I'm sure there are other places around that would be as secluded. Who knows where my future lies?

Today in the Osho literature, I read where he talked about choicelessness. That sounds the same as embracing uncertainty. I have no idea what I will be doing when I leave here. I don't need to have a plan. I'll wait and see where existence leads me.

Tonight, I may have discovered a possible way to get out of Evening Meetings. I'm formulating my plan now, and it will take a few days to set up.

Day Twenty-six – Missionaries of the Woo-woo

Today, I find out that I'm getting a new, temporary job. Chandra calls me into her area this morning. She tells me that she is taking a one-week meditation facilitator training, and that I will replace her while she's out. It should be a good change and a good experience. It is only for one week.

Chandra hands me a job responsibility document and starts going over everything with me. Trouble is, she is an awful teacher. She doesn't start at the beginning; she expects me to know information that is unfamiliar to me. When I question her about something alien to me and specific to the ashram, she responds, "Of course!" She acts like it is something simple that I should have already known. It would make me feel bad if I didn't recognize her ineptitude. Also, this whole place is a joke to me.

As I work with her, I realize how sarcastic and critical she is. During her explanation, I yawn. That drives her crazy, so she turns on the air conditioner to wake me up. Finally, I say, "Can you turn that off? I'm freezing."

Chandra says, "Well, you know it's on all the time in March."

I say, "March is hot!" Duh! Sometimes I wonder if I'm going to last another week in all this craziness, let alone another two months.

Chandra does explain something for me today during her poor teaching session. She says something about them "doing Osho's work." That is the secret. That is why she and the others have no misgivings about working seven days a week. These people are like maroon garbed missionaries. They are spreading the word. They are missionaries of the woo-woo.

Tonight while I wait to go into Evening Meeting, I watch an interesting event. There is a forty-foot walkway you need to walk across to get to the pyramid. This man starts walking down the walkway, stops halfway, squeezes out a loud fart, and then continues walking toward the pyramid. The rules are different here.

I've completed my plan how to get out of Evening Meeting. Now I have to see if my plan is possible. I don't know if they will catch me at this or not, or if I can get back into the ashram. During Evening Meeting, the ashram locks all the outside access gates. Also, if I know someone at the gate, then I can't do it, either. Today, I know the guy at the gate. I'll see what happens. I need to get out of it, though. This mandatory attendance annoys me.

74

Day Twenty-seven – Evening Meeting and Volleyball

Sporadically throughout the day, I set my regular job aside and learn pieces of the new job. With the learning comes more condescending lessons from Chandra. I start fighting her on some issues, today, though. I am not going to put up with her abusive behavior. I'm not some flunky that she can push around, and I won't allow her to treat me like that.

Chandra teaches me about the emails that I have to send out. She says, "We always address our emails, 'Beloved'." I laugh. What else can I do? It's stupid!

She says, "Parvati, why are you laughing? That hurts me."

I say, "I don't even know this person. How could I love him?"

She looks down dejectedly and says, "Address it however you want."

Something comes up today about cats because someone in the office has a cat, and people come to her with cat problems.

I say to Prana, "So you can have cats here."

She says, "No, you can't. Girl, you have to learn not to ask permission. Just do it and get forgiveness later. That's the way it works here." All right, then. Someone else told me that was Osho's idea. You don't ask permission because they can say no. Just do it. I can live with this.

I've mentioned before the coughing restrictions while in Evening Meeting. The other night as I sat close to the door, someone would creep through the sitting throng and open the door. I looked out to see where they were going. Two steps away from the door, they would begin coughing. How they held it while stepping through the crowd and then cough uncontrollably outside is beyond me. It happened with several different people, too.

My first year in college, I needed to take a physical education class. Since I was late signing up for class, my only choice was volleyball. Playing volleyball three times a week for an entire semester was more than I could handle. Every day, I would go into the gym area, change into my gym clothes, and go outside while they took roll call. Then I would go back inside, dress in my regular clothes, and leave. Although I only played one game of volleyball the entire term, I received a "B" in the class.

There are a hundred of us in the Residential Program that have to sign in every night for Evening Meeting. Tonight, I walk over to the auditorium earlier than usual, watch the bats for a while, and walk across the walkway and up the stairs. Then, I put my shoes in the rack by the door, wait while someone marks my name off the list, and I walk into the auditorium.

After speaking to Dilasa for a minute, I sit on a chair at the left side of the auditorium. I wait for less than two minutes when a rush of people come through the door. Then I start coughing and slip out the door past the people coming in. Discreetly, and coughing all the while, I make it over to my shoes on the rack. There are several people between me and the person who watches the door. So I hurriedly put my shoes on, walking on the tongues, and slip down the backstairs. When I get to the landing, I put the shoes on correctly and pull my shawl over my head partially covering my face.

I walk out the door and down the stairs. When I get to the Meera eating area, I see Prana! Luckily, I catch myself before I make eye contact and acknowledge her. I hope that she doesn't realize it is me. Then I go through the gate, and as I wait for cars to go by, I see Sakra waiting to cross the street from the other side! I hope he doesn't see me. I don't know if I can keep up with all this intrigue anymore. I'll find out tomorrow if they caught me.

My floating job at the pyramid gate starts tonight. It is across the street from the back gate, which leads to the main part of the ashram. On my way there, I decide that I will have a great time tonight. So, I sit at my appointed post and watch as locals go by on motorcycles, bicycles, or walking. I look around admiring all the foliage around me. As I am thoroughly enjoying myself, I look at my watch. Seven minutes after nine. Ah oh. After what feels like an interminably long time, I look at my watch again. Nine twenty-two. It's going to be a long night. At nine-thirty, tiredness sweeps over me and I start getting cold; and I still have two and a half hours to go.

As the course of the evening wears on, there are many bright moments. A woman from my Fast-Track group stops by and talks to me while she waits for someone to pick her up. She tells me about her experiences at the back gate, when she caught people trying to sneak in.

I wonder if I'd make the effort to catch them. Sometimes, the people flash their cards so fast, it's hard to see the date on it. I might have seen an occasional person whose date had expired, but I'm not sure. Where I sit, I can barely see the cards they show me, anyway. It is mostly dark.

After she leaves, another woman from my group stops by and talks to me for a long time. She tells me the book that I'm reading is against the rules. You can't read while at the guard post. She also tells me about the groups she has been attending. They are similar to the one we attended together. In her groups, for two hours they sit opposite different people and ask questions like, "What is truth?" It cost nine hundred rupees to discuss truth with a stranger. It's not my thing.

Shortly after she leaves, Geet, the older Indian man at the back gate across from me, wants to take a short break. Since his post is more important than mine, I sit there. Dilasa comes by shortly after Geet leaves. Tonight, he's not too impressed with my cobra stories. He's excited that he has secured permission to clean Osho's Rolls Royce. He proudly shows me the key.

Dilasa is as close as I have to a friend here. Because he is an Osho-ite, I feel like I can't trust him. However, I trust him more than I trust anyone else around here. I've told him how I feel about some happenings here, which I probably shouldn't have. But, nothing happened to me - - so he must be trustworthy. He doesn't live or work here - - he stays down the street and hangs out at the ashram all day.

Then Geet comes back from break, Dilasa leaves, and Geet tells me to take a break. I go to the Plaza and order some hot chocolate. Since I haven't had any since I arrived here, I have a hankering for some. It cost thirty rupees.

I've never discussed how one pays for items here. No money is ever exchanged. You buy these "voucher cards" for a thousand or five hundred rupees at the main gate. Then, you use the cards to purchase meals, robes, whatever else you need at the ashram. Instead of money, they cross off the amount you spend on your voucher card. So, I give her my voucher.

She says, "No, I need a night voucher," and she shows me one. I have never seen one before. Finally, after some discussion, she marks out thirty rupees on my day voucher. This place is so weird - - night vouchers - - what is up with that?

When I return from break, Geet tells me to stay with him at his gate so we can talk. When I mention that I am trying to learn Hindi, he offers to teach me after we get off work. He also keeps hugging me, so I know what he wants! He asks about children and marriage, and I tell him I'm not looking for love right now. At least not here, but I don't tell him that part.

Geet's only been here a couple months, but he says he wants to stay for thirty years. I ask about working seven days a week, and he likes it. I ask about meditation, and he doesn't do any. When I ask why he came here, he says because of Osho. These are not my people.

After a while, I go back over to my gate and huddle into myself trying to keep warm. I'm wearing a one-piece maroon long underwear jumpsuit, plus pants on top of that, and my maroon robe on top of that. Also, I wear a maroon shawl pulled up over my head because the mosquitoes keep annoying me. Even with all these clothes, I'm still chilly. I make it through to the end. Then, I go back home and go to sleep.

Day Twenty-eight - Paranoia or Not?

Although I had set my clock for nine o'clock, I wake up before that and start to meditate. However, I keep falling back to sleep. At five minutes to nine, Chandra calls into my room as I'm finishing the end of my meditation. She keeps ragging on me to hurry, but it is ten after nine and she is still in her room! At nine thirty, I amble into work. No one says anything.

I finally meet with Andre and we have our coaching session. He asks if the workshop I had attended helped me at all. I tell him that it didn't resonate with me. Something comes up in the conversation and I tell him that I'm not a sannyasin. He asks what my definition of sannyasin is. Correcting myself, I say that I'm not an Osho sannyasin, but I am a sannyasin. Sannyasin in Sanskrit means truth seeker. I tell him that I am a meditator and a sannyasin. Anyone around here who says they are a sannyasin, means they are an Osho-sannyasin.

He asks, "Then why are you here?"

I say, "To experience it . . . ." Then, I waver between telling him the whole truth and what he wants to hear. Around here, I don't know what would happen if they knew my true thoughts. I have to protect myself.

Andre talks about the ashram as a club, and about not belonging. He says the "experiment" is scientific. Several main players around here have thrown around the word scientific. I don't buy it.

He says, "You're not giving it a chance. You're afraid of the unknown."

I say, "I'm not afraid of the unknown! I came to India!"

He says, "You have one foot in and one foot out - - because that is safe."

We talk about Evening Meetings, and he thinks I should listen differently. According to Osho, you shouldn't listen to his words as much as just be and experience them. I tell him I'll try it tonight. What I should probably do, though, is take part in the whole program - - the dancing, the gibberish, and the lying down. I'm awhile from letting that happen, though. Perhaps I need to listen to that electronic beeping sound a little while longer!

When I mention that I do my own meditation, he wants to know what it is. I tell him silent sitting. He scoffs at my meditation. Waving his hand in the air to dismiss it, he says, "Oh, no, no, no, no, no. That is not meditation." When I ask him what meditation he does, he answers

Evening Meeting and occasionally Kundalini.

Evening Meeting is not stillness. I've asked several people here if they meditate. Most of them have said that they only do Evening Meeting. Maybe I'm not enlightened enough to understand this. Then again, judging Evening Meeting as not a true meditation makes me as judgmental as they are. Watching a dead guru on video doesn't feel much like a meditation to me, though.

The weird electronic beeping that I have mentioned before - - none of the regulars around here hear it at all. Every time I ask, they say, "What beeping . . . ?" Chandra hasn't heard it either, but at least she said to tell her next time I hear it. When I stop hearing it, that's when I'll get scared!

Today, an unknown woman comes into my office and reprimands me. She says, "The cleaning crew told me that you have food in your room. That can attract ants and huge Indian cockroaches. I don't think you want those! If you get those, then we would have to fumigate the whole building."

I say, "I usually buy two apples and keep one for the next day."

She says, "If you want to do that, you have to keep it in a plastic container."

What do you call paranoia if it's real? I have one major problem with her story. The cleaners come Saturday, and today is Friday. Why would she wait a week to address something so supposedly serious? I'm trying not to assume the worst here, but this does feel suspect. I may experiment with this a little to confirm or relieve my suspicions.

While crossing the street today, I run into Phani. He says he saw me last night at the gate. He works some long hours every day of the week. The rickshaw costs him one hundred twenty rupees every day. If he takes a day off, he still has to pay one hundred twenty rupees. That's more than three dollars. It doesn't sound like much, except the average rickshaw ride is fifteen rupees. That's many rupees to cover each day. Phani is a good guy, and I like him.

I tell him I need his phone number again and ask him to write it down for me. He stops two guys walking down the street to borrow their pen. After he uses it, he says, "Thank you" to them. I say thank you in Hindi, "Shukriya." Phani, the two guys, and I all have a big laugh at that. He uses English, and I use Hindi.

Tonight at Evening Meeting is the first time I don't see any bats at all. The last couple of weeks I watched some interesting bat behavior. They landed in the trees. It was too fast and too far away to see exactly how they landed. When I saw them, though, they were hanging upside down. I expected them to sit on top of the branches like birds. I know they sleep upside down, but I didn't expect them to be like that when awake.

The first several weeks I watched them, the bats would only fly by. Lately, I have watched them playing in the wind currents like you see eagles or seagulls do. Occasionally, they'll do flying maneuvers, tilting over from side to side almost flying upside down - - Jonathan Livingston Bat! I've also watched one or two small bats flying erratically to catch mosquitoes over the water by the pyramid. They fly fast; they are here and gone again before you know it.

After the dancing, I lie down at Evening Meeting tonight and stay that way the whole time. As Andre suggested, I try to experience Osho's words instead of listening to them. It doesn't make a difference. The jokes are good, but often I can't hear the punch lines because everyone is already laughing.

Nobody mentioned me skipping out on Evening Meeting last night, so I guess I'm not caught. I might try it again tomorrow or the next day. At first, I thought to try it only on nights I have gate duty. But, if I can get away with it, I might do it more often. I enjoy feeling like I'm getting away with something, and the luxury of the extra time.

Day Twenty-nine – Indian Friends

During our lessons this morning, Chandra says something about break time. Break time? What's that? No one ever mentioned break time to me. Prana, who sits across from me, talks about teatime and disappears around eleven o'clock. She has been here forever, though, and does her own thing, anyway. Of course, like a good Osho-ite, she mostly does what she's supposed to.

I have been going out at eleven o'clock every day and feeling good about getting away with something. That is always more fun. Now, I find out that it was my right to take that time. No one ever bothered telling me. My first few weeks here, I spent glued to that chair for four hours. That's a little rude. Another reminder that this is a different place with different rules.

While sitting in front of the computer, I find a spider crawling on my monitor. It is that black, jumping kind like I found in my bathroom last week. I say, "Prana, do you have anything I can catch it with?"

She gives me a cup and says, "They don't live outside. It won't know what to do out there."

I catch it in the glass and put it outside. I think it will figure out what to do. Once back inside, I ask Prana, "Do you want me to rinse out the glass?

She says, "No, I live here. I'm used to this place."

This morning I meet a woman named Revatii. She has worked here the longest, has here own private office, and is catered to. According to Chandra, she has as much power as Sakra. My guess is that she has more. Revatii asks me about "putting something up," so I ask, "What is putting up?" She laughs like it is obvious. It involves copying articles and putting them up on a bulletin board in the main part of the ashram. Yeah, obvious. Being around her reminds me of an incident from my teenage years. I've never told anyone about this.

When I was sixteen years old, my mother had wrangled a job for me at a local religious establishment. It was close to our house, and I could walk to it. It was a perfect first job for me. My job was to use one of those old-fashioned switchboards where you plug and unplug each extension. I learned fast and liked it. The people I worked with were friendly.

On my second or third day, a woman called to speak to a certain clergyman. I asked who was calling. It was my job to ask who was calling. After becoming furious with me, she told me who she was and I connected her.

The next day they fired me. The nasty woman's husband, the clergyman, was dying of cancer. I had no idea. My job ended abruptly, and I felt like I was fired in disgrace. Intellectually, I realized what had happened. Although, how intellectual can a vulnerable sixteen-year-old be? It bothered me. Judging that I've never told anyone about this, I felt bad and a little ashamed.

This woman, Revatii, gives me the feeling she could be vindictive like that. That's what brought up this long ago memory. I will try to avoid her as much as I can.

There are several facets of my new job that I haven't learned yet. Chandra kept saying, "I'll show you Saturday or Sunday." Now it's Saturday afternoon, and there are still many gaps. She will be unavailable once I start. If I have any questions, I'm on my own.

As bad a time as Chandra has given me as she teaches me the details of this job, it feels kind compared with how she treats the moving crew today. She called them over to move some furniture around upstairs. It is almost embarrassing the way she treats the guy, ordering him around, no please, no thank you, nothing. I'm thankful she's not like that with me.

Without asking anyone, I leave work almost ten minutes early. Since I need to go outside the gates, I want the extra time so I can get back early. Hurrying home, I change into my jeans and maroon long sleeve shirt and go through the back gate. I find Phani and ask if he will take me to German Bakery for ten rupees. He does, but he's not happy about it. Usually I walk, but I feel tired from not getting enough sleep again the last two nights. Also, I don't want to see Gowri, Manik, or Tanul on my way there. I need to get my errands completed before I visit with anyone.

I stop at the Ayurvedic store that someone told me about. They don't have valerian. So, I walk around the front of the building and go into the pharmacy. They have valerian, which will help me sleep at night. It is something that I regretfully neglected to bring with me. Thank goodness, they carry it here. I didn't bring enough milk thistle, either, but I can do some research and find the Ayurvedic equivalent. While I'm at the pharmacy, I also buy an Indian herb called triphala. It is only two dollars, and I can use it sometime later. I can't resist a bargain.

After cashing a traveler's check from the money exchanger behind German Bakery, I walk next door to a travel agency where I buy a Pune street map. I have wanted one for a while now. It should give me the

freedom to go other places. At least I'll know how far they are and how to
get there.

When I come out of German Bakery area, Manik waves to me while I wait to cross the street. I'm getting better at crossing streets now. It's easier by German Bakery because there is a median. I can comfortably go halfway and then wait for the traffic on the other side to stop. That is the way you should do it even when there is no median. With cars, rickshaws, and motorcycles all coming straight at me, it scares me when I'm standing in the middle of the street with no protection.

I get there and Manik shakes my hand and gives me his chair. While I talk to Manik, Tanul comes over to say hello and he shakes my hand. He only stays for a few minutes, because he has to take care of his father's shop.

I have a long talk with Manik. He has six brothers and two sisters. Manik is the youngest at twenty years old, and his brother, Tanul, is twenty-eight. Although Manik still lives at home, he has been supporting himself selling gemstones since he was ten years old!

I tell him all about the ashram, Sam, and Sheba. Showing him the pictures in my camera, I tell him about my cobra experiences. He offers to take me in a car to the snake park! Wow, I can't believe that! It is too far away for a rickshaw, because that's too scary. And, I have been considering calling the guy who picked me up at the airport to see how much it would cost to drive out there. If you're wondering if I would go with Manik, oh yeah! I didn't come to India to be fearful; I came here to experience life.

He also tells me that he had seen me down the street and called out my name, but I didn't hear him. I explain that I wouldn't expect anyone here in a car to know me!

Then, I walk over to visit with Gowri. Every time I see her, she mentions what's wrong with her eyes and how much it will cost to fix them. When I offer to give her Reiki, she says she doesn't want it. I'm beginning to think she is trying to ask me for money.

But, I think she honestly likes me, too. Some women stop to buy something, and Gowri tells them that I'm trying to learn Hindi. They don't look like locals - - I thought they were from Europe somewhere. I stand up to talk to them in English, and Gowri sits down and takes my hand!

Here is another point about culture. You often see women and women, and men and men holding hands or with their arms intertwined with each other. Even fifteen-year-old boys will walk down the street arm

in arm. Can you imagine that in America? I don't think so! It's common here.

Leaving Gowri, I start walking toward the corner and home. A man selling little tom-tom drums stops me. He says they cost four hundred rupees. Since I'm not that interested, I offer him one hundred rupees. When he says three hundred fifty rupees, I walk away. But, he keeps coming after me. He says, "Okay, how much?" I say, "One hundred rupees," and he gives me the drum!

I say, "I can't believe you're giving it to me for one hundred rupees."

He says, "Business is bad."

Carrying the drum, I walk to the corner and see a camel across the street. I wait for him to cross. Who can turn down a camel ride when you're in India? The camel man wants one hundred rupees and I say, "No, I've already ridden a camel, only fifty rupees." When I start walking away, he says he'll take the fifty. Then he tries to get the camel down on its knees, and it doesn't want to go down on its knees. It keeps straining at the halter and making a braying sound.

It feels like a warning; I think that I shouldn't ride this camel. But, the poor camel has so much trouble getting to its knees, it's too late to say no. Fate intervenes. A policeman on a motorcycle tells the man to take the camel away and tells me not to ride the camel. I feel bad for the poor camel that had eventually gotten down on its knees although it didn't want to. So, I follow the guy and give him ten rupees. I'm a sucker I know, but I can't help it.

Then I haggle with the guy on the corner and buy some small items from him for a couple dollars. I'm getting good at bargaining with these guys. It's fun, too. If you're willing to walk away, and I usually am, then you can get good deals.

On my way to Evening Meeting, I go in the back door so I can put my shoes at that end of the pyramid. After I check in with the person at the door, I sit at the far end on the floor against the wall. Two minutes later, I fake a cough, stand up, walk past the woman at the door, and walk to my shoes. I hurry and put them on like I did last time, and walk down the stairs. At the landing, I put the shoes on properly, pull my shawl up over my head and across my face, and walk back to the main gate.

I don't like the way the guy at the gate looks at me, but he isn't someone that I know. I've seen him before, but he doesn't know me. I hope that I will get away with it again. It does scare me, though. I don't know what will happen if they catch me. This isn't something I can do often. Tomorrow, I may try to bring my iPod with me.

Day Thirty - Learning

When I arrive at work this morning, I find an Osho calendar on my desk. I ask Prana, and she doesn't know. Than I ask Chandra. She acts like she put it there. So, I stop asking. Then Surabi comes in and tells me she gave it to me because the calendar wanted to go there. I love the calendar. Although I had wanted one, they sell it packaged with a book that I didn't want. Surabi and I have had a couple little bonding incidents, but I don't feel close to her. She is too much into this place.

This morning, as Chandra teaches me another procedure, she again starts from the middle instead of the beginning. When I ask a question, she says, "You need to write it down."

Raising my voice, I say, "I don't need to write it down. I need you to start at the beginning."

Before this, I had told her that I had no memory and had to write everything down. Sam always told me that I tell people too much. It is difficult to get away from my policy of absolute honesty. Another lesson learned?

During this incident, I fight her on this until she admits she didn't start from the beginning. I must have shocked the people around me - - quiet little Parvati standing up for herself.

On and off all day, Chandra and I get into it. At one point, I tell her not to treat me like a stupid child, because I have a genius level IQ. Sometime later, I ask where the scissors are. She says, "You're a genius, you figure it out." I walk away, and she comes after me.

She says, "I don't like your attitude."

I say, "I don't like yours, either."

Our disagreements heal later in the day when I stay over to help her with some of her work. Sakra asked her to come in every day after her meditation training. I tell her she needs to take care of herself.

Prana and I talk about me reading so many of Osho's discourses, and how I can now quote him better than other people who live here. She thinks I was chosen for this position. I agree. Someone on the "other side" wanted me to have this job; and I think Osho had some say in it, too. I'm sure that is sacrilegious and scandalous to say, but I believe it is true.

Dilasa and I have a long talk. He agrees with me that most of the people here are robots - - at least the major players. He also uses the word "fundamentalist," which I agree with. Osho fundamentalist - - an odd combination.

Dilasa tells me that even with all the issues, I can still learn here.

And, I am. I have learned so much about myself, already. I have achieved so much more flexibility. And I am learning not to make hasty judgments.

Toward the end of Evening Meeting every night, Osho says, "Okay, Maneesha." That was always the signal that you could leave. With the new program, after the Maneesha part, Osho starts clapping and everyone in the auditorium joins him. I've been trying to leave right at the "okay" part, but tonight someone catches me. Literally. A fat Osho-ite sitting by the door grabs my robe and tells me to sit! When the clapping stops momentarily, I stand up to leave. He again tells me to sit! The crowd resumes clapping for a few more minutes. This controlling behavior annoys me.

When I leave Evening Meeting, though, I get a gift. It is a clear enough night for me to see Orion again. This is only the second time I've seen it since I've been here. We are all under the same sky.

A friend of mine wrote to me saying, " . . . you pay to live there . . . you have to buy your own food . . . and you work for them every day free . . . you are a slave." She's right. Sometimes I feel like a slave, too. Luckily, I have my friends outside the gates to sustain me. Not to mention the cobras!

Day Thirty-one - Gibberish

Today is the first day of my receptionist/administrative assistant job. So far, it hasn't been too bad. Nobody knows who I am, so they don't give me work that they would have given to Chandra. Later in the week after they see me here every day, I imagine I will have a ton more to do. I hope the rest of the week will go as smoothly. The job feels good so far. It is something that I'm good at and mostly like. However, it is also something that is not good for me and usually develops into something I hate. A job like this is why I came to India!

I've mentioned before about how you have to show your pass at all the entrance gates to the resort. Some gate people act as though you are invisible. They give no nod of the head, or anything else to let you know you can enter. Some of them will raise their eyebrows or blink their eyes - - any acknowledgment is welcome. When I did the gate last week, I tried to thank every person who showed me their card. Whether they were American or English or Danish or Japanese or Indian, I thanked them all in Hindi. It is India, after all!

When I thank, in Hindi, the locals who work at the resort, they laugh or smile, and I think they appreciate it, too. They correct my pronunciation and teach me new words. Few people here learn the language. Some people in America demand that everyone speak English. Yet, when they go to another country, they don't bother to learn the native language. I'm trying not to be that arrogant; I want to learn as much Hindi as I can. I thought I was ahead of the game because I knew so many words in Sanskrit. But, nobody uses Sanskrit here. That surprised me.

Dilasa and I have another long talk today. I want to know how to get out of Evening Meetings. He says there are hundreds of ways. Unfortunately, since I won't lie, there aren't many choices. And, it isn't only the lying; it is lying about your health, which I won't do.

The only real suggestion is not to go for a while and hope they don't look at the computer sheets until the end of the month. It is too early for me to take a risk like that. I'll probably fake the cough one or two nights a week, and then not go at all on my gate night. If they speak to me about it, I'll say what Dilasa suggested - - that my meditation is important to me; and I don't have time on those nights. I've also decided, "If I can't beat 'em, I might as well join 'em!" Perhaps I've been listening to that beeping for too long.

Tonight, I decide to try something different. While everyone dances, I do yoga. First I do lying down poses, then sitting up poses, then standing poses, and finally I do several sets of Sun Salutations. I place myself behind a big pillar in the back, and nobody says a word to me.

After the discourse, during gibberish, I do it. Yes, I participated in the whole gibberish piece. During gibberish, everyone uses hand gestures, so I let my hands go wild, as well. I liked it. I tried it for thirty seconds or a minute back home and thought it was effective at keeping thoughts at bay. Tonight, though, I notice some thoughts floating around in the background. Altogether, though, it is a good experience and I will probably do it again.

After gibberish, I even do the lying down part of the program. However, I skip the clapping and screaming "Osho!" That is going too far for me. I've had enough.

After Evening Meeting, I normally retreat to my room and stay there, or else work on the computer. But, another new decision: I need to experience this place to get the most out of it. Starting tonight, I will venture out at night and see what is going on out there. Time to move on and try something different.

Tonight is a good night to start. They have arts and crafts in the plaza area. I work on a painting for a long time, not realizing that they also offer collage and jewelry making. Both of those would have been more enjoyable than the painting. But, I have a good time and much fun.

Day Thirty-two – Shopping Center

Today is a rotten and stressful day at work. I'm glad this is only one week. I didn't come to India for stressful work. I came to India to see cobras!

The stress feels so bad right now, I can't think. I have another encounter with Revatii, and it is like the first one only worse. She also teaches worse than Chandra. Chandra is my peer, and I can laugh it off and fight back. With Revatii, she wields power like a gang member wields a knife. She is dangerous.

Stress like this is why I came to India! This stress isn't the kind that goes away. It slowly fades, but hides away in your body to come back another time when you don't expect it. The stress I feel when I ride a rickshaw in traffic is momentary. It disappears like smoke in the wind after the ride is over. The stress I feel now, I don't need. An hour of meditation a day is not enough to combat this work-a-day stress.

If I'm honest, part of the reason Revatii bothers me is that she makes me feel like an idiot. That's not the honest part, though. In the past, I have treated people like she does. She is smart, like I am. She expects everyone to "get it" as fast as she does. That doesn't leave any room for individuality.

I hope that I'm over treating people like that. Maybe this issue is a reminder that I need to be aware of my tendency to do that. My mother used to say, "It's easy, if you know how." That is so true, and I need to respect it.

When I talk to Dilasa in the afternoon, he says, "I'm going to play therapist. We are here to learn lessons. Maybe there is something in your encounter with Revatii that you need to learn."

I say, "What I need to learn is that I never want to be in a position like this again." Truthfully, I never want another job - - but, I don't tell him that.

After work, I want to go to a shopping place that Kanti told me about. Unfortunately, I can't remember the name of it and I can't explain to the rickshaw driver how to get there. He drops me at German Bakery. The big street that I have to cross has a light, so it doesn't worry me. Big mistake. Lights don't make it any easier to cross here. This intersection not only has a light, but also has a policeman directing traffic.

I stand there five minutes trying to figure out a way across. A woman starts crossing, and I curse myself for not following her. But, she isn't paying attention. She goes against the light and strands herself in the middle of heavy traffic. Thankfully, I didn't follow her.

Finally, I decide to walk down the street, instead of across it. Traffic clears in the middle of the block, and I cross easily where there is a median.

When I get across the street, I see many stores there: a small grocery store, a digital camera store, a photo place that looks like it develops film, and a couple others. When I turn around to walk back down the block toward the corner, I see a cool contraption sitting on a street cart. I don't know what it is, so I ask a couple people on the street. They patiently explain it to me. I love these friendly people.

One man feeds raw sugar cane into the press part of the machine. It looks like one of those old fashioned washing machines where the clothes squeeze between two rolling bars. Another man walks around the cart, pushing a horizontal pole as he goes. The sugar cane goes between the rolling bars and comes out as fresh sugar cane water. People on the street buy glassfuls.

After watching the sugar cane machine, I continue down the street and turn at the place where I tried to cross earlier. I find myself on a narrow, one-way street with apartment buildings on the side. It doesn't look like a place to find a shopping center. So I ask some people on the street, and they assure me it is there. They say to keep going. On my way, I pass a man in a small stall at the side of the road. It looks like he is making or repairing purses with a sewing machine.

The narrow street ends at a major street, and there is Pune Central! I walk to the middle of the block where I can cross the street without much trouble.

It is a large, exclusive department store spread out on three floors. The prices are high even for America - - for India, they're outrageous. I walk around and find myself in the luggage department. A friend told me that I could buy luggage cheap in India. This store is too expensive for cheap luggage.

About to leave the luggage department, I thank the guys in Hindi. That gets them all excited. So, I give them my whole Hindi vocabulary. One of them shakes my hand! He says, "It helps us if you speak Hindi."

I say, "It helps me if I speak Hindi!" When I bid them "Namaste," they say, "Salaam." When I repeat it, they help me with my pronunciation. Salaam is the Muslim greeting, instead of namaste.

There is an ice cream place with bright colors and flavors, but I'm not sure if it is all right to eat. I pass it by and take the escalator up to the floor with the grocery store.

As I walk in, I stop at the nuts counter and ask if they have any packaged mixed nuts. The man points to a container and says, "These are better than packaged because you can taste them and see that they are fresher." He opens the container, sticks in his hand and pulls out a handful of nuts, offering them to me. When I say no, he continues saying how fresh they are.

As I walk away, I say, "No thank you."

He says, "I don't think I've convinced you that they are fresher." I laugh and agree!

This store has many more products compared with the little grocery stores that I was in before. I choose a couple packages of crackers and a small package of cookies. They also have many western cereals including the sugared kids' varieties. The store has fresh produce, but someone told me not to eat any. So, I only eat produce at the ashram, where I know it is safe.

When I finish looking around, I take my crackers and cookies to the checkout counter. My items total sixty-two rupees. I didn't even know rupees came in ones. While I pay the cashier, another man comes over and puts everything in a plastic bag. He doesn't ask "paper or plastic." Then, he puts one of those hard plastic ties on the top and hands it to me.

When I leave, it is late and I don't want to walk. Approaching a rickshaw driver, I ask him how much to the Osho Ashram. He says, "Thirty rupees," so I tell him I'll walk. He asks how much I will pay and I say twenty rupees. Five minutes later, I'm home. I understand this rickshaw business now! Once I made the move to ride in one, I knew it would be easy after that. The rides don't scare me as much now, and they give me more freedom.

I leave early for Evening Meeting. Halfway there, I realize I left my identification card with my camera. After I retrieve my card, it's still early enough for me to attempt my Evening Meeting escape.

When I get close to the auditorium, I see Prana sitting and waiting in the eating area while people file by her. I don't know what she is waiting for, but I want to remember that she is there. After walking up the backstairs, I leave my shoes in the rack and sign in. I enter the auditorium, walk over to the left side, and sit on the floor. Less than two minutes later, I start my gentle coughing routine. Standing up, I hurry out, cough, put on my shoes, cough, walk down the stairs, tie the laces, put my shawl over my head, and walk rapidly back to the gate.

The gate guy allows me in with no problem. I recognize him, but he doesn't say anything. The problem is the more people I get to know and the less anonymous I become, the more difficult this will be.

Quickly, I walk home taking the back route by the laundry. Unfortunately, I run into several gentlemen outside my building. It's almost dark, and I think they are all hired Indians, but I see one or two Osho-ites dressed in maroon. As I walk by, I think I hear one say, "Hi Parvati." I hesitate for a second, but I don't stop and don't respond. I hope this isn't the incident that gets me busted!

Before I go out at night, I always leave a dim light on in my room, because I don't like coming home to a dark room. Tonight, I almost forgot. Luckily, I didn't because I would have had to sit here in the dark the whole time Evening Meeting is in session. I can't risk turning on a light. As I'm waiting for the computer to finish something, I try to read a book by the light of the computer monitor. It is the high tech version of reading by candlelight.

Day Thirty-three – Rescued by a Stranger

Last night was a quiet night, and I wanted to take advantage of that so I went to bed early. I had a hard time falling asleep, and woke up in the middle of the night and couldn't go back to sleep. I only slept three or four hours. Sleeping has been difficult since I've been here. I'm not sure why. If I have to take my herbs so I can sleep every night, I will, reluctantly, but I will.

Today is another horrible day at work. It starts with a new woman with a bad attitude. Some of these Osho people don't know how to treat people with even a hint of respect.

Then, I have to call Nalini to ask her to give me more DVDs, and she says later in the morning. Of course, by the end of the day I still don't have them. The rude, new woman has nothing to do all day.

Later, I have more conflict with Revatii. She asks about the scanning, and I make some excuse. So, she asks for the folder back and says she will get it done elsewhere. Fine. The less I have to do with that woman, the less stress I'll have.

Some of these people need a day off, or a lesson on courtesy with their fellow employees. Thankfully, I only have four more days of this left.

When I see Sakra, I mention to him about considering me if there is an opening in the bookstore. He says there will be no openings for a couple months. That's too bad, because I wanted that job. Whatever is meant to be.

I want nothing to do with filling in for Chandra in the future. If they force me into that, I might turn into a rude person like the ones I have complained about. I'm done with this job. Well, not yet done - - I still have four more days.

As tired as I am today, I decide I need the solace that I get from Gowri and Manik and Tanul. So, I change clothes and leave the ashram for the outside world.

First, I see Gowri and sit with her for a while. She always makes me feel good. Then, since neither Manik nor Tanul is on the corner, I cross the street and walk toward their store. Since I can't remember where the store is, I have to ask a couple merchants. With so many beggars that are missing eyes and limbs and looking sad, it is an emotionally difficult street to walk. It breaks my heart, and I hate walking by them.

I walk slowly along looking for the store, when Shareef, Manik's father, sees me walking and calls out to me. He invites me into his shop

95

and shows me some cool crystals. I tell him that I had a bad day at work and want to visit with Manik or Tanul. He commiserates with me on my job and the ashram and says I can come in there anytime to visit. Then he offers me coffee or tea. He is always so kind. Also, he says that Manik will take me to the snake park on his motorcycle. I hope that Manik can somehow get the family car that day. I would ride the motorcycle, but not without a helmet.

After buying a small handful of crystals for a hundred rupees, I leave. As I walk back toward German Bakery, I see the merchant who directed me toward Shareef's store. Something in his shop window looks interesting, and he invites me in. On a shelf inside, I find a tiny Shiva that I have been looking for.

The merchant's name is Hassan. Behind the counter, he sits on a cushion on the floor, and I sit on a small stool. He shows me some beautiful wall hangings. When I say that I like the Shiva with a red background instead of a black background, he says it has better energy. Then, he says something about my day and wonders if something is wrong. I say, "Yeah, I had a horrible day!"

After asking my birth month and day, he closes his eyes. He takes my hand in his and places his thumbs on my open palm. Then he starts giving me Reiki, because he says I need it. He has an intricate crystal wand that he says he designed himself, and he waves it around me. I feel the energy.

Then, he asks if I will take my shoes off and sit behind the counter with him. So, I do it. Hassan gives me Reiki without touching me, uses the crystal wand, and then asks about sound. When I say I like it, he gets a large singing bowl, has me close my eyes, and taps the bowl at different places around my body. I feel warmth surrounding me.

Between these actions he talks to me, and more than once tears come to my eyes. I can't believe he is doing this for a stranger.

As he moves the crystal wand up and down, I feel the energy. It feels palpable. It is an incredible and profound experience, and I am not doing it justice here. He keeps talking about giving, and my needing it. What an incredible man.

Before I leave, he gives me a tourmaline crystal and says it will ground and protect me. All I buy from him today is the tiny Shiva, but I will return to buy other items.

Afterward, I feel a remarkable deep peace and a lightness of being. All the stress from the past two days has melted away to nothing. It has disappeared. What a gift.

I continue down the street and see these two adorable Indian boys playing on a cart. They say hello to me as I pass, and I ask if I can take their picture. After snapping the shot, I show it to them. They like the picture and want a copy. Then they ask me for money! I smile and start walking away, when one of the boys says something about being hungry and wanting an apple.

A few meters from the boys is a fruit and vegetable vendor. I buy two apples and bring them back to the boys. I'm a sucker for cute kids. One boy takes the apples from me and puts them on the cart. He says, "I lie to you, lady. I just lie to you. We're not really hungry, I just lie to you." Laughing, I head toward the ashram.

Now it's getting late. Hurrying back to my room, I squeeze in my meditation and don't even mind going to Evening Meeting. I walk there with a smile on my face.

The peaceful feeling lasts throughout Evening Meeting. The time passes almost too quickly to notice. I don't do yoga or gibberish; I sit there in peace and leave when it is over.

Day Thirty-four – Beggar Business

I still feel peaceful from yesterday, and I'm not letting anything get to me so far. Only three days and two hours to go for this job.

Work today isn't as bad as it's been. Revatii isn't too bad, or I don't let her get to me - - I'm not sure which. I talk to Prana and mention how people treat me. She says, "We are all here to learn lessons." I also say that I thought some people needed a day off, and later she tells me she thinks that is a projection. Maybe I need to say something abrupt to Revatii, but I guess the time isn't right or perhaps I don't have enough nerve.

When I talk to Dilasa about my experience yesterday, he says, "He was just trying to get in your knickers!" Although I tell him Hassan is young, I'm not so sure.

After work, I go out so I can thank Hassan for what he did for me yesterday. As I approach the busy corner, something feels wrong. The shoe vendor who is normally on the corner is missing. The other vendors down the block are missing. Then, I pass the friend of Gowri's who always talks to me. She says the police have chased everyone away. She is starting to put her stuff up again.

Gowri is also out there, with all her stuff lumped in a big pile behind her. Usually, everyone has their wares strung out on a clothesline. Gowri shows me a picture of her grandson. He is a cutie, and I thank her for bringing the photo for me. A couple minutes later she says, "Tomorrow you bring me two hundred rupees."

I don't think I hear her right, so I say, "What?"

She says, "No business. I am hungry. You bring me two hundred rupees." When I stand up to leave, she asks if I will be back that way. I avoid the answer and walk away floored and broken-hearted, thinking, "I should have known better." Although I feel badly about this, I set myself up for it.

Then I cross the street, using the median that is across from German Bakery. Immediately several beggars surround me. By entering the German Bakery area and then walking out the back door, I lose them.

While walking down the narrow street, I run into the guy and his brother who, a few weeks ago, wanted to show me the snake for twelve hundred rupees. When I show him my cobra pictures, being careful not to show the guy holding the cobra, he says he will do it for two hundred rupees. It's probably the same snake. Then he asks me to buy him and his brother some tea. That's when I say good-bye and walk on.

Although I have to avoid several beggars on the way, I have no problem finding Hassan's shop. He invites me in again, and I thank him repeatedly for the generous gift he gave me. Then I offer to give him Reiki on his back, because he mentioned yesterday how it bothered him. As he sits on a cushion on the floor, I sit behind him. First, I put my hands on his back, but the way I am sitting makes it uncomfortable. So, I take my hands away and continue sending him Reiki for several minutes. He feels it and is grateful.

Then we talk for a while, and he says I am his friend. I ask him, "Is it safe for me to go to the burning ghats by myself?"

He shakes his head, no. He points to the camera bag around my shoulder and says, "You shouldn't even walk down the street with your camera. Guys on bikes may try to grab it and keep going."

I say something about the beggars, and he says, "The ones on this street are not real beggars. They keep having kids and people say to them, 'Why do you keep having kids if you can't afford to feed them?'"

"We have the same problem in America," I tell him.

He says, "Most beggars here are like professional beggars."

"What about the lady that looks blind?"

He says, "It would be all right to give to her, but she's the only one. But, if you give to one, the next day the other beggars will surround you." Before I leave, I give him twenty rupees to give to the blind lady for me.

As I walk toward home, someone calls to me. Turning around, I see Manik at the back door of German Bakery. He introduces me to an Indian friend of his named Anderson! Manik says something about calling him when I am coming to visit. Then he bums a cigarette off his friend. Seeing him smoking makes me feel weird - - almost a bad feeling, but I can't define it. He also tells me that he is going to join the ashram for the meditations, because he needs it.

Tonight, I skip Evening Meeting - - I don't even pretend to go. Since I will not have a mark by my name for this night, I wonder what the consequences will be. I'll deal with it, because I thoroughly enjoy the time off.

I have gate duty tonight. When I relieve the woman who watched the gate before me, she asks if I have had dinner yet. That is so sweet. Phani stops by and I ask him about "renting" the snake. He goes on and on about how expensive it would be, and I finally say, "And you wouldn't make as much money, either, huh!" Then he laughs. He lives close and walks home from here.

For my break, I go to the office to check my email. While there, I run into Kanti, the friend of my brother and sister-in-law. When I tell her my sad story about Gowri, she says that I shouldn't take it personally. Gowri can't help it - - this is India. I still feel bad. I tell her the funny story about the little boys saying they lied to me.

She tells me about a little girl she liked, and the little girl used to hold her wrist tightly. Kanti didn't know why she did that, until her watch went missing! She never saw the little girl again. That is a terrible story!

The guy who watched the gate across from me tonight is the cute Australian guy from my office. When we finish, he gives me a hug and a little kiss on the head. So many men here are affectionate. Dilasa always holds my hand or puts his arm around me when we walk together.

Day Thirty-five – Talking to Osho-ites

Work today isn't too bad. Only two more days to go. Sakra asks me about the scanning, and I tell him the problems I have been having. He asks if I am willing to try it again, and I say yes. Revatii brings the folder back to me. Oh, joy.

Nimisha calls me today to say that Sakra has asked me to volunteer at a group with him on Monday. She wants me to come see her to have something entered into the computer. I give her the information and then say something about giving her a private yoga class.

I say, "You saw me at my worst: an advanced class, different Sun Salutations, and my first time doing yoga in a robe." Surprisingly enough, she says yes. Now I have to prepare a class for her.

The title of Sakra's group, Hypnosis and Relaxation, concerns me because I do not want anyone here to hypnotize me. When I speak to Dilasa about it, he says it's gentle, easy, and not deep. He says not to worry. My concern is that I read where you have to be careful who hypnotizes you, because it is a direct link to your unconscious. If I start spouting this Osho crap, you'll know what happened to me!

After work, I hear a noise outside my room that sounds like a cat meowing on a loudspeaker. I look out the window. There is a peacock on the roof of the building next door! For a while I watch him, until he flies to the roof of my building where I can't see him anymore.

Later in the afternoon when I get some fruit from the Zorba restaurant, I see three peacocks there. When I ask someone about the meowing sound, they say, yes, that is the peacock! I put my hand out with nothing in it to attract the peacock over. He comes to me and pecks my hand. Bonding with a peacock!

After buying an orange, I see Adhanya, an older woman who works with me, sitting there. I go over to ask her what I can wear to Celebrating Sannyas tonight. After she tells me, she asks me to join her. I tell her I have to meditate and I walk away. Then I think - - why not stay and talk?

So, I go back and talk to her for a while. Then Chakori comes along and joins us. She also works with me now, and is the new person who I referred to as rude. I talk to both of them for a long time. Then I leave to go meditate. If I'm going to be here, even if I don't agree with most of what goes on, and although I don't believe like they believe, I can still establish relationships. That will be good for me. It should make my time here easier, also.

I've noticed that most of the people around here - - the regulars, anyway - - are introverts. That could be why none of them make eye contact or smile as I walk down pathways. They are all damaged in one way or another. I am damaged, too, but in different ways. Is part of their damage what drew them to Osho initially? I don't know.

Tonight, I had planned to go to Celebrating Sannyas. When I walk into the auditorium the music blares loudly. I'll try it another time with earplugs.

Day Thirty-Six – Mosquito Attack

In the middle of the night, mosquitoes attacked me repeatedly. I awakened to the sound of buzzing in my ear. Waiting until I felt it land on my head, I swatted at it. They land with a thud, like they forgot to put down their landing gear. Five minutes later, it was back. This went on for hours. Every time I fell back to sleep, the buzzing would wake me again. I thought it was one persistent and lucky mosquito. When I got up this morning, I found four dead bodies by my pillow. I didn't get much sleep.

Consequently, I feel exhausted and cranky today. I don't want to be here, I don't want to do this, and I have a headache as well. They cleaned my room today and sprayed something bad inside. The window is open now, but it will get cold, so I'll have to close it after a while.

When I'm tired like this is when I feel lonely. A few days ago, I met a German guest here and I am smitten with him. Although I have no idea how old he is - - probably thirty-five! When I saw him sitting in the plaza and didn't have the nerve to sit with him, it made me feel bad and lonely. As much as I would like a companion, I don't want an Osho-ite! That limits my chances while I'm here. I need to get my profile up on an Internet dating site and see what comes of that.

I wait in the plaza a long time to meet Sakra to help with his group. While I sit there, Anugyan asks me to help with something, and it is fun. It is a silly, little job, but there are several other people all working together, and I enjoy it. Anugyan starts helping us, but then becomes the guy who convinces other people to do the work.

When I finally come back to the office, I discover they had canceled the group. Nobody bothered telling me. Oh well, I had fun in the plaza while I waited. It is always a treat being out of here!

I read an article today that Revatii gave me to scan. It said something about having a strong ego. If someone is hostile to you, it shouldn't bother you. It is their problem, not yours. I disagree with that. If someone is abusive - - and that is often what the hostility is - - that IS my problem. I have to deal with the abuse and the negative energy associated with it. This is another example of the propaganda around here.

Tonight, I go to Evening Meeting and use the coughing trick to get out of it. A woman from my office recognizes me as I walk out. Coincidentally, she is also the woman who caught me surfing the dating sites earlier this week. The less anonymous I become here, the more trouble it will be.

As I walk home from my aborted attendance at Evening Meeting, I pass through the Meera eating area and spot a blue heart on the ground. Although I am in a hurry to get out of there and get safe, I stop and pick it up. I think that is how love will come to me, unexpectedly, and sudden. The love that will sustain me.

There is a party in the plaza, and I have a raging headache. So, instead of returning to my room, I'll sit at this computer for as long as I can. The party doesn't end until after 11:30, so I have a while to go.

Day Thirty-seven – Different Rules

Last night I had another battle with mosquitoes. They cleaned my room yesterday and they leave the door open while they clean. This morning, five prominent mosquito bites cause my face to look like a battlefield. I will need to take a double dose of my Ayurvedic herb today.

Perhaps I was a little hard on Chandra when she told me how everyone sends emails addressed "beloved" and signed "love." The water heater for my room needs fixing, and they left a note on my door about temporarily turning off the water. They addressed it "Beloveds" and signed it "love." It strikes me as weird in a place where smiles are rare and abuse is acceptable.

Today is cleaning day in the office again. On Saturdays, I used to help Chandra prepare all the cleaning supplies. Yesterday, I did it all myself. This morning I arrive at work twenty minutes late. The lights are on, and everybody is busy dusting and scrubbing away. I find the whole exercise rather manipulative.

Later in the day, I talk to Dilasa about cleaning on Sundays and how I feel it is manipulative. He says, "Who else would do it?"

I say, "Sudexo." They are the company who hires local Indians to work here doing the dirtier jobs.

Dilasa says, "In the days before there was a Sudexo, everyone always cleaned their own area. Now, not everyone does." Then, he mentions someone's name and says she would never clean her own office. Coordinators decide who cleans. Dilasa is good for me. He sometimes commiserates and sometimes clarifies my thinking.

Then Dilasa says, "So what's the good news?"

My answer is, "Only two more months to go!" And, I raise my arms in victory. It's disgusting that he should have to ask about the good news. Am I that much of a complainer? I am with him. I need to stop that. The next two months could be positive months, so I shouldn't look at it like I have two more horrible months to go.

Someone told me to set up a workstation for a girl who was to start today. Sakra isn't available, and so it doesn't happen. Someone tells her that she has the day off. She says, "It's Sunday. What am I going to do? All the shops are closed."

I say, "Several are still open." Then she says something about not being a shopper. Complaining about having a day off? These people are so clueless. It's like they can't be by themselves, and that's why they need to work so much. That's why they need Osho - - because they can't be alone.

Here is another example how the rules are different here. I am a person who has to be punctual. When I first started here, I was always on time. Usually, I was the only one in the office for five or ten minutes, sometimes longer! Also, I was always the first one back from breaks. I always left for lunch on time.

Times have changed. The rules are different here, and I am willing to play by the new rules. I'm usually on time in the morning so I can answer my personal emails before work. At lunch, I leave early because of hygiene issues. When it gets busy in the restaurant, all manner of disgusting acts happen. I've seen them. I've experienced them. I'm done with them. Dilasa suggested I take longer breaks, and I will do that. Today, I read a chapter during my break time. Tomorrow, who knows? Rules have changed and times have changed. I have changed.

I read an article today that I thought Revatii had written. It had a slightly hostile, abusive edge to it. Osho wrote it! What surprised me is the essence of the article was to embrace uncertainty.

He said that people who didn't feel confused were idiots, and if you felt confused - - uncertain - - then you were intelligent. Many of his tirades are like that, calling people idiots, stone heads, coconuts, and the like. Also, he often makes fun of certain groups. He may have done that to manipulate people, or deliberately make them angry. That's not the way I want my guru to be. I've had enough abuse in my life. This impresses me again that he is not my guru, nor will he ever be. I'm not the guru type, anyway - - I've always preferred finding my own path.

Something that I realized is that although I am not desperate for a man, I am desperate - - for a friend. The first clue was when I answered friends' emails and gushed about how happy I was to receive them, and how important it was to me. Then, I wouldn't hear from them again! The second clue was when Yama, a new woman at work who is always friendly to me, shied away from me when I told her emphatically how good it was to see her. I've backed off since then. She's friendly again, but it was a lesson.

People don't like that. Not just men, but everyone. Once, I knew a little girl who emanated neediness. It felt scary being around her. I didn't want anything to do with that desperation, and I knew then it was a lesson. Now, I realize it's not only men who feel that desperation. Anyone can feel it and it puts everyone off.

Evening Meeting tonight went back to the Rebel discourses that they played when I first arrived. I like those much better. During the dancing part, I do yoga again and no one says anything. And, I chant a mantra instead of doing gibberish.

After Evening Meeting, I spend awhile at the variety show, but it isn't that great. I find another mosquito in my room tonight and can't catch it. I'm hoping it doesn't have any friends with it.

If this journal does become a book, I'd like to name it, What Would Osho Say. With his current broader perspective, I thought he might admit that he may have been wrong about some of his ideas. Now, I'm not so sure. He might just raise his arms and shout, "Osho!"

Day Thirty-eight – Osho's House

I hate to start every day off with mosquito news, but I have become the new fast food spot for local mosquitoes. There are so many bites on my face and my hands, I can barely count them. The bright red ones on my face make me look like I have the measles!

My laundry came back late a few days ago. Normally, it is back in three days. This time it wasn't. That scared me. Then I found that my maroon robe was missing. I looked at a bunch that didn't have tags on them, but it wasn't there. Later I went back and found it. I'm glad I don't have to buy another one.

Chandra came back to work today and rescued me out of that terrible job. On her first day back, she comes in fifteen minutes late. The rules are different here.

Instead of going back to work early after lunchtime, I go to Silent Sitting Meditation at Chuang Tzu. I believe this is where Osho used to live; and I think his ashes are under his bed. That was his request!

As I walk through the door, a big Rolls Royce fills the space off to the left. You must remove your shoes immediately and place them in a small rack by the door. They require you to wear white socks in this area. If you don't have any, they provide them for you. Luckily, I have my own white socks - - I wouldn't want to borrow theirs.

A facilitator sits just past the chairs where you put your borrowed white socks on. She or he also watches the doorway leading to the meditation area. After going through that open doorway, I walk down a hallway lined from floor to ceiling with filled bookshelves.

Then I turn into another hallway and walk past Osho's dental chair. Osho must have had teeth issues, because the chair has a prominent place in his past. The passageway reminds me of a maze-like house of mirrors, because mirrors line the path to the meditation area.

At the end of the passageway, I reach the large, round meditation room. With marble floors, and marble and glass walls, it is beautiful. Tall marble columns adorn the room. A chandelier on the ceiling has crystals draped over recessed lighting. The glass panels are reflective glass. From where I sit, I can see a waterfall outside.

People sit on cushions that line the floor in rows. There are also some of those back-jack floor chairs. I try putting a cushion by the wall. The facilitator says no and points me toward the back-jacks.

A bell rings to start the meditation, and the room goes silent. It is peaceful and relaxing as I do my own meditation. Another bell sounds at the end of the half hour. I walk contentedly out of the mirrored passageway and put on my shoes. As I step out the door, I see a beautiful swan behind a fence. It sits on the walkway in front of the water. What a gift this is.

After meditation, I return to work twenty minutes late. Either no one notices or no one mentions it. I may do this again. An extra half hour of meditation a day would serve me well in this place.

Today after work, I go outside the gates. As I walk past the lone rickshaw driver, I nod hello to him, and he says, "Snake woman, eh?"

I walk down the opposite way I usually go, so I can try to find a stationery store. I run into Omar, the merchant I bought items from a month ago. He says, "Where have you been?" Then he invites me into his store. We sit on the floor. He opens out all his beautiful wall hangings for me. I'm not interested, because I think he overcharged me last time. If I buy anything else, I want to buy it from Hassan. I may come back here if Hassan doesn't have the same items.

Tonight is a spectacular Indian music concert. Two Indian musicians and two Austrian musicians join for a fusion of East and West music. It is more East, though, and I love that. Three Indian dancers move as one with the music. It is beautiful to watch.

Day Thirty-nine – Another Workshop

Early this morning, I give a yoga class to Nimisha. It goes well. She isn't familiar with one pose. She has to ask where her head should be. That is my fault for not teaching correctly.

Nimisha likes the gentle class I gave her, and I leave the rest to the universe. I'm happy to do so. Right now, there are no openings. In the future, who knows?

I do something bad, though. Nimisha asks me how I like the program. In telling her it is fine, I also mention that I am not a sannyasin. Why do I do that? There is no reason that I have to do that. It could hurt my chances to teach yoga. Sometimes in the name of truth, I go too far. Too much information.

After giving the yoga class, I have to go to the Inner Skills for Work and Life workshop. Like everything else around here, it begins with dancing. Fatima, the facilitator, says it is to wake us all up. But, I think it is to get the extra energy out, so we can listen and participate fully. After dancing, we do a short session of gibberish.

Then, we sit in a circle. Fatima talks about how our conditioning when we were children has shaped our lives in many ways.

The person next to us becomes our partner. We tell them how our families conditioned us as children. I talk first. It is always difficult for me to fill the allotted time. It's not easy to talk about something that doesn't engage me - - something someone TOLD me to talk about. (Don't tell me what to do!) It doesn't bother me, though - - it is one person, one stranger, who I tell the information to. Then, my partner tells me about her conditioning.

Next, we have to introduce our partner and tell the group about our partner's conditioning as a child. While it is absorbing to listen to everyone else's story, the exercise makes me feel violated. When I told my family "secrets," I didn't expect them to be exposed to the group.

After that, we are to "step into the shoes" of who we might have become if we would have listened to that conditioning. We had to decide our name, and then walk around the room and introduce ourselves as that person.

I choose Dr. Hill, a holistic veterinarian. When I think about this later, my family didn't condition me for that. I had told my partner that intelligence and education were important for my family. There's more to it than that. For me, my family talked about going to college to get my "MRS" Degree - - get married. That is a compelling mini-revelation.

On our break, I speak to Sajeev, an Indian guy who was in my last group. He was my partner who cried during that one exercise last time. He tells me about his wife and family, and I ask him if it was an arranged marriage. Sajeev says it was arranged with love. When he was in his early twenties, his family wanted him to meet the beautiful sister of his brother's fiancé. Sajeev, not interested in marriage, didn't want to meet her. Then, she came to the house for a party. When he saw her, it was love at first sight. What a great story!

Back as a group, we discuss how in all our families that cleaning was the lowest job one could do. So, our next project is cleaning. There are cleaning supplies outside the room, and each of us grabs something and starts cleaning. I grab a cute, little Indian broom that you have to bend over to use. Since it is a game, the cleaning doesn't bother me. The ending bell rings quickly.

Then, we have to clean with awareness. I am so aware, that I find something that needs cleaning. Next, we have to clean in groups of four while two of the four gossip, and the other two have to block it out. Then, the same exercise without blocking it out. This time we let it go by.

Afterward, our discussion about this helps me. Fatima talks about how if you fight against something, it not only takes more energy, but you are giving energy to whatever you are fighting against. I realize that I have been giving my energy to those two women at work who I find so difficult to work with. In my struggle with their abuse, I gave them more power.

Right before lunch, Fatima plays a quote of Osho's where he talks about how important non-doing is. It occurs to me that when someone forces you to do something - - such as Evening Meeting, which they call non-doing - - then it becomes doing and crumbles the whole idea of non-doing. It's almost paradoxical. At least for me it's like that - - but, I am a rebel. Perhaps it's not like that for the rest of the robots around here.

During lunch break, I try to eat with awareness, as instructed. Usually, I eat as fast as I can to get out of the area and back to my room. This time, I eat slowly with awareness, trying to taste each morsel of food. I find I fill up quicker than usual. Normally I'm not paying attention - - I'm shoveling it in so I can leave the area.

After lunch, I go to Silent Sitting again. This time - - CAUGHT! When I get back to the office, Chandra tells me that I can't do it again because I have to be at work. That would have been a good time to point out that when she attended Silent Sitting the other morning, she was fifteen minutes late to work. Alas, I don't do that.

Chandra says, "I have another group to attend. You will fill in for me again."

I say, "I hope they aren't grooming me for your job. If I have to do it full time, I will probably kill someone." I probably shouldn't have said that!

She says, "It is for this class only and on other special occasions. This job is my karma, so I have to keep it."

I will refuse to do Revatii's scanning. That will take the pressure off.

Chakori, the new woman in the office returns after attending the lecture by Dwami. She has a different take on it than I did. Dwami had been her hynotherapist many years ago, and she said that today his voice calmed her and put her in another place. So, to her he wasn't abusive at all. Of course, she is abusive, so she probably wouldn't have noticed, anyway.

Part of what I don't like about Osho is that he is so on the edge. That is also what I don't like about many of the people here. A woman in the office had a problem with her computer being slow. I ask her if she had restarted it recently. She snaps back, "I always do what I'm supposed to." Later that afternoon I walked by her computer after she had left, and she had logged out but not turned it off.

That edge bothers me. Osho exemplifies it. Tonight during Evening Meeting, there is a comment about this woman being jealous of other people asking questions. Osho told her she was sick and needed help, and went on and on with what was wrong with her. He went too far. But, maybe that's what these people need.

A friend and I have discussed people who don't know what to do with themselves if they have free time. That describes these people. They need the guidance. They need the demands on their time. They would dissolve or go ballistic if they had to make a choice of what to do on their own. I go back to my assessment that they are damaged in one way or the other. Again, I say that I am damaged, also, but in a different way.

Tonight during Evening Meeting while everyone dances, I do my yoga. Since I have no other time for yoga, I like the opportunity to do this. While I am on my knees doing six directions of the spine, Dwami walks by right in front of me! He doesn't say anything.

When I was at Silent Sitting Meditation this afternoon, I had wanted to surround myself with white light again. Instead of white light, a rainbow of light came down all around me. I don't understand this until later. It comes to me now, in Evening Meeting. I think Osho sent me that rainbow. It doesn't change too much for me, though. I still don't agree with everything he says. But, I don't think he would want me to, either.

Tonight at Evening Meeting, Osho told a Sufi story that was elaborate and a little convoluted. The essence of it was one of my mother's favorite pieces of advice. She told it like this: If everyone hung their troubles on the line and you could choose whichever batch you wanted, everyone would run for their own troubles. I thought it was fascinating that Mom and Osho would share this story. I know it sounds wacky, but I think Mom and Osho are both up there guiding me on my Osho-journey.

The Osho police are active tonight. A man a few feet away from me opens a candy and crinkles the cellophane loudly. Out of nowhere, someone in white (everyone in the auditorium is in white) appears at his side and tells him not to do it again. Sometime later, during Osho's discourse, someone comes from the middle of the auditorium and sits beside me. That same large Indian fellow who grabbed my robe last week, comes over and escorts her out. The Osho police! You never know who they are!

Day Forty – Learning and Growing

This morning I wake up at an ungodly hour and can't fall back to sleep. Finally, I decide to do my meditation, and when I finish it is 7:00. I have wanted to return to Osho Teerth Park in the morning like someone suggested. This is a good time to do it.

I expect a guard posted outside to allow only Osho-ites in the park this time of morning. When I arrive, there is no guard and I see several joggers inside the park. I'm barely inside when I see a little, white heron on a rock. Although I want to take a picture, the sound of turning on the camera scares it away.

I keep walking and find another heron, but he doesn't want his picture taken, either. After walking most of the way to the end, I turn around and come back. Finding the first heron again, I take some pictures, but they are all blurry. Finally, I put the camera away and enjoy watching the heron hunt for food.

Today is the second day of my workshop. First, we dance again, and the whole beginning of the workshop is relaxing, breathing deeply, and trying to stay in awareness.

The next part is dealing with people. We each have a partner, and we have to repeat a sentence four ways: in frustration, in anger, in manipulation, and in fact. The sentence is: "I need two people this afternoon, or I'll never get the job done." For this exercise, Fatima encourages everyone to speak in their native language if they want. My partner is a Russian fellow. He says the first sentence in English, and the rest in Russian. The anger sentence doesn't come across - - he is too considerate about it. The manipulation message, however, comes through clearly. It is interesting how it comes through even in a language I don't understand.

Later, we have another exercise about arguments. My partner is my friend, Sajeev. He tells me about how he handled a condescending colleague effectively and without emotion. He still got his point across. He had to stand up for himself several times. I tell him he is my hero.

I usually get so affected by the negativity or abusiveness of the situation that I am unable to speak up. It puts me back into the same helpless place as when I was in an abusive relationship many years ago. Although I left him long ago, I still react by cowering under treatment like that. Perhaps that is one of my lessons I need to learn here. I have already learned much. This workshop has been valuable to me.

Many of my personal issues stem from not being assertive enough.

Today, during lunch, the line is long, and all I want is a coke (because I have to get in another line to order my pizza). Finally, I say "excuse me" and push into the place to grab a coke. Normally, I would have felt frustrated and waited. Of course, I could have done it sooner and not had to wait as long as I did! At least I did it. Everyone has to start somewhere!

After lunch, we have another short session. We get in a circle, cover one eye with one hand, and with the other hand make like a telescope. Then, we turn around and face the wall. When Fatima taps someone on the shoulder, they announce what they see. Then, everyone else agrees or disagrees.

It is an exercise based on a Sufi story of Osho's about five blind men and an elephant. Each man would say what he thought the elephant looked like. One man held the leg and said it looked like a large tree. Another man held an ear and said, no, it's round and flat. One man held the tail and said it's like a skinny snake. That story says so much about one's perspective, and I love that.

During a part of the workshop, everyone in the room is walking around, mostly in a circle. Deliberately, I walk the other direction. I do not want to get in any groove that everyone else is in. I'm my own person and I'm proud of that.

Chandra goes over parts of her job with me again today and is benign about it. Maybe it scared her when I said I'd kill someone! During our conversation, she recommends Kundalini Meditation. I tell her how badly it made my hands feel last time. She shows me how to do the shaking differently. I will give it another shot. Why not? I need to have as many experiences here as I can.

When I tell Dilasa about my mosquito problems, he tells me I should ask for a mosquito net. Later, I call the help desk. Now, I'll see what happens. I'm hoping I'll get one. When I lie down now, I feel like I'm offering myself up as a sacrifice.

I mention to Dilasa about forcing someone into non-doing, and how it becomes doing. At least for me, I tell him, but maybe not for the rest of the robots. He says, "What if I gave you ten million dollars to go in there and non-do? Could you do it?" I say yes! Although I see his point, it still feels like a paradox to me.

Someone once told me about a job she had at a spiritual place. She said that it put your karma through a washing machine. I almost feel like that's what's happening to me. Until now, I'd stuffed away parts of myself that needed working on. Incidents that I had forgotten about were still affecting my psyche. Although I don't always like what goes on here, it is helping me in ways that I hadn't anticipated.

I also know that I am in the exact right place at the right time. Several times at work I have gone over some of Osho's words, and then the same words pop up in the novel I'm reading. The universe is exactly the way it should be, and I am exactly where I should be.

Tonight I have gate duty at Meera gate, across from the main gate. I brought a book because I thought I'd be at the back gate. Although I'm at the busier front gate, I don't want to give up my opportunity to read. Carefully, I pull the book out and put it in the folds in my robe. Every once in a while I sneak in a paragraph or two.

It reminds me of when I was a kid and would read after my mother put me to bed and turned out the lights. Our house had a long hallway, and I could hear footsteps coming toward the bedroom. I learned the pattern of everyone's footsteps. When I heard someone coming down the long hallway, I would act accordingly. If it was my mother, I'd turn out the light immediately. If it was my youngest brother, it could go either way. Sometimes he'd tell on me and sometimes he wouldn't. If it were my older brother, I'd leave the light on and keep reading.

Everyone in our family is a book lover. My mother used to tell a story about when she was a kid and her job was to take care of the baby. She would read with one foot on the cradle rocking it. One time her mother came in screaming, because the baby was crying and my mother had been too involved in her book to notice! Our family reads like some families drink.

Day Forty-One – One Hundred Dollars

The final day of the workshop starts with dancing again. Some people come in late, so we extend the dancing to include them. The music is too loud for me, so I put toilet paper in my ears. Next, each of us talks about how the workshop has helped us in our jobs and the challenges we still face.

For our first exercise, we draw with crayons on a big piece of paper. I'm no artist, but I have the drawing arranged how I like it. Then, Fatima asks us to move down one seat. My drawing! It is an exercise on change - - which I don't mind - - but it is MY drawing! Possessiveness kicks in. Then, we share one drawing among four people. After that, we go around the room and draw on any picture we want.

The next exercise involves little, colored pieces of plastic. We have to trade to match different colors and match different shapes. After that, Fatima gives us a bag full of cool items. She tells us that we can do anything we want with them. All I feel like doing is to give them all away. So, I give one item to each of the people who made an impact on me during class. Then, I walk around with nothing until other people start adorning me with their items.

The last part of the class is a play - - where you do the same act unconsciously and then consciously. It feels stupid. Mostly, though, it is a valuable workshop, and I profit from it.

When the workshop is over and I finish lunch, I decide to go to Silent Sitting again. Chandra and Sakra had both planned to be out of the office. As soon as I walk in, I see Chandra. She starts asking me questions, but never mentions that I am almost twenty minutes late.

After work today, I run into Phani. We have a long talk, but I only catch half of what he says. Although I have another prospect for a snake, I tell Phani that I don't trust the guy. The guy wants to take me to his house with his two brothers. I tell Phani that I want him to take me to the house and stay with me. Phani says he'll be my bodyguard! He's a funny guy, and I enjoy talking to him.

Then, I walk over to German Bakery to change some money. I walk by Gowri without stopping. Although I say hello, I keep walking. At German Bakery, I run into Manik and he's smoking again. I tell him that if I were his mother, I'd tell him to quit. He says that he has decided to go to London, and it will cost twelve hundred dollars. I hope he's not trying to ask me for money like Gowri. That would break my heart again.

I receive an email from my Osho-itc brother today. He talks about how this is a place of transformation, of beautiful people, and meditation. Except the meditation, I'm not sure we're talking about the same place. He also says that if I like it better outside the gates, I should leave. My brother finishes the email by telling me he bet his wife one hundred dollars that I won't last three months. I write back and say he must not know me if he thinks I'm such a wimp.

Although I was already determined to stay the three months regardless, after what he said, I'm really determined! I hope they won't kick me out for being a "re-bel," as Osho puts it! But I think Osho likes me - - and will protect me. No, they haven't indoctrinated me yet.

I want to say more about the so-called beautiful people here. At least in the office that I work in of thirty people, some of them never say a word. Of those who do, the words are often curt or rude. They don't have any people skills. But, as this is a place to learn your lessons, something interesting happens to me today. Someone asks me something. After I answer, I can see her "back-pedaling" - - I had answered her curtly or rudely! Another lesson learned? I complain about their rudeness and then act the same way. Wow.

Last night made me rethink my perceptions and expectations. When I did gate duty, I noticed that some people didn't want a thank you. My saying it didn't offend them, but it wasn't something they needed. That is the opposite of how I feel. I like the acknowledgment, and I always feel a lack when I don't receive one. Perceptions and expectations - - everyone is different.

One reason I like the acknowledgment is that I don't like feeling invisible. Most of the people here treat the local Indians who aren't Osho-ites like they are invisible. I'm not pointing the finger at these Osho-ites, though, because this behavior is rampant everywhere.

During an Ayurvedic conference I attended in Colorado, one speaker talked about how the hotel (a fancy, expensive hotel) staff loved having the Chopra people there. We treated everyone the same. There were no "servants," no "masters," only people. We are all people, each on our own journey with our own lessons to learn.

This lesson hit home with me many years ago. I worked for a large corporation. The cleaning crew came in each morning to clean while we were in the office. My colleague, Joe, used to say hello to them by name. What a concept! They have names! I started using their names and it changed my perspective. It was an important lesson. Before that, they were invisible to me. Thank you, Joe.

Day Forty-two - Mosquitoes

SEVENTEEN. Last night the sound of mosquitoes buzzing in my ear woke me at 3:30 in the morning. They kept me awake the rest of the night. I now have seventeen mosquito bites on my face. This is getting serious. I call the help desk about the mosquito net again. They say, "They haven't done it yet?" I also have a line on somebody official to help me, Yuthika, but she is out today.

This morning I have breakfast with Chakori. When I ask if it is okay if I sit with her, she hesitates. She says that she likes her solitude, but she also likes my company, so it's okay. She talks about her mother, and how beautiful she was. Chakori says that beauty is a curse.

After working up my nerve, I ask her about Osho's derogatory comments toward homosexuals, and if it bothers her. I say, "I'm not even gay, but it offends me."

She says, "You have to understand the time he said that. It was when AIDS was getting widespread. He was afraid because of all the sex going on at the commune. He also makes positive comments about homosexuals, especially lesbians."

During our conversation, she also tells me the old men at the commune constantly hit on her. That makes me feel bad - - men have only hit on me three times. I'm not any more interested in them than she is - - although for different reasons. It still makes me feel bad.

This morning, Chandra asks me to lie for her to Sakra! I say, "You want me to lie for you? I can't even lie for myself!" The request surprises me.

Another event happens today with me telling the absolute truth. Dwami comes in with Jiadore and wants to put her in the editing room where Chakori was going to sit. After he leaves, the computer guy is in there setting up a computer, and I ask him who it is for. The woman in there, Tattva, speaks up and asks, "Why are you asking?"

I say, "Chakori should sit there."

She says abruptly, "All seat changes in the editing room have to go through me."

Maybe I'm too sensitive from not enough sleep, but these people are rude and short and not "people" persons! I say, "Chakori needs to be downstairs."

She says, "It is altruistic of you to protect her."

Then again with my absolute honesty, I say, "It isn't totally altruistic, because I don't want her taking my desk!" I don't want

119

something that doesn't belong to me - - the compliment of being altruistic.

It is another exchange that feels bad. Whenever I deal with most of these people, it feels bad. They don't know how to relate to people. It's becoming increasingly obvious to me that's the situation.

I talk to Jiadore today. Jiadore has been in both my groups and has been my partner several times. She wants me to go to lunch outside the ashram. I tell her I am nervous about that. Later in the conversation when cobras come up, she says, "You're not afraid of cobras, but you're afraid to eat outside the ashram?" It's true, it's true.

Jiadore is not an Osho-ite. She is only in her late-twenties, but we have much in common. Although, she is into the life here and goes to Dynamic Meditation and Kundalini every day. When I tell her that I don't have enough time for myself, she says that is the way it's supposed to be here. I tell her that it isn't for me.

EIGHTEEN. I'm in Evening Meeting with five hundred other people, and the mosquitoes still come to me. Another reason not to go! They still haven't put a mosquito net in my room. I'm hoping tomorrow.

Day Forty-three – Lunch Outside the Ashram

More mosquitoes attacked last night. Fortunately, they didn't start bothering me until 5:30. I call the help desk right away, and they send the carpenters to meet me at ten o'clock. They say they need to talk to someone. When I call back later this afternoon, they say they can't do it. Then I call Yuthika, whose job is to fix problems like this. Her advice is to buy my own mosquito net. I will, but it is not right. Also, I have to endure at least tonight without a net again.

Later, I speak to Andre, my coach, to see if he can help. He says he'll make some calls. If I do have to buy the net myself, I will take part of a day off to do it. I'm covered with mosquito bites and angry at this.

I have a new adventure today! It is scarier than a striking cobra! I eat someplace besides the ashram! Jiadore and I take a rickshaw to Bukhara - - a local Indian place filled with Osho-ites.

There is no menu. After we sit, they bring us the food. It consists of a large scoop of rice, some stir-fried green beans, and some stir-fried cauliflower combined with something. We also receive Indian tortillas, called chapatis, and a cup of soup with potatoes and mushrooms in it. We can have as many helpings as we want.

A spoon in the soup is all the silverware we receive. I want to use the spoon to eat everything else, but Jiadore says no. She says to break up the tortilla with only your right hand, and use it to eat everything. I struggle, but I mostly get it. At the end there is no more tortilla left and I still have some rice and vegetables, so I cheat and use the spoon.

The lunch is excellent. Surprisingly enough, it only cost thirty-five rupees! I thought it would be expensive, but it is so cheap I can't believe it! At the ashram, it costs forty rupees for one bowl. My lunch there usually runs one hundred twenty-five rupees. Jiadore tells me that she rarely eats at the ashram because it is so expensive. I'm hoping she shows me some other places to eat. I could learn to love this!

There is no rickshaw to take us back, so we start walking. When we get to North Main Road, it is busy as usual. As traffic speeds by, Jiadore steps off the curb and says, "Now!" Cars race toward us, and I stand like a statue. She grabs my arm and pulls me between lanes. The cars stop as we go by. Standing in the fast-moving traffic like this terrifies me. Somehow, we make it across safely.

After work, I walk to German Bakery and splurge on a large chocolate brownie for twenty-five rupees. It would have been forty-five or fifty at the ashram. It is a little dry, but it has nuts in it and tastes good.

Chocolate isn't the same here. They add some ingredient to keep it from melting in the heat. But, you know what they say - - even bad chocolate is still pretty good! I eat the brownie in front of the bakery, and several beggars stop to beg. I try to ignore them, and it is so difficult, because I feel bad.

That little boy with only one foot is out there. Since I've said no so often, he leaves me alone now. He sits on the curb next to a parked rickshaw. Leaning over, he picks up something out of the gutter. It is a round white object that looks like a ball, so he tries to bounce it on the curb. But, it isn't a ball and it won't bounce, so he loses interest. This moment gets to me. It makes him so much more real. He's a little boy who wants to play ball, like any other little boy. But, he was born in India without a foot, and begging is his life. It breaks my heart, honestly.

After I finish the brownie, I walk down the road beside German Bakery. When I get to the end, I turn right and find the Osho event that I have come to see. It is at that new Muslim Temple that Devika took me to a month ago. Some rich Indian Osho-ites put on the event, according to Dilasa. Many people kicked out of the ashram will be here. I walk up the steps and there is a huge picture of Osho on the stage, with yellow ribbons draped over it. Loud music plays, and some people dance. Most events that have anything to do with Osho include loud music and dancing. It doesn't interest me, so I don't stay. Then I walk back toward the ashram.

Gowri is out in her usual spot, and I sit with her for a few minutes. She asks, "Have you been busy?"

I say, "Yes." She doesn't say anything about money, though. I don't stay long. A man sells flutes down the way, and I want to buy one for the cobras. Someone else is there, though, so I don't stop.

On my way home, I stop at another street vendor. This is the place where I bought my maroon purse a few weeks ago. They have a maroon hat that I want. In Hindi, I ask how much it is by saying, "Kitna?" She says something that I don't understand.

I keep saying, "What?" And she keeps repeating it. Finally, I say, "I'm sorry, but I don't understand."

She says, "Then why did you ask in Hindi?" This is the first negative response that I've gotten with my meager Hindi vocabulary. It doesn't surprise me. She is always in a growley mood, and her husband is, too. I'm not going to judge this event. Unfortunately, it is the only maroon hat I've seen!

A woman in my last workshop had a sneezing, blowing, coughing cold, and I caught it. My throat hurts, and I'm starting to get the sniffles.

Eighty-eight degrees, and I'm getting a cold. I still go to Evening Meeting. As I sit there, my throat bothers me and I feel like I have to cough. I think about it, and if I wait and accidentally cough later, I will have to go to the "coughing Evening Meeting," which they moved outside. That isn't too appealing: outside where it's chilly when I'm catching a cold, and out with the mosquitoes when I already have eighteen bites on my face.

So I stand up, cough, keep coughing, get my shoes, and walk outside and back across the street. Normally, when I do the fake coughing routine, I am much earlier than this. The two guys at the front gate know me, unfortunately. They ask where I'm going. I say to my room to get more to wear. One of them barks, "You have five minutes." Sighing loudly, I hurry off.

Now, I'm in my room and my throat still hurts. I can feel the cold coming on. I'm glad it's a cold, though, because Chakori had strep throat, and she sat at my computer. I've been hoping that my sore throat wasn't strep.

Day Forty-four – Her Problem, Not Mine

I'm not making excuses for my rude behavior yesterday, but I felt tired and cranky. Now that I have identified this flaw, or re-identified it, how am I going to fix it? Two ways. First, I'll use a suggestion from an old friend who I worked with many years ago doing telephone tech support. He said to smile when you talk, because people can "hear" a smile in your voice. I always make an effort to smile when I walk around, but I don't when I'm inside working. I get too involved with what I'm doing, and not aware of smiling or not smiling. Second, I am going to buy myself a bindi.

A bindi is a red dot that many Indian women (and some Indian men) wear on their foreheads. To my understanding, the bindi has two meanings. One is that it represents the third eye. The other is that it signifies a married Hindu woman, like a wedding ring. Or it could mean married person, because my rickshaw driver, Phani, always wears one. I have been toying with the idea of getting one - - the stick-on kind, but thought it might be annoying feeling something alien on my forehead. Now, I'm going to use the awareness of it to help me to remember to smile while I'm at work. I'm practically fixed. Can I go home now?

I go to lunch with Jiadore again, and she has to grab my hand forcefully and pull me across the street. I panic more than once as cars and motorcycles race straight at us! This feels much scarier than cobras. We eat at another small Indian restaurant, and lunch cost us thirty rupees each. We both have fried noodles. Although they are good, I'm going to buy a slice of papaya after work, because I'm still hungry.

On my way to wash my hands, Revatii stops me and asks who is doing reception today. When I tell her that I am, she says that so-and-so had asked her to tell me that he wouldn't be in today. It is a multisyllable Indian or Sanskrit name spoken in Revatii's heavy Indian accent. I ask her to repeat the name for me. She walks away looking angry and offended.

This is where that workshop that I attended helped me. I realize this is not my problem. Normally when an incident like this happens, I feel like an idiot. Intellectually, I know I'm not an idiot. Emotionally, this is a sensitive area for me. Today, I realize what an idiot she is. When I get back to the office, she walks by and I ask her to spell the name for me. She shakes her head and walks away. Not my problem.

I speak to my coach, Andre, today to see if he has gotten anywhere with my mosquito net. He is kind and holds my hand while he tells me to talk to Yadgar. When I find her, she visits my room to check it out and suggests putting up a mosquito net right inside the door. She will try to arrange that, but if it doesn't work, then I will have to buy my own mosquito net. I'll see how that goes.

I'm reading a book about a prison camp now and I'm reassessing my opinion of how it felt when I had that lecture from Dwami. It felt more like the orientation for a prison camp. But, something intriguing has surfaced. Dwami is Jiadore's coach! She wants to go to that Evening Meeting talk again. Hearing her say that shocks me so much, that I ask if she can find out if I can go a second time, too. Jiadore obviously didn't feel about it like I did. Maybe I misread his intent or his tone. I'd like to know for sure. Maybe going a second time will alter my perception of the whole experience.

I run into Sajeev tonight on the way to Evening Meeting. When he asks how I am, I tell him that I am sick and feeling poorly. He says something about feeling better in Evening Meeting, and then says something about feeling the energy in there. I say that I don't feel it. That is what Osho talks about, too: why we wear the white robes and that once you experience it, you understand. Honestly, I think it is all a suggestion on his part. I am empathic, and aware of subtle energy, and I have never felt anything in there.

Once inside the auditorium, Evening Meeting goes okay, but my cold has hit me hard. Only during loud music or gibberish am I comfortable enough to blow my nose.

Day Forty-five - Conversation with Strangers

Nimisha calls today. When I first hear her voice, I think it is to ask me to do a yoga class. It turns out to be something even better. She tells me to call Yuthika about a change of space. They are assigning me a different room! I call and leave a message because she isn't there.

Later in the morning, I stop by her office to see her. Yuthika says I'm getting a new room in the pyramid section of the ashram - - a quiet area. I am to pick up the key tomorrow after work. She said to call her during the day, and she will let me know when I can pick it up.

After talking to Yuthika, I go to see Yadgar.

"Thank you for your suggestion about turning on the light," I tell her. "And thank you for arranging the room switch."

She says, "I presented it to the space team."

Although Andre took the step that made this happen, there is so much involved. Yuthika had already told me to buy a mosquito net. If she hadn't been sick, Andre couldn't have gone to Yadgar, who I had already done a favor for. Everything fit together perfectly for this to happen. Whatever the reasons are, everything came out in my favor, and for that I am grateful.

I have no idea who my roommate will be, but I'm hopeful we'll get along. I haven't seen the room yet, but it has a relaxing, peaceful place to sit outside. Yesterday when I walked by the area, I saw some cool birds.

When I tell Chandra, she says my new room must be in Omar Khayam, because that's where they have shared bathrooms. And I thought, how cool is that - - then I can skip Evening Meetings, and go back to my room without going through the gates. It's good that it didn't work out that way, though, because I should go to some of them.

The back pyramid area is the quietest place to be. It's far from the laundry and food, but with more sleep I'll have more energy. It is exactly what I've wanted. I hope there will be no mosquitoes there.

I have another two-hour workshop this afternoon with Sakra. It is a follow up on the three-day workshop I had last week. First, we watch an Osho video on awareness at work. It is enjoyable, and I may even try to buy it at the bookstore. Afterward, we talk about it, and then we have to write out answers on a question sheet. My one insight about Revatii isn't applicable to any of the questions. After Sakra says the information is for our personal information only, I write it down.

Lastly, we get into groups of four and discuss our answers. The three men I am with all have customer service jobs and deal with many people. They were all more successful at being present than I was. When it is my turn to talk, I say I lose all awareness as soon as I walk into the office and get behind the computer.

After work, I hurriedly put on my jeans and rush out to find Phani. He isn't there, so I go to the office to call him. The phone rings for a long time before he answers. He tells me that he is sick and has been sleeping. Then I go outside and walk down the street hoping to find the snake guy.

As I walk toward the area where I usually find him, two well-dressed Indian men stop me. Their names are Deep and Ram. Ram does most of the talking. He excitedly tells me he has recently gotten a new "gourmet" job. At least, that's what it sounds like. I say, "Like a cook?" It takes many words and much patience on everyone's part for me to figure out that he said, "government!" Ram also tells me he is going to school to become a lawyer.

We talk about many subjects. Hinduism comes up, and I say, "I like it, but don't agree with the caste system."

They both say in unison, "No, no, all men are equal." They tell me women are also prominent in the Hindu religion as most of their gods have significant others. Shiva and Parvati. Ganesh and sometimes Laksmi. Ram and Deep also tell me how important it is to be a vegetarian. They are happy when I say that I am.

Both Ram and Deep are married, and Ram's wife is having a baby in four months. I ask them about the bindi, because Phani wears one, but neither Ram nor Deep have one. It is difficult to understand the whole answer, but it sounds like different regions have different customs. I always nod my head many times in my conversations, because there is so much I don't understand. They did say that married women wear a gold necklace.

Talking to these two guys is a treat. Indians are so friendly and helpful. Ram says that is part of their culture. I love these people.

While I talk to Ram and Deep, the snake guy walks past. He points to the corner and says to talk to him later. It distracts me so I forget to take a picture of Deep and Ram. But, Ram gives me his address because he wants me to send him a Christmas card. Also, he gives me one of those tiny wallet pictures of himself.

At the end of our conversation, the three of us shake hands and do the "knuckle bump." Doing that with these two Indian gentlemen starts me laughing hysterically! What a great experience this has been.

After saying good-bye to Ram and Deep, I walk over to where the snake guy is. He is with several other Indian men sitting on a log, and he invites me to sit with them. There are several cloth bags, and I point to them asking, "Sanp?" That is Hindi for snake. But, they aren't snakes. I sit next to an elderly, grandfather-looking gentleman who is his Uncle Makeen.

Uncle Makeen has a commanding presence and a charismatic manner. He wants to show me a magic show. He starts with two silk scarves, knotting them together. I look at the snake guy and say, "Where's the sanp?" The snake guy shakes his head and looks at Uncle Makeen. And, Uncle Makeen keeps going with his performance. At one point, the knotted together scarves are in my hand, and I think maybe he will pick them up and leave the cobra behind. But no, he only does his trick. It is cool, but not what I am looking for. I say, "I can see magic in America - - I want to see a cobra!"

Uncle Makeen continues. I keep saying, "No magic! I want sanps!" Finally, he puts the scarves away, and we start talking about the snakes. First, I have to get it across that I want a cobra only. Then, we talk about the price. I want it for two hundred rupees, but we finally agree on two hundred fifty, although he isn't happy with that.

After we have settled it, the snake guy and I walk away from the others. He says, "Come on, I'm just a country boy."

So I say, "And I am NOT a rich American! I can get the other snake for two hundred fifty rupees." It ends that he will bring it on Wednesday. He says not to tell anyone. The good part is that I will see the snake outside the ashram. Now, I don't have to go to his house and pay Phani to be a bodyguard.

Day Forty-six - Woo-woo Days

My new room is twice the size of my old room. I missed having a chair in my old room, and this one has a chair. It also has an air conditioner, and shelves inside the large closet. The Plaza with its constant music is now far, far away. The new room is close to my office, and more importantly, quiet, quiet, and quiet. My new roommate is Bhava, someone I know from my groups.

As I stand in my old room and look out the window for the final time, a little down feather floats by. A gift from my mother! I go downstairs to look for it. Although I can't find it, I still feel like it has special meaning for me. My mother may have arranged the room change. Or, maybe she's letting me know that she approves of it.

After packing the last of my belongings, I'm about to lock the door for the final time at my old room. When I hear someone knocking, I look around and see no one. But, I keep hearing the knocking. So I say, "Yeah?" The guy two doors down from me answers. Someone had locked him into his room as a joke! Since most of the rooms lock with bolts across the door and padlocks, it is easy to lock someone in.

Today I have to go to the stationery section to get some paper. There is a sweet, little Indian girl there named Rasha. The other day (when I was having one of my famous "bad hair days"), she suggested that I use henna. She told me it would turn my hair maroon. Since I wear maroon, she probably thought I'd like that! I asked how to get it darker like her black hair. She explained how to put coffee or tea in it to make it darker.

When I see her today, she says, "You didn't use the henna yet!"

I say, "I looked it up on the Internet, and indigo might work better to make my hair dark." She doesn't think that is right and again describes the henna.

Then, I ask her, "Where I can get those stick-on bindis?"

She says, "I get them for you!"

I say, "No, no, I'll get them myself."

Rasha says, "Why can't I get them for you? We are friends, no?" What can I say? Her salary in India can't be much at all, and yet she offers to buy me something. I doubt if they are expensive, but still, the thoughtfulness and generosity of these people amaze me.

Rasha also helps me with my Hindi. Different people pronounce words differently, or even have different words for the same object. It must be because there are so many languages here. I'm learning, though.

129

Aap kaise hai? How are you? Theek houn. I am fine.

Jiadore tells me an entertaining story today. While she sat at a table at Zorba Restaurant, some guy asked if he could sit with her. She says he talked and talked, and then she asked him one question. "Why are you here now?"

And his answer was, "To have sex with as many women as possible." So, this place is still a sex haven. I'm glad I'm celibate.

An Indian guy who I've said hello to for a while, suddenly ignores me. It is weird. He is the one I ran into New Year's Eve. He wasn't happy when I told him I wanted to go back to my room. Maybe he is sensitive about that, but I thought he had said hello to me since then.

Woo-woo warning! I've thought about Uncle Makeen a great deal. He made an impression on me. I feel he was a general, a king, and perhaps even a master in his previous lives. He gives off an aura of royalty. I feel like I should kneel at his feet - - this old, poor street magician. Also, I get the feeling that it wasn't that he did something bad and this life is a punishment. It was more that he chose this life for other reasons.

It might be my romantic musings (not romantic as in love, but romantic as in castles and kings and faraway places), but I think the old coot has some heart. I'd like to see him again to see how it feels the next time. If he is a Hindu and I told him this, he would probably understand. But, if he is a Muslim, and I think he is, he would think I am crazy - - which I probably am.

And while we are in the woo-woo arena, I might as well interject this. When I told an acquaintance about some of my cobra adventures, she said, "I wonder what past life this is coming from?" Since my brother is a biology teacher and always had snakes and spiders at our house, I never considered that. I always thought it was part of my upbringing. That doesn't explain, though, why cobras have always fascinated me. My brother never had a cobra. I start researching on the Internet, and it turns out that snake charmers, in the "olden days" were also herbalists and healers. That, I can identify with. I've been here before. I have held a cobra before. No wonder it is so important for me to do it again.

Day Forty-seven – Good Transaction

Last night I had my first shower experience in my new room. Every night before I shower, I do an Ayurvedic procedure on myself called abhyanga. It is a head-to-foot oil self-massage. On this evening, I do my abhyanga and then turn on the shower. The right knob says H and the left one C. So, I turn on the one labeled H and wait for it to warm up. It doesn't.

Meanwhile, I'm dripping with oil and shivering from the cold, waiting for the water to warm up. Then, I think maybe they reversed the knobs, so I turn on the left one. It is even colder! So, I turn the right knob back on. While I wait for it to heat up, I try to wash as much of me as I can in the sink. Washing my hair isn't too bad, but washing the rest of me isn't easy. I run over to the shower and douse myself with cold water, and then run back to the sink to warm up with the warm water there. It is only a few steps, but dripping with cold water and oil, it feels like a mile. This procedure takes forever, and is not much fun. This morning, I ask roommate-Bhava, and she says they reversed the knobs - - that this is India.

Today is a nature day. As I cross the street on my way to lunch, I notice the wind blowing the leaves from the trees. The small leaves float gently through the air and remind me of the snow that I miss so much. The leaves fall to earth at their own quiet speed, so peaceful, so beautiful. Then, as I wait for my pizza, I look up to see some of those beautiful birds of prey circling in the sky. Two of them dodge back and forth right at each other. Then in the tree, is a beautiful, little yellow bird the color of a goldfinch. Then, two butterflies flit by. What wonderful sights!

The way they serve the pizza and anything else you order is efficient. You order and pay at the cashier, who hands you a slip of paper and a small, round device. Then you turn around and hand the slip of paper to the cook behind you. After five or ten minutes, the device goes off with red blinking lights and a buzzer. Then you trade it in for the pizza, eggs, spaghetti, or whatever else you have ordered. It's a cool system.

At work today, someone calls the reception desk about a problem with her light. She says her name, but I don't catch it. Then she jokes about the light and laughs. I thought it was Revatii. Since I had never heard her laugh, though, I doubted it! Later, when I deliver Revatii's mail to her, she points out the problem with the lights. So, she can laugh, after all. Now, I've seen a new side of Revatii.

There is one possible badness with my room. Bhava's boyfriend uses the bathroom. When I went to the bathroom today, the seat was wet. Unfortunately, I didn't realize it until I stood up! I'm hoping it wasn't from him not picking up the toilet seat! Later, when I went in to the bathroom I found the toilet seat up, so that probably wasn't the case.

The other badness is that I left my towel in the bathroom. When I went to use it later, it had a suspicious brown mark in the middle of it. I'll have to keep my towel in my room. Not such a big deal. Whatever it is, I can deal with it. Bhava is a great person, so I know it will be fine.

After work, I walk down the street to where I am to meet the snake guy. He sits there with one of his brothers and several other Indian gentlemen. He forgot the snake. The guy who owns the snake is there, and now he wants to bargain. I stand up and say, "I already have another snake I can see for two hundred fifty rupees, so let's forget it."

The snake guy, Zakir, who is more like a snake middleman, says, "Sit down, it's okay."

The snake owner then says, "You can see one snake for two hundred fifty rupees, and two snakes - - one big, one small - - for five hundred rupees."

I say, "I only want to see the one big one for two hundred fifty rupees." I also show them the picture of me with my snake. I'm not sure if it impresses them or not! However, when they talk about what snake to bring and I say it has to be a cobra, they finally understand. If they don't forget, tomorrow is the new snake day.

My rickshaw driver friend, Phani, is still sick. It worries me. For these guys to stay out sick is a huge deal. They still have to pay for the use of the rickshaw when they are out sick. I hope he's all right.

Since I didn't see the snake and tonight is gate duty, I decide to go to German Bakery to get some chocolate. I walk up there, saying a brief hello to Gowri on my way. I cross the street easily with the median, go in to German Bakery and buy a piece of chocolate pie. It is rich, moist, and delicious! This will give me such a sugar-high that I will never get to sleep tonight. If someone said that to me, I would answer, "Argue for your limitations, and they're yours."

On my way back, I stop to see Gowri, and she puts something on the ground for me to sit on. She says that I always come and go and come and go and come and go. Then she pulls out a beautiful wall hanging. Once I had mentioned to her that I like those little mirrors on wall hangings. This one has the little mirrors, and embroidery of people and animals.

I tell her it looks expensive and ask how much it is. Gowri says, "You tell me."

I say, "Two hundred rupees," knowing that is too little.

She says, "Okay," and wraps it in plastic and hands it to me. Something feels weird. I'm not sure if she is trying to make up for when she asked me for money or if it is something else.

I say, "No, that's not enough. What would you normally get for it?"

She says, "Five hundred fifty rupees." Of course, that is the starting price and it comes down from there.

After digging into my pocket, I give her three hundred rupees. Her eyes light up and she says, "One hundred rupees more?"

I say, "Yes!" And we both laugh. I say, "You knew I would like this one, didn't you? Because of the mirrors? Did you save it for me?" She shakes her head, yes, and I think she probably did. It is a good transaction, whether or not it is a good deal!

I show her the picture of me at twenty-five years old with the snake around my neck. She has a long conversation in Hindi with the street vendor next to her. Each of them sprinkles the conversation with the word, "cobra." I keep saying, "What are you saying? What are you saying?" They both laugh. So, I ask them how to say crazy in Hindi. It is pagal. So, I point to myself and say, "Pagal, cobra pagal."

Gowri says, "No, no, no." The three of us laugh.

When I walk by the crabby woman vendor who was rude to me the other day for asking in Hindi, I stop to talk to her. I say, "Aap kaisi hai?" That is Hindi for how are you. She answers me in Hindi and asks me how I am. I answer, "Theek houn." That is fine in Hindi. Then we both laugh and I walk on. That felt good.

Although I've been skipping Evening Meeting on gate duty nights, I decide to go tonight. I feel so grateful for my new room, I shouldn't try to get out of it. At least tonight!

Gate duty isn't too bad. It would be almost enjoyable seeing all the people and everything going on, if it wasn't for the pollution, the mosquitoes, and three hours of my time!

There is a cute dog close to the gate. Someone must have trained him. When he sees people, he makes a bow to beg for food. Dogs here are engaging. There are many of them wandering all over the streets. Although they are skinny or maybe half starved, homeless, and some are mangy, they all are generous with their tail wags, and always have a smile on their faces. My cousin warned me not to touch them. I haven't, but I would like to. It wouldn't take much convincing for me to gather these stray dogs and stray children and bring them all back home with me. They all have such character that I can't help admiring their attitude and their courage.

Day Forty-eight – 1984 Revisited

I couldn't sleep last night because of that delicious chocolate pie that I ate. The sugar raced through my body and kept me awake most of the night. At least it wasn't mosquitoes!

When I go to brush my teeth this morning, I unbolt my side of the bathroom door and pull. Nothing. Someone locked the bathroom door from the inside! After uttering a few expletives, I laugh. This is what I did to Chandra, my old bathroom roommate, when I first arrived at the ashram.

I run into Bhava later at the water filling station at the bottom of our stairs. I tell her we have to make a deal about the bathroom door. She suggests that we don't lock the door, but always knock before entering. Fine with me. It's not as "free" as it was with Chandra. That's okay. Flexibility is one of my lessons. The problem is that Bhava's boyfriend uses the bathroom. Whatever, it will be better now than it was.

I go to Silent Sitting today and enjoy it as usual. Inside that meditation room, I feel the presence of Osho. Although I wasn't going to go today, I felt like he wanted me to. I become peaceful in there and almost fall asleep.

Although Chandra told me I couldn't go, I wouldn't let that stop me! When I come in fifteen or twenty minutes late, she doesn't suspect anything and never says a word about it. As long as I don't confess on my own where I was, I think I'll be okay if I only go occasionally. Especially since she comes in late in the morning and after lunch most days.

When I see Rasha today, she says, "Wait a minute! I go get them for you!" She disappears, to reappear a minute later. Looking around carefully, she hands me two different packages of bindis. She says, "Don't tell anyone." Someone else walks up at that moment, so I can't ask her why. I wonder if she can get in trouble for associating with the Osho-ites.

The Osho text I'm working on doesn't match the audio files. The files were recorded when Osho was still Bhagwan. In the text, they are changing Bhagwan to Osho. I write a note saying that although I am a newcomer and ignorant of the Osho ways, I feel that it is Orwellian, like *1984*, that they are trying to change history. Osho used to be Bhagwan and that is a fact. Are they planning to redub his voice in the spots where he called himself Bhagwan? I don't think Osho would approve of that.

Zakir was going to bring the snake today and he stood me up. Although I go out there several times to see if he is only late, he never shows up. It disappoints me, because I thought I might get to hold a cobra today. Now, I have to start again. I'm going to have to go back to the other guy from the train station.

Something has been on my mind, lately. There are many instances here with old, gray haired men with young, vibrant women on their arms. They are not "only" old men, though. They are facilitators - - they wear the black and white robes. I can see how young girls can see them as charismatic. I guess. Yesterday, I saw Dwami with a young woman. His girlfriend. He is around seventy. She is twenty-four, if that. She brought him a coke and opened it for him. In the lecture of his that I attended, he surprised me with his aggressiveness. With her, he was soft as a child. Gentle and kind. An amazing transformation. Of course, she is young enough to be his grandchild, so I guess it's appropriate!

Now, I'm sorry, but I have to add this in. I read it on the Internet. The difference between a sixty-year-old woman with a thirty-year-old boyfriend, and a sixty-year-old man with a thirty-year-old girlfriend, is the sixty-year-old woman knows she looks like an idiot.

Day Forty-nine - All the Snake Charmers Went to Bombay

When I see Rasha this morning, I show her that I'm wearing a bindi. She says it is very nice, but I have it on upside down! It's narrow and looks like an ankh. That's the Egyptian symbol meaning life, which looks like a cross with a circle on top. It must be something else, though, because it's on wrong. Unfortunately, since I can't feel it on my forehead, I can't use it to help me be aware.

When I walk down to where Zakir and those guys usually hang out, Zakir isn't there. Instead, I run into his cousin, his brother Khalid, and Khalid's cute little son. The cousin calls Zakir from his cell phone. Zakir tells him that all the snake charmers went to Bombay. We arrange to meet on Monday, when the snake charmers will be back in town.

Khalid proudly tells me that his son will be attending English school. From what I have learned, it costs money to go to school here. That would be an accomplishment for a street magician. The boy looks preschool age now, so it will be awhile before he goes to school.

Since they called Zakir from a cell phone, I have to talk about cell phones here. While they are not as ubiquitous as in the United States, they are more common than you'd think. I've seen street vendors with them, and even my rickshaw driver, Phani, has one. I find it all so comical. When I first saw a street vendor with one, it shocked me so much, I asked to take his picture!

Tonight, Evening Meeting goes back to that other format that I can't stand. First, the woman, Maneesha, asks a long, detailed question. Then Osho slowly, and I mean slowly, repeats the question. It drives me crazy. I'm going to have to figure something out, because I think too many people know me now to pull anything shady.

Last night during Osho's discourse, he talked about gibberish and he said something about being a coward. It felt like a dare, so of course I had to do it. All this time I thought I was thirty years old emotionally, now I see that I'm only fourteen after all.

I like doing gibberish. Tonight I even do it without the dare. I swing my arms, spout made up words, move my whole body, and get right into it. If I like it, I'm not going to stop only because I don't want to "go along" here. That is stupid. I need to do what I want to do, regardless. If I want to do something that happens to be something they want me to do - - that's all right, too.

On my way back from Evening Meeting, I run into Bhava, my bathroom roommate. She has a new floating job - - counting the people

137

with a clicker as they come into Evening Meeting. She says it is usually between five hundred and seven hundred. Wow! And I thought I was exaggerating when I said five hundred. I ask her how she likes the job. She says, "I like it, but now I can't skip, if you know what I mean." I'm not the only one! I am so happy to hear her say that. She is into all this, too, and she still wants to skip.

An hour after Evening Meeting, I dress in my jeans and go to Celebrating Sannyas in the pyramid auditorium. First, they have live music and dancing. The music is excessively loud even with toilet paper stuffed in my ears. My body feels the vibrations from the music although I sit at the back of the auditorium.

Shortly, an announcer comes on and says if you want sannyas, you need to write your name on the list at the desk. He says, "If you have discovered Osho through a friend, or books, or the Internet, and you are ready for sannyas, come on down. Or if you just have something to celebrate, you are welcome, too."

After a couple more songs, the lights go dim, and everyone sits on the cold, marble floor. Several cushions are placed in the center of the auditorium. The announcer calls some names, mostly Sanskrit names, and those people sit on the cushions. Then a piece of Osho's discourse plays, and then a second piece of him talking about going inward. After that, soft music comes on and everyone except the people on the cushions stands up and starts dancing again. The people on the cushions get up slowly - - I guess they have to let everything soak in.

The next song is faster, and people dance together or in groups, sometimes holding hands and dancing in a circle, some people hugging. A guy sitting in a chair a couple seats down from me holds up the palms of his hands toward the crowd while I am there. He also clasps his hands together in prayer position and holds them at his third eye. He alternates this with holding up his hands. These people scare me.

Day Fifty - Trouble with Camels

For the first time in a couple weeks, I got plenty of sleep last night. I feel great! I'm grateful to be alive! I'm grateful to be in India! I'm grateful for the new experiences I'm having! I'm grateful that I turned a corner this morning and a beautiful, turquoise peacock approached me!

I finished my work project and I will move on to something else. It doesn't sound too bad the way Sakra describes it. But I also have to do the photos. The two projects together should keep it from getting boring. Also, I have been breaking the guy at the cyber cafe. That is cool, too, because I can surf the Internet while I sit there. It's busy, but I have plenty of time between customers.

My maroon robe somehow finds its way into the toilet again today. I hate when that happens. Now I have to wash it again, and I barely got it out of the laundry.

I wear a bindi again today. This time I wear a small, circular red garnet-like one. I can't get this one upside down! It's interesting that these Indian men who used to pay me no attention, now smile at me. And Gowri has told me that wearing a bindi means that I'm married.

After work, I go outside the gates again. When I get to the main road, I hear a drum playing. Across the busy street, a man has set up a tightrope. While a little girl walks across it, he plays the drum. I watch for a minute and walk on.

The man with the flutes is back, so I stop and ask him how much they are. He keeps picking them up and playing them for me. I tell him I don't want to play it, I only want to take a picture with it, so I don't care how it sounds. He doesn't understand me.

We finally agree on sixty rupees, and I point to one inside a cellophane wrapper. He starts unwrapping it! Shaking my head no, I point to one still in the wrapper. Finally, he understands and gives me a wrapped one. I pay him seventy rupees. Bargaining is fun, but ten rupees, maybe a quarter, means much more to him than to me.

When I get down the street to Gowri, she saw me with the flute and was laughing at what happened. I tell her that I wanted it for the cobra and he kept playing it. So, she calls him over! She has a long conversation with him in Hindi, pointing to me, saying cobra, holding up her hand like a cobra, and pointing to me again. When she does this to me, it always fascinates me. The way it ended is that I think the guy is going to bring a cobra a week from Sunday. At least, I think that's what's going to happen.

Then I walk down to German Bakery to change a traveler's check. Thirty-eight rupees for a dollar. One rupee more than I can get at the ashram. While I'm there, I buy a chocolate bar, in case I can't get back there before gate duty night.

I am such a kid, and sometimes my innocence and naiveté get me into trouble. When I come out of German Bakery, there stands a camel waiting for me to ride. Of course, I can't resist. I say, "Fifty rupees?" He surprises me when he accepts so quickly, because usually they try to get you to pay more. I should have known something was amiss.

Then the camel leans down and allows me to kiss him on the nose. Well, I would have to admit, that is worth the fifty rupees right there. The guy says, "You can pet him. His name is Raja." And the guy stands there. My fifty rupees have disappeared, and he stands there like the transaction is over.

I say, "What about the ride?"

And he says, "Oh, you want to ride?" Then he asks the camel, Raja, to go down on its knees. Raja is a tall camel, and I have to boost myself up to get into the saddle. We walk up and down the street, and he asks Raja to get down in front of German Bakery where we started. When I'm off, he says, "One hundred fifty rupees for the ride."

I say, "No way. I've ridden twice before and it was fifty rupees."

He says, "It's one hundred fifty rupees to ride the camel."

I say, "I'll give you twenty rupees more." Although I don't think he should get any extra money, not having had an encounter like this before, I don't know how to handle it.

Then, another kind and helpful local saves me. While I'm arguing with the camel guy, a man in a suit comes up and talks to the guy. He asks me, "He didn't tell you that in advance?"

I say, "No."

He says, "Well, you might want to give him something," and he starts to walk away.

I say, "I already gave him fifty rupees!" So, the gentleman turns around and talks to the camel guy again. Then, he tells me to come inside because the guy is trying to cheat me.

I follow him into German Bakery, thank him, and then go out the side door. Unfortunately, the camel guy is at my favorite crossing place by the median, where I can cross easily. There is much traffic today. Somehow, I wait long enough for a break on both sides of the traffic and run across.

It reminds me of when I started scuba diving off the coast of

California, and you had to wait for a break in the waves. The only difference is that if you missed with the waves, they would pound you into the sand. If you miss with the traffic, well, you don't want to miss with the traffic.

Day Fifty-one – Losing My Friend

Dilasa is going home! I'm upset that he's leaving, because he has been my one voice of sanity here. He is the one I have confided in. He has commiserated and counseled me. Who will listen to my tales of rebellion? What am I going to do without him? I will miss him.

Rumor has it that he's an outcast and has a bad reputation. That's why he has been hanging out here and not working. That would explain why I get along with him! But, it couldn't be true. They would not have given him the keys of Osho's Rolls Royce, if it were true.

I have asked many Osho-ites if they meditate. All of them either give excuses or tell me Evening Meeting is their meditation. Dilasa is the only one who meditates every day - - the way I do - - sitting quietly in silence.

But, I do find it odd that he's leaving, when he was going to stay through March. He told me that Dwami wouldn't let him sit at his usual place anymore. That and perhaps more have something to do with it. Ah, well. I'm on my own now, but I have a couple "kind of" friends, although they are Osho-ites or near-Osho-ites.

When I tell Prana about my brother making that bet against me, she thinks it is cruel. When I tell her there would be no way I would leave now, she says maybe my brother mentioned the bet as incentive. That would be too benevolent of him.

My new project at work has me thinking. I like everything spelled out, so I know exactly where I am. Now, they have given me a convoluted and confusing new job. Normally, I don't do well with projects like that. Instead of complaining and struggling with it, I have decided to accept it. Maybe it is another lesson I need to learn.

Since the project was hers before, Chakori gives me some information today. She says, "Look at all this that was done with volunteer labor. It's pretty miraculous, really." She is right. It does surprise me how into "doing Osho's work" these people are.

I am doing that, too, but in a different way. Shortly after I started, Prana said to me, "I think you were chosen for this job." Yes, I was. And, I think Osho chose me. It's my destiny to write this book about Osho and my time in the ashram. That is why I was given the job of going through his books, so I could get a feel for him. Now that he is in the place of all knowing, he may have recognized the flaws in some of his ideas. He wants those flaws made public. With any luck, that's exactly what I'm going to do.

I'd like to say something about safety. In America, we take it for granted that we will be safe. I'm not talking about crime; I'm talking about getting hurt. If you walk down the street, you know you will not fall in an unmarked hole. If you walk on a path in the dark, you know that lights will shine on any stairs. I've said it before - - the rules are different here.

A friend of a friend has this huge scratch on his leg. It is so big that when he tells me it is from a tiger, I believe him! I'm gullible, though. The sidewalks here sometimes have these removable cement "plates" on them. I'm not sure why. I've seen plates like them in cities in America, and there are meters underneath. As this guy walked down the street, he stepped on one of the plates. It cracked under his weight (not a big guy). His leg went a couple of feet inside the hole, scraping it as he went down.

I have been walking on those plates every day I go outside the gates, and now I will always walk around them. There are holes everywhere, and rubble - - rocks and broken cement. Even in the clean and first class ashram, it has poorly lit stairs. When I first arrived here and before I learned where everything was, I stumbled a couple times in the dark. Luckily, I never fell. Even now, I have to be careful. The rules are different here. India is not such a litigious culture as the United States.

For tonight's Evening Meeting, I have something new planned. First, I prepare everything by putting a slit in the pocket of my white robe. Then, I color about a foot of the earplug cables dark so they will look like hair, and run them from the pocket up my back. Next, I put my black iPod into two white socks to cover and protect it. I slip it into my pocket and plug into the earphones. Before I leave my room, I set up the iPod to play my favorite songs.

When everyone starts dancing, I put the earphones in, but can't hear my music because the music in the auditorium is so loud. When I put my hand in the sock to adjust the volume, the little light on the iPod comes on. Quickly, I cover the light with both hands! I make it a little too loud. During the silences right before Osho comes on, I keep looking around thinking everyone can hear it. But, they can't. This is so sacrilegious that they would probably throw me out of India if they catch me! But, oh, it makes Evening Meeting go so quickly.

Day Fifty-two - Kicked Out!

It has been freezing here - - only seventy-five the last two days! I am shivering in my shoes! When the wind blows and the temperature is "only" seventy-five, it feels chilly. I heard some other people complaining about the cold. One said, "Well, it is winter in India!"

When I go into my room at lunch today, I immediately realize that someone has been in it. Today is not my cleaning day. They didn't make an effort to conceal their presence, because they left a couple items obviously out of place from where I had left them. They even used the bathroom. Outside my bathroom door, I had a little foot towel that they tossed aside and put down a new one. Also, they didn't lock the bathroom door from my side of the room. And I hear the toilet making that weird sound when you don't flush it right.

I tell Prana at work about it, and she says I should call security. They don't answer. Later, while doing work errands in the ashram, I go in to see Yuthika. First, I tell her how much I love the new room, and then tell her what had happened. She says that sometimes Sudexo sends their guys in to make sure you're keeping the room tidy, and that I shouldn't worry about it. It bothered me, but I guess nothing is missing. After this, though, I will make sure to keep everything locked up.

For lunch, I go with Jiadore to a new place that Prana suggested. We take a rickshaw there. At first, the driver wants twenty rupees, and we walk away until he calls us back. You have to do that.

The restaurant advertises itself as "fast food." There are no golden arches, however! They have a menu, but we eat thali. That is one plate of food with many different items in small tins. On the plate is white rice, two kinds of chapatis (Indian tortillas) - - crisp and soft - - and then several little tins of other food, including some vegetables all squished together, some soup with beans in it, and a couple other Indian dishes. It is all spicy hot, except the white rice and vegetables. I keep getting the hiccups from the heat. I have to order a coke so I can finish eating. It is wonderful, though, and I enjoy it. And, I am stuffed afterward. For both of our lunches and one coke it is ninety-five rupees. That's two and a half dollars. The lunch is thirty-five rupees, and the coke twenty-five rupees.

We both have another afternoon seminar today and we walk in ten minutes late. Luckily, all we miss is dancing and loud, earsplitting music. We walk in and the music stops! Yippee.

Komya is the woman who wears the black and white robe of the facilitator today. She tells us that she has just finished her training, and this is her first class. We start by getting into groups of four or five and discuss how we have maintained awareness at work this week. Small groups like this used to bother me, but I think I am getting over that. Another lesson learned here.

I tell my group how I got a bindi, hoping the pressure on my forehead would make me more aware of my surroundings and my actions. They all like the idea. Then they laugh when I tell them the bindi was so comfortable, that it didn't work unless I touched it or crinkled my forehead. Felipe mentions that he usually needs something external to remind him - - such as dropping something on the floor, or accidentally kicking something with his foot.

Then we talk about guilt. Sajeev says that he stopped feeling guilty years ago. He says that when he does something he shouldn't do, or doesn't do something he should do - - it is not deliberate, so why feel guilty about it. It's an accident. He says that even forgiving yourself is indicative that you did something wrong. If you didn't do it deliberately, then it isn't wrong and it isn't something that needs forgiveness. I like most of Sajeev's ideas. He is a gentle spirit and a wise man. What is he doing here at the ashram?

A new girl who recently arrived at the ashram is in our group. She starts talking and then bursts out in tears. Felipe tells her the first fourteen days are difficult, and that many of us have gone through that. I wish I would have known that. It would have made it easier for me.

Next, we watch an Osho video of him discussing the difference between workaholism and loving to work. The main difference according to Osho was workaholism is if you do it without awareness; and loving to work is if you are total and do it for Osho. In a Tom Sawyer moment, he talked about how people like doing work for him, and that it serves both of them. It serves Osho because they do his work for him and it serves the other people because they like doing work for Osho. He was proud that he gets people to do work for him. Can you be proud and enlightened, or does one cancel the other, I wonder? I like Osho - - I think he's wise - - but some of his ideas are simply ridiculous.

Osho also talked about how the Japanese never used to have a day off, and they liked it that way. Then the government decided to give them one day off a week, and they resisted. "What could we do?" Osho mimics. It reminds me of the woman a couple weeks ago who was given the day off and didn't want it. Osho was unintentionally talking about his own people! They don't know what to do with themselves if they have a day off.

After the video, we do an exercise where we do four simple tasks. We are also to take five conscious breaths as a "neutral gear" between each task. The breaths create a separation between each of the four tasks. Komya says this is another tool we can use at work. I like this and realize that I have done this myself before. I like and need that neutral gear between tasks. And I have known this about myself for years.

Next, we do an exercise where we act like workaholics. When Komya says freeze, we stop and see how it feels. After that, we do the neutral breathing. Then we do another complete series (including feeling the feeling and neutral breathing) with acting with awareness, achievement oriented, and finally celebrating ourselves. For the celebratory gesture, I raise my arms signaling a touchdown (or an Osho! motion), but nobody else does that.

After the seminar, I go looking for Zakir to see if he brought the snake. He didn't. I used to think of Zakir as a slimy used car salesman, but now he has dropped the fake smile and most of the used car persona. Today, he asks, "Do you want to kiss the snake on the mouth?"

I say, "I could."

He says, "You shouldn't."

I ask, "Can I hold it?"

He says, "It is all right to hold it, but you shouldn't kiss it on the mouth because it is poisonous."

I'm not sure what this odd exchange is about. I'd like to think that I've been hanging around him so much, that he's beginning to like me. But I don't want to be that naive, and I'm sure it's more like him protecting his investment - - because I told him I want to see the snake many times.

I'm still disappointed that he didn't bring the snake today, so I say to him, "For a guy who is really into rupees, you are missing opportunities to get my money."

And very philosophically, he says, "No, no rupees. What is important is people." Just when he has me, he adds, "And when you go back to America, you can give me something then." Ah, Zakir, you could make a fortune selling used cars in America! Or beachfront property in Arizona.

On the ground in front of where we sit, is one of their pink magic bags. When I walk by it, it makes a noise. When I look at Waseem, he says it is a bird for the magic show. After we sit there a while, I ask, "Is it too hot for the bird in the bag?"

He says, "No, it is a very small bird." I'll have to see the magic show sometime.

146

As I sit with the brothers, Zakir points to the old man next to him and says it is Makeen's brother. I had once asked if I could interview Uncle Makeen, and Zakir says I can interview them together. I tell him I only want Makeen. The brother is an old Indian man missing his front teeth. He's a pleasant guy, but doesn't have the commanding presence, the charisma, or the power that Uncle Makeen radiates.

Osho's brother works with me in my office. He's in a different area, but I run into him now and then. He looks similar. He is a sweetheart of a man, quiet and soft-spoken. But he, also, has none of the charisma or power or presence of his brother.

Jiadore tells me something amusing today. I have mentioned before about the mixed-up rooster that crows at odd times during the day. When I run into her at lunch today, she says she didn't hear the rooster. I ask, "What rooster?"

She says, "Oh, come on!" It turns out there is a fake rooster that crows at certain times. Tonight while I meditate, I hear the rooster crow. I open my eyes momentarily to see what time it is, and it is exactly six o'clock. So, I will have to be more aware of the rooster to see when it crows.

Chandra finished some training. I ask, "Does it bother you that you have to pay for training, and then use it to help the ashram?"

She says, "I can use it when I go back to Chicago." These people don't think of it as spending money for the ashram's benefit. I believe they are glad to take part in something that is doing Osho's work. It is such a curious mindset that I can't get past it. In some ways, it reminds me of buying condolences to get to heaven. Are these people buying the training to get closer to Osho?

Tonight at Evening Meeting, as I listen to my iPod and not paying attention, a tiny, little cough escapes my mouth. The woman sitting next to me touches my arm and motions me out. I motion back that it won't happen again. The next second, that big Indian by the door jumps up and starts toward me. Immediately, I gather my belongings and walk out the door.

In the entranceway where the shoes are, it is dark like in the auditorium itself. There is someone out there with a flashlight. It is a woman I recognize from work. In my haste to leave, I accidentally drop my back-jack on the ground and it makes a noise. She looks horrified as she clasps her hand over her mouth. I whisper, "Sorry," put on my shoes, run down the stairs and out the door.

After taking a few steps, I realize I don't want to go anywhere.

Carefully, I open the door again, enter, and close it as quietly as I can. Then, the woman with the flashlight leans over the top railing, so I leave.

Slowly, slowly, I walk through the Meera eating area and out the other side. I don't want to go to the "coughing" place. I stop in front of a foliage area so I can listen to the crickets. Well, listen to them as best I can with my iPod music still in my ears.

Several Sudexo guys walk past me, but no one says anything. Sitting on the wall, I wait. After a few minutes, I figure I'd better go, so I head toward the gate. After only a few steps, I look up and see the locked gate! So, I sit back down by the crickets.

A few minutes later, a guard approaches me and says something that I can't hear through my music. I tell him the gate is locked. He motions me to follow him and pulls the gate open. It is only closed, not locked.

The new coughing area is at the entrance to the ashram, right off the street. As I walk toward it, I see many shoes lined up outside the door. There is no way I am going to leave my good tennis shoes outside, not to mention walk in there without shoes. So, I go in and plunk myself down close to the door - - with my shoes still on. No one says a word. I am only there for a half hour, but I get mosquito bites all over. Probably because I can't hear them through the music of my iPod!

It is one of those interminably long Evening Meetings. When the clapping starts, someone in the back slips past me and out the door. Hesitating only for an instant, I jump up and follow. They let us through the front gate with no problems. After walking through the main resort, I reach the back and see the closed pyramid gate. I ask if I can get in, and they say yes. Ah, finally back in my room.

What an ordeal this was. I had thought about deliberately coughing to have the experience of the "coughing place," but this spontaneous experience is much better. Awful, but better. More spontaneous. More outrageous. More mosquitoes. They put sick people who are coughing and sneezing out in the cold with the mosquitoes. Smart move, Osho-ites!

After Evening Meeting, they have "Creativity Night" in the plaza. I hoped it was that painting, collage, jewelry making event like they had a couple weeks ago, but it isn't. There is a Japanese woman who had done eight beautiful, paneled paintings titled Eight Seasons. While everyone looks at the paintings, she plays the flute and someone else plays the keyboard and drums. It is soft and beautiful music. Then, if the urge strikes you, you can go to Buddha Grove - - around the corner - - and do some painting. I go home and go to sleep.

Day Fifty-three - A Day of Dangerous Stupidity

This morning I wake up early so I can attend Zen Archery in Buddha Grove. The facilitator is a patient, older woman. She says Zen Archery has a different goal than "western archery." The goal here, like most everything else at the ashram, is to remain total - - in the moment. One does not strive to hit the target in Zen Archery. One strives to remain meditative while you do it - - which should allow you to hit the target easier.

Since it is my first lesson, we start by doing several easy yoga, tai chi, and chi gung movements. I enjoy it immensely. It makes me realize how much I miss doing my yoga. My body misses it, too. Some of the simple ones today stretch me in slightly hurtful ways.

Next, we move into exercises for the archery movements that we will do. Then we progress to practicing with a small practice bow. The bow consists of a twelve-inch long piece of wood, equipped with a thick rubber cord strung between the two ends. We practice pulling back the "bowstring" and releasing while keeping our bodies in the correct alignment, vocalizing, and throwing our right hand out to the side. We also watch the other more experienced archers' techniques, good and bad.

The facilitator tells me the palm of the hand is an energy spot. That's why some of the meditations include clapping the hands. This archery might tempt me again. But, I can feel the exercises, including working with the practice bow, in my sore shoulder and in my neck.

I go for a quick visit with Rasha today. She comments how good my bindi looks and that it is on properly! Then she shows me a beautiful flower tattoo on her arm, created with henna. She says that after putting it on, you leave it for a couple hours and then wash it off. It lasts a couple weeks. Rasha wants me to come to her house so she can give me a tattoo.

I run into Sakra at the laundry. He tells me that he won't be in today or tomorrow. So, I surf all day, answer my email, and write in my online journal. Should I feel guilty? I don't think so!

While walking back from lunch, I come across a beautiful, black butterfly. It is a dull black color, with yellow spots on the bottom of its wings and a speckled body. While I watch one butterfly, two more flit by alternately playing follow the leader and then dancing with each other. The dance is beautiful, and I watch them and their shadows. Then they go their separate ways, and one flies around and then toward me, and then away again. One time it comes straight toward my face and turns away at the last second.

I go to Silent Sitting again today. As I come out the door, I see the swan stand up, stretch its wings, and vocalize. How cool is that!

When I get back to the office, I don't say anything and Chandra doesn't say anything. She probably thinks I am just late. I'm sure that she would never guess that I would go to Silent Sitting after she told me not to.

This afternoon, I do something incredibly stupid. Thank goodness I learned a lesson from it and nothing bad happened. I have not seen a cobra for more than two weeks and I feel "withdrawal." It is like an addict. And, like an addict, I put good judgment aside to get my "cobra-fix." I have become too cocky and too comfortable with my so-called "friendships" on the street. Today it almost came back to bite me. And it wasn't the cobra doing the biting!

After work, I go to the corner to see if the snake would be there. No. The only person there is Zakir's young cousin, named Sandeep. At first, he tells me that he is going to Bombay. Then, after talking a while, he asks if I would come to the house with him to see the cobra. After yesterday with the three brothers, I felt that although they were conmen, they were harmless and the next time they asked me to go to their house, I would. So, when Sandeep asks, I say yes.

We start walking there, and he looks me up and down and says, "How old are you?"

I say, "Forty-eight. How old are you?"

He says, "Twenty-one."

We get down to the end of the block, past Osho Teerth Park, and start walking to the right. I say, "I think I've been here before." He stops like he's considering something. We talk about the cobra for a few minutes, with him telling me again not to kiss it on the mouth. He says that he will bring the cobra tomorrow. Then he hugs me! Tight. A full body hug.

When I pull away from him, he says some word in Hindi that I don't understand. It sounds like gala. Then, with his hands, he mimics petting a cobra. Since all I'm thinking about is the cobra, I don't get what he is saying. Suddenly, I understand. The kid wants to get laid! This young punk could have raped me! I should feel flattered. He's not a rapist - - he just wants to get laid. And he's probably heard about ashram women.

I can't believe I agreed to follow him to his house! Having cobra on the brain overrode any caution that I might have had. This is a good lesson for me. It turned out harmlessly enough, but the experience gets its message across.

After I recover my senses and realize how stupid I've been and the serious trouble that I have almost gotten myself into, I need to talk to someone. The first person I see is Phani. I confide in him all the messy details of the adventure with my young friend.

He listens patiently and then comments, "Muslim people no good. Don't trust them."

I ask, "Are only Muslims snake charmers?"

He says, "Yes."

I say, "But I thought Hindus consider cobras sacred."

He says, "Yes, but they don't keep them in their houses!"

Osho often talks about the conflict between the Muslims and the Hindus. So, this piece of "real life" prejudice intrigues me.

Probably, I shouldn't have confided in Phani. It's not something one usually tells one's rickshaw driver. But, he is the only ear available at the time, and I had to tell someone how stupid I had been. Well, Phani knows now, and I hope he won't get any ideas from the story!

While we talk, Uncle Makeen's brother rides a bicycle up to us. He shakes my hand and wants to shake Phani's. Phani shakes it reluctantly. The brother says he will have the snake here tomorrow. I hope that's true.

Tonight while I meditate, I hear what sounds like a man urinating in the bathroom. I remember the last time I sat on the toilet seat and it was wet. So, when I go in there and see the seat is down, I feel it. Sure enough, it is soaking wet with urine. How disgusting is that! I wash and wipe it off. It will be uncomfortable for me, but I have to talk to Bhava about this.

When I leave for Evening Meeting tonight, I don't bring my iPod or my back-jack. Arriving early, I have to wait until they open the door. I go in, sign in, and walk into the auditorium. After sitting on the floor, I almost immediately start fake coughing. Walking out, I put on my shoes and leave. I pull my hair behind my head so I won't look as recognizable, and rush out.

I have to make both gates before they close. It's harder to do this, now that I live in the back with the pyramids. Also, I'm more nervous than usual, because so many more people know me now. But, I make it through all the obstacles and arrive safely back in my room.

The white robes that we must wear for Evening Meeting have reminded some of the Ku Klux Klan. Evening Meeting is also called the White Robe Brotherhood! Sometimes, instead of people saying something about "Evening Meeting" they call it, "White Robe."

One would think that head movements for yes and no are universal. Well, not exactly. I don't understand it myself until the novel I'm reading, *Bridge on the River Kwai*, mentions it. It talks about a head movement that is like no, but instead is yes. I have experienced this, and it is confusing! Yes is moving your head up and down. With no, your head pivots from side to side. The yes here is similar, but instead of the pivot, your head tilts right and left. It's more of a flowing movement. Rasha shows me how to do it. It's not an easy movement to master. Other Indians that I have seen do it move the entire head and neck and it looks like it "rolls" one way and then the other. Yes looks so much like no! You have to pay attention to tell the difference.

Day Fifty-four - Sex and Gurus

Last night, I saw a beautiful butterfly on the floor in the hallway. It looked like a perfect leaf that had a bite taken out of it. You could even see the veins in the leaf. It was a perfect design by nature to protect it from predators. Unfortunately, not perfect enough to protect it from itself when it entered this man-made structure.

In the morning, the poor butterfly is still there, but lying on its side. It is so sad - - this beautiful, little creature. When I see it there, I keep thinking, who else will grieve for this beautiful creature? I don't want anyone to step on it, or sweep it up. So, I bring down a piece of paper from my room to get it out of the building and into the foliage. When I go to pick it up, it flutters! The night and morning cold had slowed it down, but not killed it. I get it outside and off it flies, a beautiful sight.

For lunch today, Jiadore and I walk over to German Bakery. It is busy for lunch and we have a long wait. Luckily, we find a place to sit. I order a veggie burger and fries, and the incredibly wonderful chocolate pie. The veggie burger and fries are good and a welcome change from the Indian food I've been eating. Although I love Indian food, once in a while a burger is good, too!

It is too much food for me, so I offer Jiadore half the burger. After eating most of the chocolate pie, I feel slightly sick afterward. I have to buy a coke to settle my stomach when we get back to the ashram. Then, for most of the afternoon I feel my insides vibrate from all the sugar I had. Now I feel exhaustion setting in. And I have no idea how I'm going to stay awake until midnight for gate duty.

Someone I met online says something bad about Osho that is not true. So, I find myself in the curious position of defending Osho! It feels a little funny, but it also feels right.

Today, I find out that Osho was not celibate. I thought he had "transcended" sex like he talked about. Not only did he insult the question-asker, something he often does, but he went on and on with the answer. He said that just because you are enlightened doesn't mean you can't have sex. He said sex is fun.

Then he told the story of what happened when he first became enlightened. He thought he couldn't have sex anymore. Reconsidering, he thought that if enlightenment is so fragile that having sex would destroy it, then it wasn't worth having anyway. So, he had sex and afterward found himself still enlightened.

This discovery feels huge for me. So many of the self-proclaimed gurus have been so sexual. And I have found myself attracted to Osho when he gives his discourses. Osho is a charismatic and charming man. I can see how women would fall for him - - not so much as a spiritual master, but as a man. He is attractive. My guess is that in person, he would have had the "womanizer" ability to look at you and make you feel like you were the only woman in the universe. Who could resist that?

This knowledge makes me think less of him as a spiritual and holy man. It almost puts him in the category of Jim Jones and David Koresh. Their sexuality defined both of their kingdoms. Isn't sexuality what defines Osho's kingdom?

Tonight I skip Evening Meeting. I heard that they compile all the check-in sheets at the end of the month. So, I will see how much trouble I get into. I hope they won't throw me out. I don't want my brother to win that bet! And, I want to last the whole three months here, so I can say I did.

Tonight is gate duty. Chandra stops to talk to me. I tell her about the big Indian throwing me out of Evening Meeting. She knew exactly who it was. She laughs about that and about how he grabbed my robe and made me sit down. When I complain about getting mosquito bit while I was at the coughing place, she says, "Oh no, you don't go there. You sit someplace else."

There is a stray dog hanging around. I'm not sure if it is the same dog as last week, but it is friendly and smiling. Unfortunately, it is also limping. Its front leg is so sore, it has a hard time lying down. I send it Reiki for over an hour while doing gate duty.

There are always rent-a-cops out in front of the ashram. Tonight's cop comes walking down the street and tapping this big stick - - a dog stick. As soon as the stray hears him, the dog runs away. The cop keeps tapping his stick as he stands out in front. He reminds me of a Nazi.

A little while later, I hear a dog yelp, and a different dog runs down the street. The Nazi cop comes out between cars with his stick. I can't help myself. I say, "Why did you do that?"

He says, "The dogs are not allowed to go inside the gates of the ashram." This dog wasn't even close. We have a short discussion, and he says that he only tapped it. Since the dog cried loudly, I doubt that. Then he tells me that he had four dogs that died. Our conversation ends with him putting the stick to the side. Later, when another guy comes, he picks up the same stick. But he doesn't tap it, and he doesn't hit any more dogs.

The stray dog had settled into the street sleeping quietly by the curb. The new guy starts walking toward the dog. I say, "Please don't hit that dog! He's not doing anything and he's not going near the gate!" So, the guy turns around and the dog runs away. It comes back later and sleeps a little farther down the street, and the guy leaves it alone.

I wear a surgical mask during the busy time of the evening when all the cars, motorcycles, and rickshaws go by. The pollution is nasty there. I read some, with the book hidden in the folds of my maroon robe.

Day Fifty-five – Shopping at MG Road

I read more about Osho's non-celibacy today. It has changed my attitude about him. This morning, I talk to Jiadore about it. I say, "I find Osho attractive, charismatic, and sexual."

She says, "That isn't fair, then."

I say, "Although I'm attracted to him, I wouldn't want my guru having sex with his disciples." I see having sex with his disciples as exploiting them. If he had a girlfriend, or hired prostitutes, I could accept that. Surprisingly, I still feel like Osho is guiding me in the information that I am finding. Maybe because he feels remorseful now.

I go to Silent Sitting again, today. I love it in here. If only I could go without having to sneak back into work. In here, they don't throw you out for coughing, but they request silence. While I am peacefully chanting my mantra silently to myself, suddenly, the saliva goes down the wrong "pipe." If you have never had this happen, it's like swimming and getting a mouthful of water that goes down into your lungs. I desperately try not to make any noise. My body is silently crying out to cough out the wayward saliva. Tears run down my face as I struggle to stay silent. It takes me five minutes to settle my body down so I don't feel like I have to cough. But I am glad when the thirty minutes are over, so I can go outside.

Jiadore and I go shopping today at MG Road. Phani quotes us too high a price. We walk to Main Street and find a rickshaw driver to take us there for thirty rupees. There are shops on the street, but if you look closer, you can see more behind them. We enter a long, narrow hallway. On each side of the hallway are shops, one after the other. Shops also line the other hallways, perpendicular to the main one. This is the Indian version of a mall. We don't have time to look around too much in here, but walking through is an amazing cultural experience in itself.

There are many beggars on this street. We pass one after another, each looking sad. Some of them hold metal cups and jangle the coins inside them. One woman holds up her arm to show that she has no forearm. The beggars always make me sad And, I feel bad ignoring them and passing them by. You can't give something to all of them; so, you can't give anything to any of them. It's almost like you have to leave your compassion at home to walk down the street. It kills me.

Next, we come to the grocery store. It is much bigger and has a wider selection than the other big grocery store I've been to at Pune Central. I buy many items: muesli, cookies, toilet paper, prunes, nuts, crackers, and milk. The milk comes in an unrefrigerated container and has no preservatives in it. Once I open the container, then I'll need to refrigerate it. I'm hoping this will save money by not having to go to breakfast, but it is expensive. It costs eleven hundred rupees for all my groceries - - almost thirty dollars. I would prefer to have spent it on cobras!

After the market, we walk across the street. Jiadore says, "Just follow me." I know I can't, so I grab her arm and she mostly pulls me across the street in front of all the traffic.

On this side of the street is Pyramid Mall. Before we enter, we have to leave our bags at the door. They give us a little tag to claim it when we come back out.

As Eastern and Indian as the long hallway mall had been, this mall is modern and Western. It could have been in any American city. They have McDonalds, Pizza Hut, and an expensive department store. I love the contrast between the two malls.

On our way home in the rickshaw, I see my first sacred cow! It is walking down the middle of a busy street, as if someone placed it there for my benefit. The cow is dark brown or black and has horns. The traffic on either side of it doesn't bother it at all.

Day Fifty-Six – Kool-aid Consciousness

I have breakfast with Jiadore this morning, downstairs and outside by the fountain. I have my muesli that I bought yesterday. It is good not having to walk over to the main resort around all those people. This feels quiet and peaceful.

The information I discovered about Osho still disturbs me. I look at people here differently now. They work seven days a week, gladly, doing Osho's work. How far a stretch would it be for them if he told them to drink Kool-aid? If he promised them enlightenment, I honestly think most of them would do it.

Concerning his abusive talk and abusive jokes: I've read that he does that to get people to think. Think about what? It is abusive, period. All I think about when I hear it is how much I don't like it.

Prana at work shows me a finger exercise device. When I ask how much it is, she says she wants to buy it for me. I feel some guilt about what I might do to these people by revealing what goes on here. But, I still honestly feel guided by Osho.

Does saying that I feel guided by Osho make me an Osho-ite, or as bad? That's not a question for me to answer. I believe Osho is a holy man who . . . what? Went wrong? Was misguided? Got carried away? I don't know how to describe what I think may have happened. Enlightened? No, I don't believe so. Enlightened people don't exploit their disciples. Enlightened people don't wear hats to hide their baldness.

After work, I walk down the street to look for Zakir again. They call the guy with the snake on a cell phone. Ten minutes later, an old man on a bicycle comes riding with a woven basket on the back rack. We walk a little farther down the street to get away from the crowd.

He opens the basket. I can't believe my eyes! The cobra is HUGE! It is the biggest one I've seen since I've been here. It is at least an inch in diameter, and its hood is bigger than my hand. What a beauty it is! I take a few pictures, but the old man is paranoid of police coming by. He never does pick the snake up. I'm not sure if it is because he isn't comfortable doing so, or because of where we are. He worries because it is illegal to have snakes here. Every time a car passes by, he closes the basket.

The snake has white on its eyes, meaning that it's getting ready to shed. A snake getting ready to shed can't see well. It's like a person with cataracts. The snake will strike at almost anything moving. And strike it does! This snake isn't going around my neck! It is so beautiful, though, that I am in heaven for that glorious few minutes.

I had asked my sister-in-law if I could stay with them for five or six days in May. She says two days only! She offers to find me a room! This surprises me, but it probably shouldn't. I have no one to talk to about this. I'd like to tell Sam because he would understand. Can I do that? I miss the friendship we had. But, I don't miss the relationship we had. And, I don't miss our marriage.

Tonight after Evening Meeting, when I arrive at the back gate, there is a crowd. They have locked the gate! We stand there, helpless, in our white clan gear waiting for the gate to open. Several people leave and I have no idea where they go. Only a few of us wait. More people come. Then more turn around and I hear someone say, "The other gate is open?" Turning around, I follow the rest of the white sheep to the other gate where the motorcycles and bicycles come in. There is only a guard outside, no one in maroon. Luckily, they haven't locked the gate to the back part of the ashram, so I can still get to my room.

But, I find out something that disturbs me. They lock the gate to the back part of the ashram at night. That's where I live, and I don't like that. I don't like feeling caged in. It was fine when I didn't know about it. Now that I know, I hate it. I feel confined. I will work on finding another way out. That last sentence sounds like it should come from an espionage novel!

Someone told me about the AUM event. There are twelve stages to it, but I can only remember some of them, and they are not in the proper order:

Yelling obscenities, not to anyone in particular.
Going around the room saying I'm sorry to everyone.
Going around the room saying I love you to everyone.
Dancing and more dancing.
Everyone in a circle chanting OM.

The next instruction is erotic dancing like a porn star. It is your choice to do this with or without a partner. They allow touching. I had thought it would be a little more sedate than that.

Day Fifty-seven – Sex and Spirituality

This morning, I meet Jiadore again for breakfast in the garden. This is a wooded area with many plants and a fountain. While we talk about adult boys and girls in the ashram, several crows land in a nearby tree and start a loud ruckus. They are so loud we have to stop talking until they fly off.

Jiadore tells me that she had spoken to another woman that is in our group. This other woman told her that Osho-ite men don't interest her at all. Jiadore says, "That's three people who told me that in three days!"

Later, while I am outside refilling my water bottle, two crows land on the top of the fountain. As they drink water, one mock feeds the other. One crow flies off, and the second crow drops to the second level of the fountain where the water is a little deeper. Then, he gives himself a bath. It is so cool to watch. He doesn't know how beautiful he is or that he lives in India. He only knows the water is refreshingly cold and he wants a bath. What a wonderful, simple pleasure it is to watch him enjoying life.

Today during lunchtime, I run into Bhava. She says, "I want to talk to you a minute."

I say, "I want to talk to you, too." She says that I should go first, so I say, "How do you skip Evening Meetings and not get caught?"

"Don't worry about it," she says. "I've skipped four or five times, and it doesn't worry me. Many people are leaving the program early. The worst that would happen is that they would call us in and tell us not to skip anymore. Every night is too much!" How I agree with that!

Then she asks, "Does it disturb you when my boyfriend is over?"

I say, "Bhava, he is very cute, but he sometimes forgets to lift the toilet seat when he urinates. I have made the mistake of sitting on the seat after him, and it is totally gross."

She says, "That bothers me, too. I'm working on him."

I tell her other than that, it does not bother me at all. There is much more to Bhava than her outer appearance suggests. I take her for this timid person, but she has more guts than I do in skipping Evening Meeting! My new hero!

Today, I look up Jim Jones online. Besides the Kool-aid affair - - he was not such a bad guy. Well, he was, but he was also a good guy. He and his wife were the first white people in Illinois to adopt an African-American child. Many people in his congregation were black, and he was big on racial equality.

Why are these guys who have a touch of spirituality so sexually

161

motivated? What is up with this? Even the great Robert and John Kennedy were very sexually oriented. There is something to this, but I don't know what it is.

Jiadore and I go to Silent Sitting again today. I have to admit that I always feel Osho's presence in there, and I like it. When I sit down and put my hands on my legs, I immediately feel Reiki start flowing. It is bizarre. When we leave, I don't see the swan. But, I catch a wonderful whiff of fragrance from some newly blooming flowers.

In back of the ashram, I walk over to where the magicians hang out. Uncle Makeen sits there and looks like any other old, Indian man. Was I mistaken by what I felt last time? Was it my fertile imagination running away with me? No, it wasn't. I believe I received a glimpse of who he once was. When he showed me the magic trick with the scarves, he said, "Pull the scarf here and see how tight the knot is." His presence was so commanding, I had to obey him. Despite his ordinary composure today, I made no mistake about the man.

Jiadore told me that she called in sick one day. She sent Sakra a text message to his cell phone, and he never asked her about going to a doctor. He also strongly comes on to her. I find the difference in treatment strange. He doesn't question her about calling in sick because he's attracted to her? That's not right. It makes me want to skip work.

Day Fifty-eight – Of Kings and Paupers

This morning, I have a leisurely breakfast of fried eggs and toast. While I wait for the eggs to cook, one of those birds of prey that I sometimes see lands right above my head. I barely have a chance to look up at him, when the buzzer for my eggs sounds. He flies away before I return with the eggs. But, I see enough to identify him as a Pariah Kite. They have been known to swoop down and take food out of people's hands! They are the most common raptor in Pune, and I see them often.

After eating breakfast, I stroll over to the Plaza Cafe and order a hot chocolate, which I take my time drinking. I have the hot chocolate thinking the caffeine in it might help my headache. Well, that, and I want to make sure that I am late for work today, cleaning day. I talk to Jiadore about cleaning day. She says she has been in three different departments since she arrived here. This is the first one where she has to do her own cleaning. That said, when I run into her before work, she had gone in early to clean her keyboard.

As I walk toward work, I see some other birds playing in the trees. I step closer to get a better look. There are two crested birds with red markings, called Red Whiskered Bulbuls.

During break time today, I go to my room and open the locked closet. Then I close the closet and start to leave. Normally, I keep the door padlock right next to the door. Now, I can't find it. I have locked the padlock - - with the keys - - into the closet! I have to jury-rig the lock to get it open again. It bothers me how easily the lock gives up.

Chandra tells me today that she will transfer to the worker's meditation office. She didn't choose to go there. None of us can choose our jobs. That's in the paperwork that I filled out before I arrived. Luckily, Chandra will train someone else to do her job. Working her job would have been a nightmare for me.

Later, as I help Chandra put away the cleaning supplies, she suddenly jumps back. I say, "What is it? What is it?"

She says, "It is a lizard or a gecko." Of course, I have to find it. It is a small creature, with rough scales. It has suction cup feet that allow it to climb straight up the wall. Putting my hand in front of it, I try to guide it to a safer place. I would have liked to try to catch it, but I don't know enough about Indian lizards. I don't want it to bite me. Even a bite from a non-poisonous lizard can hurt. That's experience talking!

Jiadore and I walk to German Bakery Road to have lunch at the thali restaurant again. It cost eighty-five rupees for both of us. I put a one hundred rupee bill in the payment folder they hand us. They don't give me any change, and I have to ask for it. The guy that waited on us isn't happy about giving back that fifteen rupees. Now, it worries me the waiter might do something bad to our food when we return. I'm dodging rickshaws and playing with cobras, and my main worry is that some guy will do something bad to my food. Am I a nutcase or what?

Apparently, you don't leave tips here, but I feel bad and I want to ask again to be sure about that. Jiadore's Indian boyfriend told her not to.

On our way home, when we walk past German Bakery, who do I find there but Uncle Makeen. He starts talking to me and says something about living five kilometers from there. I don't get his point until he asks for ten rupees. It bothers me. Here I am shaking my head no, when what I feel I should do is kneel at his feet. I still feel the "royal-ness" of him. The ordinariness of him asking for money disturbs me. It is almost as if he is a king pretending to be a pauper.

I ask Jiadore if she knows anything about people leaving the ashram early, like Bhava had mentioned to me yesterday. Jiadore says yes. She says it was because they were angry at the ashram, or not happy here, or it wasn't what they expected.

Even if the incident with my brother had not happened, I don't think I would have considered leaving. Would I have considered it if I hadn't paid all the money? Okay, maybe. Is it more about the money than my strength? Where would I go if I left? There are many components involved here.

When returning from Evening Meeting, I know that at the front gate you don't need to show your pass. At the back, I was never sure. Tonight I hold up my pass at the back gate and the guy says, "You don't show after White Robe." Fine, I won't.

Kanti says something to me when I tell her that my camera is in my pocket. She says the Sufis say that if you give someone a temptation, then you are responsible for what happens. I can see that.

Day Fifty-nine - Learning Hindi With the Boys

Sakra, my boss, calls me in today. He tells me that I will temporarily go back to the photography project. That project is even more vague than the video project I work on now. He says the project might go to outsourcing. I joke and say, "Outsourcing to India?"

And he says, "Yes, that's the name of the company - - Outsourcing2India!"

Sakra and I have an appointment to meet with Dwami and Felipe at 12:45. Felipe isn't in his office, so I look for him. When I look at my watch again, it is almost 12:40. I rush over to Dwami's office knowing how he is about being late. I am the only one there, and Dwami doesn't even know about the meeting.

While we talk, he suddenly points to my forehead and says, "Did you know that Hindu women originally started wearing bindis to suppress their third eye?"

I say, "I thought it was to enhance the third eye?"

He shakes his head no, and I immediately rip the bindi off my forehead. Dwami says something about sticking it somewhere. And I say, "Yeah, I'll stick it somewhere!"

Sakra comes in then and we talk about the project. He doesn't like the suggestion I make about the naming convention. His idea strikes me as stupid. I may or may not deal with that tomorrow. What comes of the meeting is that Felipe and I will meet with Dwami tomorrow and work everything out. It is an experiment.

Prana had complained that in the pool restroom, the toilet paper dispenser is on the ceiling of the stall. You have to stand up to get the paper. When the carpenters come in, Prana has already left. Therefore, it is up to me to tell these two Indian carpenters about the toilet paper dispensers. Unfortunately, they don't speak much English. What can I do? I have to pretend I am sitting on a toilet and show them the dispensers are too high. It feels like a scene from Candid Camera.

Jiadore and I go to the noodle place today. It's a small, Indian fast food place a couple blocks from here. While we cross the street, Jiadore takes my hand, because otherwise I would never get across. We get halfway and we're waiting for traffic to clear on the left. One motorcycle is out of its lane and coming straight for us! I panic and step back without thinking that I have to look at traffic coming the other way. Thank goodness, Jiadore pulls me forward and the motorcycle avoids us. I run

165

across the street and have to recover for a few minutes. Cobras are so much simpler than this street-crossing business.

In the restaurant, we eat a combination fried noodles and fried rice plate. It is a large portion for forty rupees, and delicious, too. While we eat, Jiadore tells me about a conversation with a twenty-year-old friend of hers. The friend commented how sweet the father and daughter team of Andre and Cathy are. Jiadore said to her, "No. That's not father and daughter. They're lovers." Her friend couldn't believe it, and it took awhile to convince her.

This afternoon is my last seminar for the Inner Skills workshop. We watch an Osho video on recognition. While sitting and watching, I fall asleep. Since I have a printed copy, I will read it when I get home. For the rest of the seminar, we sit in a circle and talk about a question and answer sheet that we had to fill out. Few people talk, so the facilitator keeps calling on people who don't want to talk. I manage to avoid her calling on me.

For the last piece of class, we choose a buddy. There are an uneven number of people in the room. I prepare to tell the facilitator that Jiadore, who isn't here today, will be my buddy. Then, Nandano calls me over, so I am his buddy. He is the Russian guy I did a sequence with at the Inner Skills workshop a while ago. After talking a few minutes, we hug, and the class ends.

I go looking for Zakir to see the snake today. No snake today, but we arrange a new snake day on Wednesday. Uncle Makeen is there. He wants to know what I do in America. I tell him computers, which impresses him. He asks what my salary is for a month. I don't tell him. My guess is that I make more in a month than he makes in a year. I try to get him to tell me what he makes in a year. Either I don't get my point across or he doesn't want to tell me.

Then I want to show them my new knowledge of Hindi, so I tell Zakir, "Fear me-lan-gay," meaning roughly "See ya later." When they hear me say that, it animates everyone. Then I find myself sitting next to Uncle Makeen. When I tell him fear me-len-gay, he says, "baad me-len-gay." When I don't get it, he starts spelling it in English! Hindi has a different alphabet, with different characters. This old, uneducated street man spelling in English! These people never stop amazing me. This impresses me so much. In English, fear me-len-gay and baad me-len-gay are roughly the equivalent of "See ya later, alligator. In a while, crocodile!"

Then Uncle Makeen wants to teach me several Hindi words. He teaches me eyes, nose, ears, teeth, happy, and eating. Eating is easy for me - - han-a-ky-a - - like Hanukah with an aya on the end. All the guys try to teach me words and help me pronounce them. A little while before they were after my rupees and now they are all cheering me on. We laugh and have a great time. I feel closer to these people than I do to the Osho-ites at the ashram.

Uncle Makeen is seventy years old with seven children: five boys and two girls, all married. He learned magic when he was eighteen and he has been a street magician since then. I have a certain fondness for this likable old coot.

They want me to take all seven of them out to dinner. I'm thinking of taking Zakir, his two brothers, two uncles, and maybe the nephew out to lunch at Bukhara. It's only thirty-five rupees each. What a blast I would have with them! They are all so much fun.

I try to talk Zakir into hiring me as a woman snake charmer. "Since all the snake charmers are men," I say, "I would be a real attraction."

He says, "When you leave you can give me your watch to remember you by."

I say, "Your brother, Waseem, has a better watch than I do and you can get it from him!" As I get ready to go back to the ashram, I say, "You will miss me when I leave India." I will miss them, too - - conmen that they are - - they are still genuine human beings in their hearts. And I can feel that.

This may sound strange, but I will remember this time with them today as one of my fondest memories of India. It is evidence that we are all alike - - all of us. From the most arrogant and powerful CEO, to the humblest of shoe shine people. We are all alike; we have the same fears, the same desires, and the same doubts. Our fears, desires, and doubts may come in different packages. But, essentially, we are all the same. And, I like that feeling.

When I return to the ashram, I walk all the way to the front gate to see who is on duty. It is someone who doesn't know me. I do this in preparation for the coughing routine tonight.

So, I leave my room early and walk swiftly toward the auditorium. The front gate person has switched to someone I know! That's an unwanted surprise. But, I am already too psyched to change my mind. So, I go through with it, anyway. He doesn't even look at me. I rush past him and keep rushing until I am safe in my room. It scares me, but it is worth it. This exercise requires much energy, though, and I am running out.

Day Sixty - Muddled Meeting

I have a meeting with Dwami this morning at 9:15. Felipe and I arranged to meet before the meeting and walk over together. Since he's busy when I arrive, I walk over alone. I don't want to be late, because I have already heard the wrath of Dwami when someone arrives late. Felipe comes in shortly after me. We wait twenty-five minutes and no Dwami. I want to leave, and Felipe says, "Wait, let me leave him a note."

While Felipe collects paper and pen, Dwami walks in and says, "Oh, good, you waited for me."

Sakra comes in shortly afterward, gives us his viewpoint on the subject and then leaves for Delhi. It is an interesting meeting with Dwami, Felipe, and me, because all of us are slightly on the strong willed side. Mostly, I stay out of it. But, there are times when Felipe and Dwami get into it, that I have to visualize white light around me to keep out the negativity.

Our meeting lasts an hour. At the end, the project is as muddled, as Dwami puts it, as before we started. They've been trying to do this right for twenty years. It is still not right. Then, Dwami tells us to do something that is so stupid, I have no words to describe it. I tell Felipe to handle it any way he wants, and tell me what to do and I'll do it.

Then, Jiadore and I walk around the German Bakery area looking for a tailor. We can't find the one we are looking for, but we find another one. My sister-in-law had given me a beautiful Indian-looking purse with little mirrors on it. The zipper broke shortly after I arrived in India. When I ask the tailor how much to replace the zipper, he says thirty rupees - - less than a dollar. Jiadore has a maroon robe that needs some repair - - twenty rupees.

After leaving our items with the tailor, we eat lunch. It tastes delicious. I could eat here every day. The waiter from the other day isn't there, and the food is fine.

This afternoon, Bhava, Jiadore, and I talk about skipping Evening Meeting. Bhava is an older woman who is the sweetest looking person you'd ever see. She has skipped Evening Meeting more than I have. She plans to skip for a whole day! I want to do that, too!

Jiadore and I ask, "Are you a sannyasin?"

Bhava says, "Yes." It surprises both of us because Bhava has told us what a rebel she is. Then Bhava explains, "There are two reasons. The first is that being a sannyasin and choosing a sannyas name is like a transformation of who you used to be, to who you are now. The second reason is committing to meditation."

After work, on North Main Road, I run into Khalid and Uncle Makeen. Any hint of yesterday's fellowship has vanished. Yesterday was a small window of camaraderie, humor, and joy shared between people who were just being people. It was like being in the Twilight Zone. As soon as I walked away yesterday, our window closed behind me. Now we are back to being the conmen and the "rich" American. That's how they look at me. I will consider myself lucky if I can have one more window like that before I leave India.

Day Sixty-one - Friends in Low Places

I meet Jiadore for breakfast again in the garden. She wonders why the two of us have been "thrown together" in this ashram. It is a compelling question. In the last year whenever I find myself in similar circumstances, the person and I find some amazing commonalities and synchronicities with each other. Sometimes they are weird and unique. Jiadore and I have yet to discover what it might be. Although, neither of us are Osho-ites and that could be a start!

Dwami wrote an email this morning about not having the last file that I worked on. I send it to him immediately in the body of a new email. Then I receive a copy of a letter he had sent to Sakra saying something semi-rude. I know I shouldn't expend energy on defending myself. But, I email back that I had sent the file in response to his email. The original had gone to Sakra last week. If that gets Sakra in trouble, oh, well.

Sakra has assigned me to work in the bookstore for the next week. Today, I am there for two hours in the morning. It can be a busy place. Many times in my life, I have had jobs where I had to give change. At the bookstore, like most other shops and service places in the ashram, they only accept payment by voucher. There is no cash.

I have had to deal with them in the cyber cafe, also. People give you their voucher with some of the numbers crossed off. Then you have to use the rest of the numbers to pay for the item. Often, they don't have enough on one voucher, and they give you a second one. It sounds simple, but the numbers are always different - - sometimes fives, tens, twentys, threes, etc. Give me cash anytime!

While in the bookstore this morning, music plays in the background. They have a CD display saying, "This is what is now playing." It is pleasant - - reminiscent of Celtic music, which I love. I glance at the title, but know I would never buy it. Any music created at the ashram, I couldn't trust. I've been using subliminal tapes too long. I know how they have affected my life - - in a good way. I can't risk buying a tape that maybe has subliminal messages in it that I don't want to hear. Where did I get this idea? From my fertile imagination, of course! But, when I think about buying an ashram music CD, I feel a tightening in my stomach. Just my paranoia of the place, I am sure. Still, no need to take an unnecessary risk.

Later, I find out that I have a group scheduled for the same time I'm scheduled at the bookstore. When I call Nimisha, she doesn't return my call. Chandra calls and arranges for someone else to cover at the bookstore for those three days. I'm hoping they don't cancel the group; because I think I would like it and I think it is perfect for me. Also, they scheduled Jiadore for the same group, and I think we will have a good time together.

As I walk by the laundry today, I hear a noise. It is Rasha calling me over! I talk to her for a while. She and I talk about Osho-ites. I tell her I am not an Osho-ite, and I don't like the interaction between men and women here. She talks about husbands and wives in the ashram - - how men flirt with women in front of the wife, and women flirt with men in front of the husband. We both agree this is not satisfactory!

Then I ask her about "gala" or the word that young Sandeep had said to me that day. Gala means neck, and what sounds like galla meo, means hug. It is difficult for me to get across to her what he had said and how I think he meant it. I say inappropriate, but I don't know if she understands that.

Also, I ask her about the food. Someone told me the Sudexo people eat the same food we eat. Rasha says that they eat different food. She says they take two hundred or three hundred rupees off her check at the end of the month. She also says she hates the food, because there are no spices on it and it tastes like cardboard!

Jiadore and I go back to the tailor today to pick up our items. He thoroughly repaired the purse I had given him. He not only repaired the one spot on Jiadore's robe, but he even fixed another spot she had forgotten about.

We go to a new restaurant today. When we walk in, we see a crowd before us. We go back to the thali place. It is delicious again, as usual.

On our way back, we run into Shareef, Manik's father. He says that Manik has been busy. He'll let him know that I am looking for him, though. Then we run into Uncle Makeen and Khalid. I introduce them to Jiadore.

They don't impress her at all. She doesn't understand my friendship with these street people, or why I love them. I explain that I have more in common with them than with the people at the ashram. They make their intentions very clear: they want my money and make no pretense about it.

I don't understand the ashram people. I don't believe in their philosophy and I don't trust them. What they believe is so foreign to me that I am not comfortable with them. It's almost like they are from another planet.

My friends on the street are genuine, grounded, and understandable. They are more real than the people at the ashram. Give me the street people any day.

One last comment on this subject to better illustrate it. If I were walking across the street between Zakir and almost anyone from the ashram, and I stumbled, the person from the ashram would not notice, and Zakir would stop and help me. He may ask for rupees afterward, but first he would help me. More real, more in touch with life. That's all.

After that, it is still early. Since I plan to skip Evening Meeting tonight, I go back into town. Stopping at Hassan's place, I'm glad that he is there. I buy many items from him - - almost a hundred dollars worth, including an amethyst crystal ball from the Himalayas. Although I probably pay too much for it, I cannot resist. It has what looks like a chevron on it. It is too cool to let it go. I've never seen anything like it. Then I buy a beautiful Tibetan singing bowl, an amethyst ring, and a few other items. I'm happy with my purchases.

Today, after Hassan shows me some Osho malas, I ask if he is a sannyasin. He says he is a sannyasin if it means "seeker of the truth." That is exactly what it means. I tell him that I am also a sannyasin, but not an Osho sannyasin.

Then I go back to the shop above German Bakery and buy three purses that I had seen earlier. Now that I'm a purse person, I need purses! These are inexpensive and good quality.

Since I already know I will skip Evening Meeting tonight, it doesn't matter that I arrive home from shopping at 6:30. And, I thoroughly enjoy my time alone until gate duty.

Tonight, while on gate duty, Sajeev stops by to talk. I say, "I apologize for asking such a personal, inappropriate question, but I am curious."

He says, "It's okay, go ahead and ask."

I ask, "Do you screw around on your wife?"

He says, "No."

So I tell him, "It would have broken my heart if you had said yes!"

Then he gives me the same garbage all men say, that they can lust after all good-looking women. I tell him that women are the same. Then he tells me about the friendships he has had with women. It sounds a little suspicious, so I ask, "Do you have sex with other women?"

He says, "Well, if you put it like that, yes." Sometimes he has only had sex with them once in a year, but it is a special love relationship.

I ask, "Did you tell your wife?"

He says, "Yes, and it was disastrous."

I ask, "Has she been with other men?"

He says, "I hope not! I hate to admit it, but I'm jealous of that!" Then he has to leave.

Later, when he comes back, he tells me that he had talked to his wife for thirty minutes about the conversation we had. I ask if it bothers him that Osho wasn't celibate. First, he wants to know how I know he wasn't. I say that I had read it in the discourses. Then he tells me a story about a monk that he knew. The monk had a housekeeper who had a son. The son was supposedly the monk's. In a case like that, I see nothing wrong with what the monk did. But, Osho having sex with multiple disciples is different. Sajeev believes that if he loved them, it is okay. I don't know about that.

Jiadore and I had planned to meet after gate duty. But, I talked to Sajeev so long that I missed her. I stop by the office to see if she is there and run into Kanti. She and I have a long talk. I ask her about Sandeep, the twenty-one year old. She says that since he is a Muslim, and Mohammed's wife was older than he was, it's possible that Sandeep did want to have sex with me.

Kanti also says that so many of the men here have AIDS, that I should be careful. I tell her that I am not interested in any men in India. When she asks why, I say that I don't agree with the Osho-ite philosophy about sex. According to her, sometimes guys come here and then change their mind about it; so she thinks I should be more open. I don't think so!

Then, Kanti talks to me about Mystic Rose. She is facilitating it, and she goes on and on about how wonderful it is. I tell her that it does not resonate with me, and I don't like people telling me what to do. She says I might change my mind. She also talks about looking at the faces of the people that start the group. When you look again at the end, you will see a remarkable difference. Jiadore has said that about another group.

Kanti also says that Osho always talked about freedom and responsibility. That strikes me as ironic since the ashram allows little freedom.

Day Sixty-two - Preparation for a Group Experience

I work in the bookshop this morning. I'm still learning. There will be fewer people to help me the next time I work, so I'll be more on my own. It is bright in there, and I can see all the people walk by. The employees laugh often. I like that. It is not what I expected, though. After I feel more comfortable, I'm hoping it will feel better.

As I'm on my way to meet Jiadore in the shop upstairs from German Bakery, I see the little boy with one foot again. He always breaks my heart. Then, I see the woman with no fingers on her hands speak to the boy. As she walks away, I notice that she wears a bracelet on her fingerless hands. That touches me.

Some of these little kid beggars annoy me. Today's kids have been especially persistent. A few days ago, a little boy had his sister on his back. The two of them came at me and wouldn't leave me alone. It was disconcerting. They were in my space and wouldn't let me get away.

I don't understand why they keep bugging me. Perhaps it's because my front pockets are bulging. The left pocket hides my camera and the right bulges with a pocketful of crystals that I always carry with me.

After meeting Jiadore upstairs, I find a purse-type backpack that has a dragon on it. Jiadore helps me get the guy down from three hundred ninety rupees to three hundred rupees.

Jiadore and I have to meet the facilitator for the group we are helping in. The group was originally going to be, "Opening to Self Love." They canceled or changed that to, "Say Good-bye to the Inner Judge." The facilitator laughs and acts friendly. After lunch, we go again to the plaza, to meet the guy who organized getting the group together. It is someone Jiadore knows.

We go to the storeroom and load a cart with items for the group. Then, we pull the cart down the street among the cars, rickshaws, and motorcycles. I didn't know that this other place belonged to the ashram. It always had rent-a-cops in front of it, so I wondered what it was.

We unload the cart and set up the room for the group. The room smells like mothballs. We put mattresses on the floor, put covers on pillows, and put out tissues. I assume they expect there will be some crying. This is probably going to be one of those weird groups. See what I am doing? I am now judging a group called The Inner Judge. Maybe I need this group!

There must be a reason I'm in it. I'm glad Jiadore is in it, too.

One helper in the group is noticeably controlling, and it may be difficult dealing with her.

As I cross the street at the ashram, I run into Zakir. I smell smoke on him and give him some grief about smoking, both for his health and the money. He says they are cheap and he shows me one. It looks like a marijuana cigarette - - small, thin and pointed. The covering looks more like a leaf than cigarette papers.

While I talk to Zakir, Manik drives by and calls out my name. He turns around and comes back. He has his friend, Anderson, in the car with him. We talk a while, and he asks if I want to go with him and Anderson to the train station to meet some girls and give them a key. After my scare with the other twenty-one year old, Sandeep, I am a little more cautious now. So, I declined. But, Manik is a good kid, and I probably would have been fine with them. Probably.

Day Sixty-three - Judging the Group

This morning, Jiadore and I walk to German Bakery road to go to the India Blossom restaurant. On the way, we pass several dogs that are waking up. They all wag their tails and are happy to see us. What great role models they are for the art of living! The India Blossom restaurant is excellent. I get an omelet and an ABC juice. That is a combination of apple, beetroot, and carrot juice. It all tastes delicious.

We walk back to the ashram and meet the group in the plaza. On the way to the group room, some man asks me where I'm from. Since I usually say, "America," I don't realize his voice is American and he meant what state am I from! There aren't many Americans here, so this is an honest mistake.

Then all of us sit in a circle. The people who had paid for the course tell their name and why they are in the group. Then the facilitator, Aasar, mentions the helpers, and we have to talk. When it's my turn, I say that I want to be more aware of my inner judge. I thought the class was on being judgmental. It is, but it's about yourself, not the world around you -- unless that comes later.

Next, we have to raise our left hands and say "yes" that we agree not to disclose anything that happens in the group or the structure of the group. I raise my arm, but do not say yes; so I am under no obligation to keep it a secret. No one notices that I don't say yes. Why was my arm raised? I don't know, maybe I wanted to ask to use the restroom.

After receiving a notebook and pen, we write down different ways we judge ourselves depending on what Aasar says. He mentions our jobs, the opposite sex, our clothes, our body, our relationships, our sexuality -- and we write something down for everything he says. This stays private.

Then we have to walk around the room looking into everyone's eyes. When Aasar says stop, the person we're looking at is our partner. My first partner is Henry. He thinks he is ugly and has a bad nose, and he doesn't like his body. He is a little overweight, but attractive. His nose is fine. His face reminds me of Yul Brenner in the movie *The King and I*.

I have to talk first, and it is difficult for me. My primary issue is feeling like a stupid idiot. Then, I mention feeling old and gray, and there isn't much more. We have to go on and on for fifteen minutes. It is painful -- not what I am saying, but having to go on for so long. It is longer than I can comfortably maintain talking. After repeating myself many times, I start going on and on with my stupid idiot hang-up. I don't know if it helps or not. It doesn't feel like it.

After we each talk fifteen minutes, we line up in two rows and slowly walk toward one another saying how we feel with each step. At one point, I notice feeling a little lightheaded. It doesn't feel like it's coming from me. Then, the guy next to me says that he feels dizzy, so I know I am picking it up from him. I am sometimes so susceptible to other people's vibrations that I constantly have to remember to surround myself with white light.

Other people around us are crying and sobbing. I'm sure it is a powerful experience for them. For me - - it's not an experience that I would choose for myself. Although, I could use some help with this stupid idiot issue. Aasar says that when other people do something to trigger one of these issues, it's a mirror of yourself. I know that when Revatii looks at me like I'm an idiot, I feel like she is confirming what I already believe about myself. Or, I guess what I am afraid might be true.

At break time, Aasar suggests that we wear a "silence" badge. This is a white badge with black letters that says, "I am silent." Nobody talks to you if you wear this badge. Although Aasar only suggests it - - it feels mandatory.

I walk back to my room to eat some cookies - - I need some incentive to continue with this group! I hate wearing the badge. Part of my complaints of the gate people not acknowledging me is that I hate to feel invisible. Did it take this group to show me that? With the badge on, I feel even more invisible! Even people who always say hello to me, ignore me when I have the badge on.

When I get back, I sit with Jiadore and we have a short conversation. I say, "I hate wearing the silence badge."

She says, "It doesn't bother me at all. It's funny that you don't talk, but the silence badge bothers you. I am outgoing, and it doesn't bother me at all."

I say, "I do, too, talk!"

Then she says, "I never see you talking to anyone."

"What about the street people?" She has to agree. I always talk to the street people, and she is always impatient when I do. We are still talking at the door when it is time to go back in. Jiadore is outside taking her shoes off, and I step inside shoeless. Aasar says, "Shhhh," in a semi-threatening tone. Okay.

When it is time for lunch, Aasar comes over to where Jiadore and I are sitting. He says that although we are helpers, he considers us part of the group. We need to wear the badge and stay silent like everyone else. We step outside the gates, and I ask Jiadore if she wants to go to the noodle place again. She says yes, so we walk down there - - not in silence.

It is good food, as usual. Afterward, we look for a little grocery store, but aren't successful. We start walking back and are getting ready to cross the street, when suddenly, we hear a smashing sound. In front of us, a guy on a motorcycle slides across the road with the motorcycle lying on its side. All the other motorcycles and traffic go around him. He stands up looking shaken, but not hurt. I want to stay and watch and maybe give him Reiki, but Jiadore pulls me away. Is it an American shortcoming to want to see what happened? I don't ask Jiadore about "rubber-necking" in Czechoslovakia. Maybe it's cultural, but I have a hard time walking away.

When we return from lunch, soft music plays, and we close our eyes. Aasar tells us to feel in our bodies what makes us feel safe and secure, and place our hands there.

Then we make a list of ten traits that we judge about ourselves, and print it clearly in capital letters so someone else can read it. We stand up and walk around the room again looking into people's eyes. Then he tells us to stop and that will be our partner.

My partner this time is Rinaldo. We discuss his list, and he tells me how he wants me to read to him. For instance, if one of the traits on the list is "acting cold," the person reading will say, "You're cold!" The first couple of traits are what his girlfriend accused him of. The others are how he judges himself. When I read them, he listens and looks like a little boy who had been bad and knows it. He says he feels guilty.

The one receiving the reading has one black cushion and one pink cushion. You stand on the black cushion listening to the reading. If you can't take it, you move to the pink cushion and the person reading will stop.

Then, Aasar decides to walk us through it, so he tells the person when to stand on the pink cushion to recover. They are to put their hands on the place we discovered earlier that makes us feel better. He calls it "resourcing yourself." As we go through the ten traits, we hear people around us sobbing and crying again, and some of them yelling. One of Rinaldo's ten traits is being insensitive, so he tells me that it would be stupid of him to cry.

When we finish the ten traits, Aasar tells us to hug our partner. Rinaldo hugs me tight. Another of his ten traits is that he is cold. He is a good hugger for being cold! While I hug him, I think how wonderful it will be when I hug someone who I love and who loves me.

At the end of the group, as helpers we have to move everything in

179

the room to a bigger room that we will use tomorrow. Aasar had said earlier that we should all go to Kundalini Meditation, Evening Meeting, and Dynamic Meditation. Kundalini is at 4:15 and Dynamic is six in the morning. Right before we finish setting up the new room, he asks if any of us want to go to Kundalini. Jiadore and I leave. I had decided that I should go to it one more time. This will be a good time. But, Jiadore mentions going to German Bakery! We arrive at Kundalini right before they lock the doors.

Many people love Kundalini Meditation. First, you let your whole body shake. The first time I did it a couple months ago, I shook my hands the whole fifteen minutes. When the next stage came along, my hands had swollen from all the blood rushing to them. Chandra told me this was wrong and showed me how to do it correctly. So, I do it right this time, by not shaking my hands down! After the shaking is dancing. What would an Osho meditation be like without dancing? Sheesh. I honestly don't understand the meditation part of this. I obviously haven't been drinking enough water here! The good news is that I heard the electronic beeping yesterday - - so I'm not lost yet!

As we walk out of the Kundalini Meditation, who is sitting in front of the auditorium, but Aasar. Jiadore thinks that he is there deliberately to see who had attended Kundalini. So, I was glad I went, although I have no intention of going tomorrow.

I go back to my room, barely have time for my own meditation, and have to dress for Evening Meeting. When I arrive there, who is taking the names of the people in Worker's Meditation - - but Aasar again! Interesting. He won't find me at Dynamic Meditation tomorrow morning, that's for sure!

Day Sixty-four - Getting Rid of Judgments

Jiadore and I walk to the India Blossom restaurant for breakfast again. Today, I have banana pancakes with cinnamon lemon sauce. The pancake is larger than the dinner plate and folded like an enchilada. Inside are large slices of banana and the sauce. Everything tastes delicious. I had also ordered ABC juice and they didn't bring it. I ask again, and still nothing. We have to leave to get to class in time, and they bring it as we stand to go. When I ask if I can get it to go, they bring it back to me in a little plastic margarine container! I ask, how can I drink this? They refuse to give me my money back. The juice is now in the refrigerator at work.

Today, I have an odd thought. Probably I won't - - but I am considering staying here longer! Jiadore thinks I'm insane. She thinks I've been drinking too much water! I don't know if I'm honestly considering it or not. I'm trying out the "thought" of it right now.

The class today is similar to a type of group therapy called psychodrama. I used to belong to a psychodrama group when I was sixteen. The same brother who is an Osho-ite is the one who got me started in psychodrama. It is role-playing and other inventive ideas to work out personal issues.

Group starts today with everyone telling how they are. That is uncomfortable for me in a situation like this, because I am fine! That's not what Aasar wants to hear. Of the two people to my left, one says she couldn't sleep and the other one says she is cold. So, I start by saying I am cold. Aasar says, "It's cold outside. Everyone is cold. I am a warm person and I'm cold, too." It bothers me because he didn't say it to her, only me. Perhaps because I'm a helper, and she's not.

Next, we have to get with our partner from yesterday and finish the exercise we had started. This time, I am the one who has the inner judge yelling at me. Rinaldo has a hard time acting "mean" to me, and he wants to stop. So, I comfort him and tell him it is a gift. He starts with the stupid idiot comment. I'm not sure if he isn't doing it mean enough, or if it has just lost its sting.

After the first judgment, Aasar asks everyone how they are and how they want their partner to yell at them. Some of the people correct their partner, but I don't feel comfortable doing that. Judging someone else is not something I want to do in a group about judgment.

The second one about being old and gray gets to me. It surprises me how much it bothers me hearing that. I have tears in my eyes from this one. Sam telling me I'm old for all those years. I was so sensitive to it, and he was joking all the time. Even after he told me he was joking, it still stung. And I held on to the "old" piece and apparently still haven't given it up.

When I think back on it, Sam has made jokes about me being older than him from the beginning. So, it's not that he changed. It was that I started looking at it differently, possibly because I felt old. His jokes didn't change - - my perception of them changed.

My old-looking-hands judgment felt especially stupid today. I am judging myself based on something that a friend's womanizer ex-husband said - - a man I never met and probably wouldn't even like. Now that is stupid!

The others don't bother me too much until he gets to the last one: you are too judgmental. He adds in, "you judge everything and everyone," and it is so true that it shocks me. I do!

After each judgment, Aasar says "stop" then "resource yourself," and we step over to the pink pillow. It feels weird, but gives us a break from the yelling.

My partner and some of the others complain to Aasar that they don't like doing this to another person. Aasar replies, "Then why are you doing it to yourself?" That is a huge piece of this. None of us want to hurt the other person - - all of us have compassion - - but we find it so easy to judge ourselves with no compassion. A good lesson.

Periodically during one exercise or another, Aasar goes around and asks how we are. At one point, I say, "Okay."

He says, "What does it mean, okay?" Most of it doesn't faze me so I have to make stuff up.

After this part of the judgment exercise, it is break time. Aasar tells us to break with our partner and talk about it. Rinaldo and I get along great, and I feel a real connection with him. I enjoy talking with him. We get back late, and they have already started with listening to soft music and talking.

Then, Aasar gives us a large sheet of paper and crayons and tells us to draw our inner judge. I take a black crayon and draw lines coming out from a center point. After that, I put x's all over the page. Then I draw a heart in the center with a red crayon. The picture represents all the judgments stifling my heart. And the x's are "no's."

This time I have another partner, Henry, my partner from yesterday. I tell him that I am glad that I got him again. Since we didn't get to hug yesterday, I felt incomplete. When I show him my picture, he assumes the x's are resistance. That's his issue, not mine.

182

Henry holds up my picture and yells the judgments to the black cushion on the floor. But, I am not standing on the cushion. I walk around looking at the picture and am only a watcher.

Henry keeps yelling the stupid idiot repeatedly, although he should have been going down the list. Since I need the most work on that one, I let him do it for most of the time. Then you are to back up and see if it feels better.

Aasar asks, "Do you feel better now?"

I say, "I still have tightness in my heart area."

He says, "It's better, though?"

I say yes, but it isn't. He does that with a couple other people, too.

After both partners finish, it's lunchtime. Again, we are to go to lunch with our partner. Henry has so many serious judgments about himself; it feels hard to relate to him. Since I don't feel a connection, I find the conversation difficult and stilted - - at least on my end. I'm learning that my shyness is selective. Sometimes, I don't want to talk! I think that's okay. I tell him that he reminds me of Yul Brenner in *The King and I*. It is a difficult hour with him, and I am glad to be back to the group. It is such a different dynamic than with Rinaldo.

There are several times during the day when we sit in the circle and have to tell how we feel. Again, it is difficult for me because I feel fine! Rinaldo has the same problem. Maybe that's why we have a connection!

Then, Aasar talks about when babies are born there are no judgments. The judgments all come later. We have to revisit our list of judgments and write down where we got them from: mother, father, or society. Those are the only choices. Friends and lovers all count as society. It isn't clear to me what I should do, and most everyone else writes furiously. It turns out that we are to write down other judgments about ourselves. I don't understand it, Rinaldo doesn't understand it, and a couple other people don't understand it. Aasar says that he has never had a group so unconscious as this one. That sounds awfully judgmental! Maybe we just can't understand his accent!

After lunch, we spread little mattresses out on the floor and put the picture we drew on it. Aasar gives us a rubber hose and tells us not to hit the picture - - the judge - - with all our might. We should do it in slow motion and not hit it at all. Hitting it or almost hitting it is the act of giving back the judgments we don't want. He says it is an experiment based on the latest scientific data. He says that doing it in slow motion, getting your muscles involved, and seeing it in slow motion helps it stick with you. Maybe it's muscle memory. Regardless, I am glad we don't have to hit it.

Aasar keeps saying, "Give it back, give it back!" But, I don't like the idea of giving it back to my mother, because she didn't do it on purpose. So, I decide that I will send it into the universe where it will dissipate without hurting anyone else.

This exercise surprisingly gets to me. I get teary eyed and say, "I don't want it. Don't give it to me. Take it back." I do feel a relief or a clearing at some point. I go through all the judgments written on the paper.

Later, after I feel the relief come, I stop and sit there doing nothing. Aasar comes over and asks, "What is happening?"

I say, "I gave it back."

He says, "Keep going." My back hurts, but I keep going in exaggerated slow motion, stopping at the paper for a long time.

Finally, he says we have one more exercise to do. For the next five minutes, we are to strike the paper with all our might. I whack it good a few times. Although, after the relief I felt earlier, my heart isn't in it. When I finish, the drawing is mostly intact. Other people's drawings are in shreds.

At four o'clock, Aasar announces that we should all go to Kundalini together, go home and have a shower, go to Evening Meeting, and then meet back in the room at 9:30 to finish today's session with one more hour. And, oh yeah, wear maroon. That thrills my heart to no end. Read that dripping with sarcasm.

As we walk down the street, most of the people cross to the other side to go to the Buddha Auditorium. Rinaldo and I don't cross. When we get to the front gate, he turns to cross the street and I turn and walk into the ashram. I am probably the only one who doesn't follow instructions. I'm okay with that, too! I hope that I won't get in too much trouble, but if I do, I'm fine with that. There is no way I am going to give up another hour of my free time.

After I finish meditating, on my way downstairs to fill my water bottle, Bhava stops me. She says that she is in the final two days of the program and she's quitting. We hug, and she says she will be around. She thinks she's going to stay in Pune. Her leaving disappoints me because I like Bhava and I can confide in her. But, it will be good to have the bathroom to myself! Even for a little while.

Bhava says something that I can relate to. She says, "I'm not twenty years old and I can't keep up with all of this." She is my age, and the person who I have most discussed my skipping with. She is the sweetest person. I will really miss her.

Bhava again mentioned that many people are dropping out of the program. However, when I mention it to Chandra, she says there are plenty of new applicants. Maybe I better not get so cocky about skipping!

After Evening Meeting, I dress again in my maroon robe and walk over to Sanai for the last part of today's class. We sit in a circle, and Aasar tells us to tear our list of judgments and our drawing into little pieces creating a pile in front of us. Then we take the rubber hose again and in slow motion hit our pile of paper. We stand up and say one or two words to the pile - - like what we would say to ourselves if the judgment pops up again - - stop, no, or whatever. Aasar then puts a big garbage bag in the center of the room. One by one, we put our piles of paper in the bag.

After that, Aasar says it's time to celebrate getting rid of our self-judgments by dancing. Everybody is hooting, hollering, and celebrating, and I play along. We dance to one song. Aasar says we can only have one song, because this is a residential area. But, tonight is the party in the plaza, and he suggests we go over there together.

Since I'm not a party girl, I walk over there with everyone, but when we get close, two of the guys have to drag me inside! Not exactly drag - - but they are insistent. Once we arrive, though, there are others and we start dancing. I stay for a few songs, but I am tired and sweaty and the music is loud and not that good. So, I follow someone out and then walk home. I've had enough for one day! Tomorrow is the last part of the class.

There are moments when I wonder, how am I ever going to find someone? Then I think that maybe I should return to Sam. But, today, after Rinaldo hugged me so tight - - I want that. I need that. And Sam cannot give me that. There is no way I could possibly consider returning to him.

Now that I am only going to be here one more month, I'm starting to feel pressure of what I'm going to do next. Do I go home and stay with Sam? It would not be good for him, but it would be good for me. After I pack my stuff, then what? What is my next move? Why hasn't the universe provided?

Day Sixty-five - Graduating from Judgment

It doesn't look like I'll be staying longer. The universe got in the way. Sometimes when the universe guides you it is in a booming voice like a loud speaker. My trip to India was that way. I wasn't getting out of it. Sometimes, the universe whispers softly in your ear. If you're not quiet and paying attention, you might not even hear it. I heard it, so most likely I will move on when my ninety days finishes.

The group feels different today. When we arrive, we sit in a circle and share our experiences and how we feel. Since I don't think that everyone has to talk, I am last. Getting out of it didn't work! I say that I feel lighter and brighter today. That is the truth. Then I say that I feel like someone lifted a weight off my shoulders. Although I thought that was for Aasar's benefit, it is honestly true, also. Everyone else said more than me.

At break time, I have to go back to the office to check my computer. While I'm on the phone at the front desk, Revatii comes in. She is the person I've had the most issues with. She asks if I am the receptionist today. I tell her no, I am in a group and only using the phone.

Revatii mentions the scanning or me doing the reception job. I say, "You are a perfectionist and I am a perfectionist. It doesn't work with me doing the scanning for you."

She asks, "Did you not want to do it because of me?"

I say, "It is my issue."

Then, she says, "No. I'm working on myself, too, and I know I can be impatient." We go back and forth, and she apologizes and I apologize, and we both apologize and hug. It's an amazing experience that I owe to the workshop that I've been in. It started with the last workshop, and this one made it even better.

When I get back to the group, I'm happy to find Aasar alone. I tell him the great catharsis that I had with Revatii. He says I should tell the group because it will help them and reinforce their experiences and their transformation. He says that I didn't share much this morning.

After everyone else comes back, Aasar says that I still have something to share. Everyone loves the story I tell, and I dress it up by saying she was my nemesis before, and now we are best friends. Well, almost.

During my conversation with Aasar, he said that I should reveal my heart to people and to share with them more often. He's right. I am closed - - or was. This group has been beneficial for me. The universe chose correctly.

I bring the universe into this because my original paperwork assigned me to this group from the beginning. When you start the residential program, they give you a list of activities that you have to complete: the first three days are the meditation intensive, then meet your coach, go to workshops, and then a helper in a group. Originally, they scheduled me for Opening to Self Love which was changed to this one - - Good-bye to the Inner Judge. It is perfect for me and what I needed. A friend got a group called, Zen and the Billionaire. What if I had gotten that one? No help me for at all!

Aasar gives us a list of ways to defend ourselves against our inner judge by: aggression like yelling "stop," indignation, truth, humor, agreement that is paradoxical or ironic, exaggeration, surrender, changing the subject, compassion, breathing and sensing, and active visualization like what we did with the rubber hose. He also says that spontaneity is the most powerful weapon against our inner judge.

Then we do an exercise called David and Goliath. For this exercise, we choose a partner. I am sitting next to a friendly guy named Billy. But, I think it would be more helpful for me to have the strong-willed English girl, so I ask her to be my partner. It almost doesn't happen because Aasar wants one helper to stay out, but I want her and I insist. It works out, regardless.

One person stands on the black cushion, and the other person stands on the pink pillow (your resource). The person playing Goliath will say the inner judgments. The person playing David will say, "Stop" or whichever defense that he or she chooses. I am Goliath first and as she yells, "Stop," Goliath shrinks. A couple of her judgments involve her mother, so it is helpful for her to have me - - old enough to be her mother - - as her partner for this.

Then my turn comes, and she is surprisingly not powerful in her way of saying it. Saying "stop" feels difficult at first and then gets easier. She says she feels it. It is interesting watching Goliath shrink when you want him to stop. It feels empowering.

At lunchtime, Aasar assigns us to have lunch with the person sitting next to us, and I get Rinaldo again. I am glad for that. We walk to India Blossom restaurant, but they are too busy and we don't have time to wait. So, we cross the street and go to the thali place, instead. They have no tables and set one up for us. Rinaldo isn't too happy with the place and is nervous about the safety of it. My lunch is not good - - the worst I've had there. It is a negative experience. I feel like Rinaldo isn't happy, and it feels bad for me. I can feel the negativity and I don't like it.

When we run into Manik on our way back to the ashram, I ask him about driving for me next Monday. He might have said yes, I'm not sure. He gives me his number, anyway, so I will call him. Maybe I'll run into him again before then. If I am not in the bookstore anymore, maybe I will change the date to Thursday.

After returning from lunch, we hold a pillow that represents us as a child before becoming infected with these judgments. Aasar covers us with a sheet as we hold the pillow. Then we stand and walk around holding and comforting the "child" in our arms. I picture not only me as a cute little girl, but also me as the awkward teenager.

Next, we write in our notebooks all the unique qualities about ourselves. That is difficult, as well. Then we pick another partner, and this time I choose Billy. It is good having him as a partner for this exercise.

I give Billy my top three unique-nesses or talents. He reads them off one at a time, and I receive and notice how good it feels. I'm afraid Billy does it much better than I do. Of course, that is my inner judge talking.

After that, we each take the microphone and speak of three of our good qualities. Then, everyone in the group yells that person's name and raises their arms in an "Osho!" like gesture. It is cool.

Then we namaste everyone and give everyone a hug. It is a good ending. Jiadore and I walk back to the ashram to pick up a cart. She asks about going somewhere together, and I act a little indignant. I feel rejected because we haven't talked in a few days. She came this morning to our regular spot at eight o'clock like usual, but I slept in and didn't go because we hadn't discussed it.

After completing group cleanup, Jiadore and I walk to German Bakery. Just around the corner is a Subway. Inside, the food looks exactly like Subways back home. Their menu is slightly different, with a few Indian items. They have meat there, which surprises me.

After Evening Meeting tonight, which I skipped, is Casino Royale night. I buy two hundred chips for twenty rupees, and play some roulette. I win a few coins. Then I play Texas hold 'em for a while until I lose all my money!

A man comes up and starts talking to me. He teases me about wearing jeans. When I don't have a clue what he is talking about, he says, "The discourse in Evening Meeting was about women wearing jeans!"

So much for that! He makes some negative comments about what Osho said. I say, "You must not be a sannyasin, then."

Proudly, he says, "Twenty years sannyas. You need to be a sannyasin to disagree with Osho's words." Hmmmm, I don't have any trouble disagreeing and I'm not a sannyasin!

I wander over to another table that has eight Indian men and one Indian woman. It is a weird card game called Three Card. Dealers in all card games that I know deal clockwise - - to the left of the dealer. The dealer in this one deals to the right, counterclockwise. It also has another peculiarity. When you bet, if you have not looked at your cards, you only have to match half the bet. If you look at your cards, then you have to match the whole amount. They call it, "seen," or "blind." For instance, if someone bets ten dollars, and you have seen your cards, then if you want to play you have to put in ten dollars. If you have not looked at your cards, then you only have to put in five dollars. The rules are different here! After I buy two hundred more chips for twenty rupees, the Indian guy next to me helps me play. But, I never have a hand good enough to stay until the finish. For about a dollar, I have a blast! Cheaper than Vegas!

Speaking of betting, a couple days ago I sent an email to my brother who had bet against my staying here for the entire three months. I said - - four weeks and counting - - better start saving your pennies. Today, I receive a blistering email bringing up past incidents about my mother's will and other family nightmares.

Normally, an email like this would have clobbered me. This time is different. It's a shock, yes, but not the stinging affront that it once would have been. What a jerk. Since I feel so detached from it, I can write back a non-emotional response - - to tell him to get lost!

I decide to wait twenty-four hours, though, to let it all sink in before I send the email. I feel I owe this to the work I have done here in my various groups. Yes - - India is a place of transformation. Even here in the ashram where I am a stranger and a non-believer, India can still work its magic. Amazing, isn't it?

Something I realize which surprises me again, is that one of my inner judgments is being a spoiled brat. My brother continues to treat me like the spoiled brat that I once was. That should have been on my list. Until I received his email, I didn't realize that is one of my issues. What perfect timing! That is why I can answer it mostly without emotion, although he filled his letter with venom.

189

I have decided to stay at "our" house with Sam while I'm packing. It may not be good for him, but it will be better for me. Right now, I feel that it is the right path. I will sleep in the spare room.

Day Sixty-six – Meeting with Dwami

When I go to the bookstore this morning, I find another woman working there. I ask one of the workers, and he calls someone. While I wait for a response, the woman sprays some strong, cloying perfume into the air. That is enough for me! I waltz out the door and run into Chandra. Perfect timing! Who says there is no predestination? Chandra says they have assigned the other woman to the bookstore, and I should go back to my regular job.

I return to Multimedia and talk to Jiadore. She asks if I am going to the meeting with Dwami. Yes! This meeting is the one that I complained so much about two months ago. I want to see if my opinion of it has changed.

We arrive early and wait for Dwami. There are fewer people at this one, and only one person comes in late. Dwami starts to turn him away, and then just begins his speech again.

This meeting has a different feel to it. Although I know my perception has changed, it couldn't have changed this much. Dwami tells jokes throughout the lecture, making people laugh. Last time there was no laughter. It only turns serious today when he talks about Evening Meeting.

Jiadore says it is the same speech she heard when she first arrived. I think Dwami may have been angry with the several people who came in late to my first meeting. The anger set the tone of the whole meeting. Or, maybe he was angry at something else. Today's meeting feels different, sounds different, and is different.

Here are some excerpts that he shared today:
* Don't believe anything you hear until you experience it for yourself.
* Here at the ashram, it is like many ideas that come from Osho - - easy to understand and easy to misunderstand.
* What is important is the big picture, not the details. People often get so caught up in the details that they miss the big picture.
* The purpose of Evening Meeting is to learn to be present.
* Thoughts have no energy, until you give them energy.
* Your regular working life in the 'real world' is like prostituting yourself. You are selling yourself for the paycheck at the end of the week.
*Everyone gets here at the right time.

The last one thrills me. I know I arrived here at exactly the right time.

When Jiadore and I return from the meeting with Dwami, I go see Sakra to tell him about the woman in the bookstore. He immediately says, "I will call and find out about this!"

I say, "It's okay, I'm okay being here. I'll go back to the photos."

The line is busy, and Sakra turns around with his most charming smile and says, "Oh, no. Not the photos." Then what? He says, "Reception."

This is exactly the job I do not want. I must look faint, because he pats my arm and says, "It's okay - - the only bad part was the scanning, and I will take care of that."

I say, "I don't want that job. I came to India because of a similar job."

He says, "You cannot run away. Maybe if you deal with it here, you can return to your old job with a different attitude."

So, I have the exact job I did not want. Now, it is mine, and I will face it. Yippee.

Now that I've said the universe whispered to me that I need to leave at the end of three months - - I find the universe is playing games with me. Chandra calls this morning and asks if I want to stay another month. She says they can use me. As Jiadore would say, "What to do, what to do?" Although I think I'm leaving, Osho says to be choiceless. So, right now I shall remain choiceless - - at least until the universe makes itself a little clearer.

This morning I run into Revatii. I had worried that what happened with her yesterday was like my window in time with the street people. That it was a one-time occurrence that I would not see again. But, she hugs and kisses me. We both say how grateful we are of what happened yesterday. She says, "We should have tea together sometime."

I say, "I told my group what happened with us."

Revatii asked, "How did it fit into the group?"

I explain, "It had touched one of my self-judgment buttons. That's what the group was about." The exchange yesterday and today have been amazing. What a gift from the universe!

When Jiadore and I come back from lunch, we sit on a bench in the back garden and talk until after three o'clock. We should be back from lunch at two. Oh, well. She tells me about a mystical encounter she had with a shamanic old man. Then, I tell her how jealous I am of that experience and how I had hoped for that to happen with Uncle Makeen. But, his power was from another lifetime. In this lifetime, he is only a poor street magician. She says that when I first told her about Uncle

Makeen, it reminded her of this old shamanic man she had the experience with. So, I'll keep hanging out with Uncle Makeen - - maybe our time is coming.

Day Sixty-seven – Osho Police Activity

Today while standing at the reception desk, Sakra comes over, places his hand on my lower back, and goes lower to the top of my butt. It shocks me. It is only a second, but it is inappropriate. But, since he is always after younger women, I have to admit I am a little flattered. Although, why should I be? He is my age!

I see Revatii today in her office. We talk some, and she says, "I love this clearing!" We hug again.

I'm not sure if it was her or Prana who said, "We are all working on ourselves here." It is true.

When I talk to Rasha today, I find out she is university educated and now going for her master's degree. She tutors students in English, also. When she teaches me Hindi, she looks so cute. If I pronounce a word wrong, she gets this stern look on her face when she corrects me. Jiadore talks to her, too, and found out that Rasha is twenty-one. After her older sister gets married, it will be her turn. It amazes me how it works here.

When I mention to Rasha that I am looking for somewhere to stay for my last four days here, she invites me to stay at her house. Rasha is such a sweetheart. When I say no, she invites me over after work to go to some park. I tell her I will. She says, "You're not just saying it, right? You will really come?" Yes, I will. We will go to the park with her mother and her sister. This will be an experience in the real India - - and much safer than my meanderings with the street people.

One time I mentioned to Rasha that I put something on my face to help with the wrinkles, so she asked what I used because she wanted to get it for her mother. Mine came from the Internet, but someone recommended a cream from here, so today, I give Rasha one of those. She starts writing down the information, and I say, "No, it's for your Mom." She complains and says no, no, but I walk away. She is so mad. I worried that I had gotten her into trouble because there were two guys with her at the time, but she said it was fine. They won't tell.

I say something to Jiadore today, and she answers me back in Czechoslovakian. It makes me feel weird, because I'm not sure if I heard it right or not. I say, "Whaaaat?" Then, she realizes what she has done, and we both crack up. She had been in the middle of writing a letter to her parents.

Jiadore and I take a rickshaw today to a fancy restaurant that even has tablecloths. Boy, did we ever splurge - - it cost us three dollars and fifty cents each! Jiadore orders for us: spicy fried rice, some other dish that has tofu, and another dish that she describes as having a cream sauce. Although I don't think I'll like it, I taste it anyway. It turns out to be a cole slaw type dish and tastes delicious. What a great lunch it is.

After work, Jiadore and I walk over to German Bakery. On our way over there, two women stop me. They ask if I will give money for handicapped children. I say, no, sorry, and walk on. One of them shouts after me, "Yeah, sorry!" It is rude and surprising. This is the first time I have experienced anything like that.

As Jiadore and I walk back to the ashram, I see an ice cream man walking down the street with a cart. We are in a hurry or I would have run out to catch him. Jiadore says, "No, no, no. You can't eat ice cream from the street."

It makes me smile, though, because I have such great memories of ice cream men. My first experience happened when I was five years old. We visited my grandmother who lived in a large city. What a treat! An ice cream delivered to your door. Then when we moved there a few years later, it was my nightly routine to get an ice cream from the ice cream man. My favorite was Buried Treasure. The ice cream wasn't that good. But, the plastic ice cream stick had a figure on the end of it that was "buried" by the ice cream. I collected them: a pirate, a clown, a ship, a cowboy, and all manner of creatures. I never outgrew the ice cream man.

It has suddenly become hot here. I don't want to stay any longer than my time because this heat is awful, and it's only going to get hotter. While standing in front of German Bakery, a little boy asks me why my cheeks are so red. He thinks something is wrong with me. It's my sensitivity to the heat. I have to be careful and make sure I drink enough water.

At Evening Meeting tonight, I run into Aasar. I tell him that I talked to Revatii again and it was good. Also, I tell him about getting the email from my brother. How it hit a judgment I had forgotten about and wasn't on my list, but it didn't get to me like it normally would have. After I thank him a couple times, he touches my arm and acts genuinely happy that I had gotten something important from his group. That felt good.

The Osho police are at it again during Evening Meeting. There is a man from my office who sits near me at the back of the auditorium. The last few days I have seen him escort coughing people out. Today, the woman who sits with him stands, walks to the front of the auditorium, and chases down a woman. I watch to see what is going on. The chased woman somehow managed to bring in a large maroon purse and a plastic bag of clothes past the security at the door. Immediately, the Osho police escort her out and tell her to leave her belongings outside in the lobby area. These people take this so seriously. She got in, so what? No, she can't have such a big maroon purse with her in there. Little purses are okay, but too much maroon was showing. Crazy.

This evening, I call Manik about Thursday. When I say it is Parvati, he says, "Parvati!" like he is happy to hear from me. We arrange to meet at the India Blossom Restaurant at 8:15 in the morning. I'm hoping that he shows up and shows up alone. I forgot to mention that to him.

Day Sixty-eight – Birthday Blues

I feel like I am going to Disneyland, honestly. I couldn't sleep last night with all the excitement. Part of it is that I don't know what will happen to me after skipping a whole day's work. We are not allowed to do that. But, Prana has always told me - - don't ask permission - - ask forgiveness. When I asked her about it yesterday, she said, "Don't say I told you that!" So, I'll see how it goes.

The risk that I am taking with Manik is a minor one. I have met his brother, and I have met his father - - a merchant with a store. Jiadore will have his cell phone number, and she knows where the store is. That won't be much good if something does happen, though! I know Manik is a good kid, and I will have a good time motoring around Pune with him. He has never looked at me the way that other twenty-one-year-old did. He has always been respectful. I'll be fine!

Again - - the universe provides. Manik has this Indian friend named Anderson. That concerned me, because I wasn't sure if he had planned to bring him on our little adventure or not. I forgot to specify. I don't know what to say tomorrow morning if Anderson shows up with Manik. Would "three's a crowd" be appropriate? I ask Jiadore because she is diplomatic and politically correct, but she doesn't know either.

A little while ago, Bhava came to see me. Immediately, I knew something was wrong. Her Indian boyfriend had come home drunk last night and had gotten violent. She asked, "Can I keep my luggage in your room until tomorrow?"

I say, "Tomorrow wouldn't be good because I am skipping the whole day."

She says, "The next day will be fine."

I ask, "Did you get in any trouble when you skipped the whole day?"

She says, "No, and I didn't ask beforehand, either."

Back to the universe - - I thought, why not invite Bhava to go with me tomorrow! It would be a good break for her. I figured if I were meant to run into her, I would. And, I did! And, she said yes! Now if Anderson shows up, it's fine. If he doesn't, that's fine, too. I hope Bhava shows up tomorrow. If not, I'll deal with it.

While in Zorba restaurant today buying a banana, I hand the guy my voucher and say, "panch?"

He says, "Yes, panch." Panch is five in Hindi! I love using the new words that I learn!

197

As I walk away, smiling - - I always try to smile - - a man approaches me with his hand out like a high five. Like everyone else here, he dresses in maroon, and I don't have a clue who he is. He turns out to be the poker dealer from the Casino night! I sat at his table for a while and had a conversation about Santa Fe, New Mexico because we had both lived there. People look so different in maroon robes and regular clothes!

Jiadore tells me today that her boyfriend, Arjuna, told her she is different. She said this morning while training for Welcome Morning, when people asked questions, she thought - - this is not the place to ask why. She says that scared her. I ask if she still hears the electronic beeping, and she says she does. So, she's not too far gone, yet.

With Arjuna in town again, I won't be hanging out with her for a while. That is okay. I have plenty to do here on my own. I have wanted to attend some of the other ashram offerings, and this will give me the chance to do that.

After work, I go out back to wait for Phani. He was going to pick up the snake guy at the train station and then pick me up. Phani drives up from the wrong direction and gets out of his rickshaw. He tells me a convoluted story about going to find the guy and he wasn't there, and he had to wait a long time. But, tomorrow he will be there and we can do it then. Although it disappoints me, I give him two hundred rupees because he had to drive all the way to the train station. It isn't until later I realize that he had probably forgotten about the snake appointment, and made up the whole story. It makes me feel betrayed, hurt, and out two hundred rupees for nothing.

I walk down the other direction to where the street magicians hang out. Uncle Makeen is there with a few other guys. I sit next to him on the cement log. He starts saying something, and I must have interrupted, because he says, "I am talking. You listen." And, he says it in his general or king-like voice. I listened! If he would have said, jump, I would have asked, how high? We sit there for a while talking. Then I decide I have been hanging out with these guys for so long, I'm leaving in a month and I have never seen a magic show. So, I ask Uncle Makeen. He wants his son to do it. First he says his English isn't good enough, and then he says his wrist hurts - - carpal tunnel or something!

I keep insisting, so he moves opposite me and starts the show. He is good at it, too. He speaks in thirty-six languages! At least that's what they told me - - and I heard him count to four in Japanese, Malaysian, French, and several others. His son says that when Uncle Makeen was young, his father took him to many countries. I knew there was more to him than the poor street magician. When he finishes, I give him a hundred rupees more than we had agreed on, because I couldn't help myself. I try to get a picture of me kissing his cheek, but his son says that he is fasting. What that has to do with it, I don't know! But, I wasn't going to push it.

Afterwards, Zakir and I agree to meet on Saturday to see another cobra. He will probably forget again. Then, I tell Zakir and Uncle Makeen's son that it is my birthday. They tell me that if I had told them yesterday, they would have brought me some birthday cake. I honestly do feel close to these guys. It reminds me of another sad time in my life.

In my twenties, while living in a small western town, I worked for a large hotel. Each week, these two older pilots - - probably forty-five or fifty years old - - stayed over at the hotel. I would always hang out with them when they came in. They were both married, and one was sweet on me. Since they were old and married, I had no interest in them in that way. But, I did look forward to seeing them. When I realized that seeing them was the highlight of my week, it made me feel depressed. I remember thinking, "Two old men!" That is how I felt today. These street magicians are the highlight of my life here.

While I am out there with the street magicians, Manik stops to confirm tomorrow morning at the India Blossom restaurant. He has a car full of people.

Ah, my birthday. My birthday in India. No one knows. After the disappointment with Phani, and my time with the street magicians, I come back to my room and meditate. Then I dress for Evening Meeting.

As I walk to the pyramid auditorium, I run into a group of people reading a sign. It says, "Beloveds, because of the current political unrest in Pune, it is safest to stay inside the ashram." In this crowded but peaceful city of nine million people, there has recently been some violence. I have heard conflicting reports, but it could be about a political candidate, or workers coming down from another part of India to take jobs from the locals. Although the rules are different here, some issues are universal.

Isn't it ironic that after two months of working seven days a week, I finally choose a day to skip work. And now I have to worry about accidentally stumbling into some street violence. Is this Los Angeles or India?

Inside Evening Meeting, although I listen on the iPod to a singer I love, I can't help feeling profoundly depressed. Well, maybe not profoundly, but I do feel like crying. And, it feels bad. I'm sure part of it is lack of sleep. But that just emphasizes what may have already been there.

During the discourse tonight, Osho says that all creatures are divine. As I cross the street after leaving Evening Meeting, I see a guard chasing a street dog with a stick. I feel angry all the way back to my room.

After changing clothes and preparing for gate duty, I am still angry about the guard. I march down to the office and write a note to Dwami. It is a semi-blistering email about Osho's comment and the guards getting their jollies by beating the dogs. I think his little twenty-year-old girlfriend left tonight. He may not be in the best of moods when he receives it. Regardless, I feel much better after I send it. Now, I'll suffer the consequences. Or not.

Later in the evening, I tell Jiadore that it is my birthday, and she hugs me. Then, I tell Sajeev, and he hugs me. Still, it is a sad day for me.

As I prepare for gate duty, I dress in my usual gate-duty-outfit consisting of full body maroon long underwear, maroon pants, maroon robe, and maroon shawl. I walk out the door and across the street. Suddenly, I realize something odd. It feels hot! It has gotten hot, and I don't need so many clothes on. Unfortunately, it is too late to go back to my room and change. Luckily, they have a fan at the gate for the mosquitoes. It is cool enough to get me through the night without boiling to death.

Gate duty isn't too bad. Another guard comes and yells, "hut, hut" at the dog. The dog doesn't know much about football, but it knows enough to run away. Later, another dog comes close to me. It smiles and wags and I can't help myself from calling it over. I put my hand down and it licks me. What a sweetheart. It is starving, but friendly, and always in a good mood. What a great lesson.

Day Sixty-nine - Adventures in Pune

My day starts with Bhava knocking on my door, as I am about to leave. She says, "I haven't slept all night and I need to sleep today. Sorry I can't go with you." She takes her luggage and leaves.

I walk over to the India Blossom restaurant and arrive early. Devika's husband sees me in the open window and stops to talk. He and Devika live close by. When I tell him what I am going to do, he says to be careful what I eat while I'm out in the city.

Manik shows up a few minutes later and comes in looking tired. Since he usually sleeps until ten o'clock, his mother wondered why he got up so early today. I ate those wonderful banana pancakes again, and all he has is coffee. We talk about where we are going today. He says, "I don't know how to get anywhere except the snake park. I want to call Anderson."

I say, "I'm not comfortable with that." Manik assures me that Anderson is a good person. But, Anderson feels too tired to come with us.

Manik tells me that while at a party yesterday, the girl he likes danced with other boys. It bothered Manik so much he cried. When the girl asked what was wrong, he said he was fine. Manik says he didn't want to tell her and hurt her. He says he always likes to make people happy. What a good boy he is!

Manik says that he would prefer to have someone hurt him than hurt someone else. I mention the song, "El Condor Pasa" by Simon and Garfunkel. The line, "I'd rather be a hammer than a nail," is what I tell him about. It honestly gets lost in the translation. He doesn't understand it. That is always how it's been for me. Easier for me to be a nail than a hammer. Now, I don't want to be either one.

Later in the conversation, I give him a brief summary of the problems with my brother, and how we are not close anymore. He pats my hand and says, "Don't worry. Here is your brother," and he taps his hand on his chest. What a sweet kid!

After breakfast, off we go into the streets of Pune. When I put on the seat belt, Manik says, "You don't have to wear that. I am a safe driver." I keep it on!

Then he pulls into the gas station and says, "Shall we get some fuel?"

I say, "Yes."

He asks, "How much should we get?"

I say, "Fill it up." But, he doesn't. He buys seven hundred rupees worth, whatever that is. Now, it will cost me one thousand rupees that I promised him, seven hundred rupees for gas, and other expenses during the day. For fifteen hundred rupees, I could have had a professional car and driver. Although, it wouldn't have been half as much fun!

After driving for a short time, he turns off the main road and parks. Manik says, "We will wait a few minutes for my friend who knows all the temples in Pune and will tell me how to get there. She is coming by rickshaw." He mentions her caste. The only castes that I know are Brahman and untouchable. Her caste is close to Brahman. He says she is a good person, but her father beats her. I ask, "Is that common?"

He says, "Not girls. Boys are beaten, but usually not girls."

After a half hour, she and the girl that Manik likes show up. We're off again. The three of them speak Hindi rapidly, and I can't understand anything. When the girls find a beer bottle in the backseat, they toss it out the window. Littering isn't an issue here.

The girl that Manik likes sits behind him and starts pulling his hair and poking him. I have to tell her not to touch the driver. The three of them each have a cell phone and they pass them back and forth. All this while Manik drives fast, swerves, and maneuvers around rickshaws, motorcycles, and people. With the radio blaring, Manik sings along in Hindi, while the girls giggle in the back seat.

We finally make it to Parvati Hill. It is a temple on top of a hill devoted to Parvati. You have to climb one hundred eight steps to the top. One hundred eight is a sacred number in India. We stop partway up and one girl shows me what to do. You dip your third finger of your right hand into the red dust, called haldi or kumkum, and then you put it on your forehead. My right hand had the camera in it, so I touched it with my left hand. She corrects me. I hope what I did isn't sacrilegious or anything! After the red powder, she walks around this area touching all the deities. Then, we step outside, and have to remove our shoes. Thankfully, I had the foresight to wear sandals instead of my good tennis shoes.

Then the three of us (one girl stays behind on her cell phone) walk all the way to the top. They don't allow any pictures there, but I can touch many deities. Most of them have more red powder at their bases. Then the girl and I stand in line, and a man hands us some candy, dough, and flowers. We keep it in our hands and walk around the top to see more deities. Some of them look like blobs with eyes and a mouth. Later, I ask her about it, and she says they are natural and made of mud. She says they have eyes to see and a mouth to speak.

Manik says, "You should eat the dough and the candy." But I can't, so I give it to him. He says, "God will understand!"

We walk back down the one hundred eight steps (I didn't count them), and at the bottom are some merchants. Manik helps me bargain a guy down to buy an inexpensive belt. Then, Manik and the girls share some potato chips, grapes, and a coke. He says he bought the grapes for me, but again, I can't eat them.

While at Parvati Temple, Manik's phone rings, and it is Jiadore. Manik tries to hand it to me, and I tell him that I don't use cell phones so tell her I'm fine. He says, "You gave her my cell number?" Jiadore tells me later that when she heard me say that about the cell phone, she figured if I could still complain about cell phones, then I must be fine!

Next, we are off to the snake park. Suddenly, Manik pulls over in front of a weird building. It looks newly built or needing repairs, but it is difficult to tell. Manik says this is going to be his new office to sell real estate. I ask if it is to sell beachfront property, and he says yes. Then he gets out of the car, and says he will ask for directions. I tell the girls that in America, men don't usually ask for directions. They laugh about that! Some man appears by my side of the car and says, "Hi Parvati!" It turns out to be Anderson, and he squeezes into the backseat beside the girls. It must have been him on one of those many cell phone calls that they all received.

After we drive for a while, Manik pulls over and the girls get out. Manik says wait and he hands them some rupees for the rickshaw. I ask how much he gave them, and he says fifty. I tell him I'll pay him back for that, since they came to help with directions.

The snake park must be on the other side of Pune. As we drive, I see remarkable sights. It amazes me. Parts of Pune could be like any other American city. And parts of it are so foreign, it could have been another planet. Pune is a city of many different hues.

It feels like it takes forever, but then I see a sign for a university, which I know is close to the snake park. Then, Manik pulls into a parking lot. Again, I use my new Hindi when I ask for "teen" tickets to the snake park, for the three of us. It costs three rupees apiece.

Although I have high expectations, the snake park disappoints me. I never see any cobras. Or if I do, they aren't hooded up and they look like any other snake. I miss the highlight of the snake park - - the nine-foot albino king cobra. They do have a cool Russell's viper (common around Pune, and probably in Osho Teerth Park), a white tiger, and these cute little spotted deer. Now, it's time to leave. Manik doesn't feel good, and the heat makes all of us miserable.

We leave there, and Anderson asks if I want to go anywhere else. I say I'll buy them lunch at McDonalds or Pizza Hut. Back into the traffic we go, and I see more incredible sights. We wind up at the Pyramid Mall that Jiadore and I went to a couple weeks ago. Manik pulls into the paid parking lot (ten rupees), and they ask for his keys. They open the trunk and look inside. Manik isn't upset at all and says it is good that they do that. When I ask why, he says, "Terrorists."

We walk into the deliciously cool mall. There is a sign on the wall "This mall protected by electronic surveillance." A few feet down is a picture of Ganesh.

We go to McDonalds, and I splurge. I have a veggie burger, fries, chocolate malt, and a coke. The boys order fries, cokes, and some Indian food. McDonalds in India. The food tastes great, what can I say. While we eat, I thank the two of them for taking me all around. Manik says, "Don't say thank you."

I ask, "Why?"

Manik says, "Anderson will explain."

Anderson says, "Friends never need to say thank you or I'm sorry."

I say, "I have to." Later, they thank me for buying their lunch, and I say, "Don't say thank you!" I try to pay Manik the fifty rupees for the girls' rickshaw ride, and he won't take it.

We drop off Anderson, and it is still early. I ask Manik to drive by the back gate of the ashram to see if Phani is there. Manik says that I look tired, and I should go inside and rest. My face is bright red from not drinking enough water. I brought some with me, but didn't drink enough of it. Phani isn't there, so I have Manik drop me at German Bakery. He says I can make a local call there.

I call Phani. He is on MG road and will pick me up in half an hour. I start down the street to visit friends and run into Uncle Makeen. Since I am uncomfortable after trying to get a picture of myself kissing his cheek yesterday, I only speak to him for a minute.

Then, I continue down the street until I arrive at Manik's father's store. Shareef isn't there; it is Manik's brother, Tanul. He invites me inside and shows me his new computer. He shows me pictures of his son. One picture shows black under his son's eyes. Tanul calls it kajal and says it is good for the eyes. It looks like the stuff football players put under their eyes. Then he shows me pictures of some cool crystals. I ask about one crystal, and he says he had gotten it "off the 'net!"

I have to leave then to meet Phani. While I wait at German

Bakery, I run into Bhava. She tells me that she has moved into a friend's room, and will leave in a few days. Then Phani appears out of nowhere, and we walk to his rickshaw. Off we go.

We drive to the train station and pick up the snake guys. They want three hundred rupees. Phani keeps shaking his head, but they finally get in the rickshaw. They have a conversation in Hindi that I don't understand. As we drive there, I consider my choices about talking to Phani about not going to the train station yesterday. I'm not even sure that I'm right - - I only suspect it. Finally, I decide that it wouldn't serve any purpose, and I should forget it.

When we get to the place where the snake is, Phani tells me that they wanted more money, but he told them, "Money, money, money. That's not all that this is about. This is a nice lady, give her a break." Then, I am so glad I had decided not to confront him about yesterday - - truth or not.

The snake man comes out quickly with a woven basket. He opens it, and inside is a huge and beautiful cobra. He says something about it not being poisonous, so I ask if I can hold it. Although he keeps the head, I hold the rest of the snake! I did it! It isn't around my neck, and I may never have that chance again, but I hold the cobra! What a trip! What a great birthday present this is!

I get some great pictures of it standing up, but I want the back of its hood, because it is a spectacled cobra. Every time I move, the snake follows me. I keep talking to him, saying how beautiful he is and that I won't hurt him. Finally, Phani gets his attention and the snake turns his back to me, and I get some great shots of his "spectacles." Beautiful snake.

After he puts the snake away, the guy wants five hundred rupees. Phani and I work him down to three hundred fifty, but it is incredibly worth the extra money. I held a cobra! I held a cobra! How cool is that!

As we drove all over Pune today, and I had no idea where we were going, I kept thinking that I'd rather be back at the ashram, safe and secure. My job isn't so bad - - I surf often and have much freedom. What a funny thought. My one big day out, and I wanted back where it was safe and boring.

It reminded me of when my mother was in the nursing home. She always pestered me to take her somewhere. Finally, I gave in, got the car ready and picked her up. I took her around to some of my favorite places. We weren't gone long when she started complaining about her back and saying that she wanted to go back home. It astounded me because she had wanted to get out for so long, and now when I took her out, all she could talk about was going back. That's how I felt today.

Dwami never wrote back to me about the dogs and the guards. I find that curious. Perhaps he thought it was beneath him.

I'm feeling peaceful right now and ready to go back to work tomorrow. But, I can't wait to see this snake again. I hope it's the same one and I hope to hold it again, by myself.

When I get home tonight, I can feel all this grit and grime all over my face. It is gross - - city pollution and dirt.

Hoping to go to sleep early, I skip Evening Meeting. I wonder how much trouble I'll get into tomorrow for skipping work. I don't care, because I had a great day!

Day Seventy - Repercussions

While I talk to Jiadore at the front desk, Sakra walks in. He says hello and nothing else. It shocks me. I can't believe it. When I tell Prana, she says it is no big deal. The only one who asks where I was yesterday is Revatii. When I tell her that I had given myself a birthday gift by taking the day off, she smiles and that is it.

Later in the morning, Sakra calls me in and asks where I was yesterday. He is not happy. The chair where visitors sit is eight inches lower than his chair. I have never liked the "feng shui" of it. He's a big guy anyway, and towers over you. The last few times I've been in there, I sit on a pillow to make me taller. Today, the pillow isn't tall enough.

Sakra says that no one can take a day off, including him. He says that one translator (they translate Osho's words into different languages) was going to Nadabrahma meditation instead of working. She doesn't work here anymore. It sounds like a threat. It isn't good.

Now, I am back to more restrictions, after some time of relative freedom. I'm not happy about it, but perhaps this, too, is meant to be. It has become almost comfortable here, and that scares me! It's better the end of my stay at the ashram is as tough as the beginning of my stay. A full circle.

This morning when I check my email, I find one from Sam. He says, "Happy birthday. I'm getting rid of our dog." Coming home at lunch and getting up in the middle of the night to take the dog out has become too much for him. He says that he will give me the first option before he tries to find a home for her. Then he says that if I want to see her again, he will keep her until I get home. Talk about passive/aggressive.

This devastates me. I have been in such a good mood from yesterday and the cobra and all, and then to wake up and read this. It brings me down like a stone falling into a well. Plop, there I lie on the bottom.

I could hear the anger in it. Something Jiadore tells me sounds true. Sam has realized that our relationship is over, and this is his way of cutting the ties. The dog, and the house that is up for sale, are the only ties we have. He also mentioned the house in the email.

When I tell Jiadore how Sam had put it in the email, I call him an asshole. She says, "You always talk about what a good man he is." That shocks me. It is true. I always do say what a good man he is, because he is. But, to hear it put that way surprises me and makes me happy that I can genuinely say what a good person he is and mean it. Except today, of course!

Sometimes, I wonder what Indian people like Manik and Rasha think about my saying that I left my husband but he is a good man. Here in a country where love is almost unheard of in a marriage, why would anyone leave a good man? I'm sure it confuses them. Sometimes it confuses me, too. But, even when I felt so depressed the other night, I never honestly considered returning to Sam.

After giving it much thought and meditating on it, I have to cancel my plans to travel to Europe. I can't let Sam give Sheba away. Many years ago, I had to give away another dog, and I remember how the people said they'd give him back if it didn't work out. They gave him to someone else, instead. I can't let that happen with our dog. So, I'll be staying in the United States. I don't know what I'll do, but I'll figure something out. This also excludes going to that ashram in Colorado. If this is the guidance and the next step for me, then I am okay with that. It just bothers me that this came out of nowhere.

Revatii comes downstairs and asks how I am doing with the scanning. I tell her I am having a hard time. She is upset again, and I tell her that Vijay will give me a lesson. Later, I see her talking to Sakra, and neither of them looks happy. I'm sure it is about the scanning. The scanning is my undoing here. You'd think I could get this technology, but I can't make it work. I keep trying to get the scans of newspapers perfect, and it doesn't happen. So much for Revatii being my new best friend!

Later this afternoon, Vijay, the only hired Indian person at the office, comes to help me. He spends an hour with me after work. Revatii comes down and I say, "Vijay is giving me a lesson."

She asks, "What about the pencil marks?"

Sakra doesn't know about erasing them. I say, "Vijay is teaching me how. I know about erasing the pencil marks." She doesn't understand.

I'm still not sure I have it, but I have it more than I did before. Most of it is that newspapers do not scan "perfectly." It's futile for me to try to make them perfect. That's what I've tried to do. Vijay taught me many new features of the program, and I will try Revatii's work again tomorrow.

After work, I go to Chandra's to give her a Reiki session because of her back pain. We keep talking, and it is uncomfortable for me physically, because I don't have a chair. Since I only give her Reiki on her back, I cut the session to half an hour. I hope it helps, because I know she is in pain.

She tells me that her new job is also long hours - - starts at nine and ends after four. But, it requires fewer hours than Worker's Meditation that she left. I should be thankful that my job is only six hours.

When I go to lunch at Meera today, there is no Osho-ite guard at the gate. Instead, a rent-a-cop checks passes. When I go to Evening Meeting tonight, it is the same. After Evening Meeting when I leave the Meera gate, who sits there but Dwami - - wearing a white robe! So much for only using the white robe for Evening Meetings!

Day Seventy-one - Adventures with Friends

I run into Rasha in the laundry early this morning when I drop off my clothes. She says she is in trouble. When her father died a year ago, her uncle told her mother that he had a boy for Rasha to marry. Her mother said, no, she would wait for a good boy later. That angered her uncle, and he hasn't spoken to them for a while.

Now her uncle has come back and tells her mother that Rasha is involved with her older and engaged-to-be-married cousin. It is innocent -- he takes her to work and back everyday. Now the uncle, convinced of her wrongdoing, follows Rasha around. Rasha doesn't know what to do. I advise her to tell her mother the truth. She says that her mother trusts her. But, if she told her about the cousin taking her to work, her mother would wonder for a moment if the rumor were true. I understand that. It's like the Salem witch trials. It doesn't matter if it's true or not. Once someone accuses you, you might as well be guilty.

I think the uncle is trying to create a situation where Rasha has to marry the boy that he suggested. Rasha thinks that is true, also. But, that doesn't help her out of this bad situation. Although I feel bad for her, there is nothing I can do to help. I hope her mother won't make her quit working here (as the cousin works here, too), because I would miss her.

I run into the translator today that Sakra told me about. When I ask her about being kicked out, she says, "It is none of your business."

I say, "I'm sorry. It's just that I received a threat and only want information so I can protect myself."

She says, "It's all right," and then walks away without telling me what I want to know.

Three and a half weeks to go. If they do kick me out now, it wouldn't be so horrible. I've put my time in, I have my information, and getting kicked out would make a great ending. Although, it might look like seeking revenge for them kicking me out. No, that would not be good at all.

Another reason to try to make it all the way is because if I do, then I can come back and stay free. That's free plus eight hours of work a day, including my beloved Evening Meeting. So, what are the chances that I would want to do that? Um, slim to none would be my guess. Although, maybe I'll have an incredible breakthrough in my last few days here and pledge my life to Osho. Stranger things have happened!

In my last group, one guy told how he used some of what he had learned. He said that it's safe here because we are all in the same space, so it's easier to try out the tools here.

Something I thought of concerning my "stupid idiot" judgment. That judgment has a picture with it - - the picture of me at thirty years old wearing that stupid Donald Duck hat. My mother saw me wearing that hat and said to take it off because I look like an idiot. All these years I've felt like an idiot. And, the comment had nothing to do with me, and everything to do with the hat.

Jiadore and her boyfriend give me a garland of fresh, fragrant flowers. She hangs it on the wall behind my desk. They are beautiful and smell wonderful. Prana sees them and asks me if I have taken sannyas. I say no. There is no way that is going to happen. The whole idea of sannyas is so distasteful to me that I couldn't even consider doing it to experience it. No way. I had to open a letter a couple days ago at the front desk. Someone wrote wanting to give back their sannyas name. That struck me as amusing!

I go to lunch with Sajeev. Today is his last working day in the program. Tomorrow he is off work so he can pack his stuff, and he leaves on a bus tomorrow night. He wrote me a good-bye note to invite me to his home. He said that his children and his wife would welcome me there, also. I will miss him; he has been a bright part of my stay here.

While I walk to the thali place with Sajeev, we pass several of the beggars on German Bakery Road. I say, "It bothers me to see them."

Sajeev says, "It bothers me, too, but probably in a different way, since I've seen them all my life."

I learn much new information about Indian culture today. First, he shows me that the restaurant has a hand-washing place that I didn't know about! I've always washed my hands before I walk there. Then I notice that he takes a napkin and wipes his spoon off before using it. He says he has found fingerprints on them before. I ask, "Why didn't I go to lunch with you when I first arrived?"

When he sees me struggling, he shows me how to break off a piece of chapatti with one hand. You hold it between your thumb and your little finger and ring finger, and then you put it down, folding it beneath your fingers. Then you use your index and middle finger to break it off. The piece that you end with is the original piece you held in your thumb and last two fingers. I still struggle, but it is a little easier!

He asks the waiter for something. When the guy brings it, Sajeev gives him that side-to-side head nodding movement. I ask him about it. He says, "It is more an acknowledgment than a yes. To know if it's a yes, you have to watch the lips."

Sajeev has always been the picture of doing everything right - -
except his attitude about sex and his wife. Today at the restaurant,
however, I see a different side of him. He is not his usual smiling and
friendly self with the waiter. He treats him as a subordinate. One time
Sajeev told me that his family has servants at home. That might be why
he has that attitude. I'm not defending it, but I do consider it interesting.
"Never judge a person by the way they treat their equals, but by the way
they treat their inferiors."

I ask him about what Manik and Anderson told me about friends
not having to say thank you or I'm sorry. Sajeev says, "It is a saying for
twenty-year-olds. I said it, too, while I was in college. But as an adult,
you expect thank you and I'm sorry." So, that wasn't Indian culture!

Sajeev is well educated and speaks almost perfect English. I say
almost - - he probably speaks better than I do! His people skills impress
me, and I keep telling him that he's my hero. I will miss him.

After work, I run into Phani. He says something about me being
happy, and when I leave, I make him happy. The magicians, and others
have said this to me, too. They expect me to give them money when I
leave. I'll have to ask around and see how much they expect. The
magicians, Phani, Gowri, and friends have all added to my enjoyment of
being here. To tip them wouldn't be so bad.

While I walk to the corner, a young beggar woman with a child
approaches me. I say no and keep walking. She is insistent and won't
leave me alone, following closely. Finally, I have to run to get away from
her. It feels awful.

I walk across the street because I see this beautiful wall hanging
with an elephant on it. The guy wants fifteen hundred rupees. That is too
much to even bargain down. Then I ask about a smaller elephant wall
hanging. Eight hundred rupees. I ask if he will take four and he says he
can't go any lower than seven. When I say no, he asks what is the highest
I will go. I say, panch - - five. We settle on five fifty.

That is good strategy - - ask what is the highest you will go and
then add fifty on. Then we talk about my knowing some Hindi. It
impresses him that I have only been here two months. Most people don't
bother learning any, but I have had such a blast with it. Learning the few
words that I know has enhanced my stay to no end. It has created so much
joy and interesting conversations that my journey would not have been the
same without it.

Then I walk to German Bakery Road to talk to Hassan because
someone in America had asked me to buy something from him. We have

a short conversation because she wants them cheaper than he wants to sell them. Then I see a beautiful cobra pendant. It costs four hundred rupees. I ask if he will take two hundred. He won't even bargain! He says no, that he doesn't mark it up that much. I'm not a jewelry person, but this cobra is beautiful. And like he says - - it moves. I order a ring from him that he will make especially for me. Two hundred rupees - - five dollars.

I give him a deposit of five hundred rupees for the other jewelry and forget to ask for a receipt. Now, I guess I'll see what kind of man he is. My guess is that he is a good man. But I have been wrong before! And I have been right before! I'll see how this goes.

On my way back to the ashram, I stop to see Gowri. I tell her that when I leave I will bring her my maroon and white robe and she can sell them. I have some other clothing to give her, too. She has a new nose piercing today. It is a large gold pin. Manik had told me that she is divorced, but I didn't think that Indians got divorces. He says that her husband is a bad man, and that she is on her own. But, if that's true, why does she still wear the red bindi, which I thought represented "married" in the Hindu culture?

I show her my cobra picture, and she goes wild. She keeps saying I am "pagal" - - crazy. She laughs at me. I point to myself and say, "pagal." Then she says, no. She tells me that pictures of Shiva, a main deity in Hindu culture, usually show him with a cobra around his neck. So, I am in good company! I will miss her.

Day Seventy-two - Confirmation of Mastership

I wake up late and have a leisurely breakfast at Zorba Restaurant. It is still too early to go to work. I wait until nine ten and walk over to leave a message for Sajeev to come see me today. He's not working, but I figured at some point during the day he would go see his old colleagues. At nine twenty, I stroll into work and run into Sakra at the front door. At least this time he smiles.

He says, "Are you just coming in now?"

I say, "Yes, but I have a good reason."

When I tell him about my chemical difficulties, he says, "You need to let someone know so they can cover the front desk in case anyone wants anything. Remember, this desk is the action point for this office."

I think of saying that I had not chosen this job and had only accepted it reluctantly. But, my confrontational days are over here. I realize that I need to stay for the entire three months. If I am going to have any chance of doing anything with this journal, then I can't have anyone say that I wrote it out of bitterness or anger from being thrown out.

When I leave, it must be under good circumstances. I need people to be sorry that I'm leaving. Even Sakra. I'll try my hardest to be a good girl for the next three weeks. So, I will have to hide the "re-bel" in the closet for now. Since Osho pronounces rebel like the verb rebel, that's why I write it like that. From now on, I will always think of the person rebel pronounced that way.

After my accidental meeting with Sakra at the front door, I see the new woman, Mukta, vacuuming the floor. Usually, I spend excessively long doing that. Mostly because I don't mind it too much, and it gives me something to do while everyone else diligently cleans. I go to the cleaning supplies area, and run into Jiadore. Then Dulari comes in talking about Mukta putting her whole heart into vacuuming. Jiadore says that Mukta enjoys it, too.

So, what to do? I want to start dusting every little millimeter of my desk for forty-five minutes. Unfortunately, someone else sits there using the scanner. Then Mukta tells me that I can mop the floor. "Oh, no," I say, "No chemicals for me."

She says, "That's all right. Plain water is better than nothing." Oh, man. Off I go to find the water. When I get back, someone else had mopped part of the floor, so I only do half. Not bad. So much for another cleaning day.

However, I do miss one of my favorite sights. Revatii usually sweeps the stairs with one of those cute little brooms that you have to bend over to use. I would love to take a picture of that. It's an image I don't want to forget. She isn't here this morning, so no one sweeps the stairs.

Revatii is back to her cranky old self. So, I guess the window of our friendship was as fragile as the one with the street magicians. Except I honestly think the one with the street magicians was more real and more pleasing.

Just when I'm trying so hard to be a good girl, something comes up that I can't resist. Peacocks. They have been spending time by the office. I look all over for someone eating something so I can take some crumbs out to the peacocks. No luck. When they appear again at the front door, I can't help myself. I run to my room, open a new package of crackers that I have in there, and go out to find them.

They are still outside. Only one has the courage to eat out of my hand, although another one pecks at it once or twice. Luckily, Sakra doesn't walk by while I do this terrible behavior, so I get away with it.

When I stop at the ashram post office today, I see Paddya, an Indian Sudexo person who works there. I say, "I'm back to being the receptionist and I'm not happy about it."

She asks, "Why?"

I say, "These people expect me to do many different tasks and keep pestering me all the time."

She says, "It's just like that here! They yell at me, too!" Paddya has never been the friendliest sort, so this small taste of commiseration feels good. Maybe she's not friendly because of all the yelling. Sometimes it's good to know the whole story.

Most days in the plaza, they have demos. The demos are a sample of the longer workshops they offer. They can be energy work, discussion, and often dancing. Today, I run into a guy from my groups who reminds me of a leprechaun. As we approach the plaza, he says, "Oh good, more dancing." These people are really into this. He's not even an Osho-ite. But, everyone loves the dancing. What a great idea of Osho's - - give the people what they want - - loud music, dancing, and sex any time you want it and with whomever you want. Brilliant idea! Who wouldn't love that? Me.

After work, I decide to go to the grocery store at Pune Central. When I see Phani out back, I ask, "How much to Pune Central?"

He says, "Thirty rupees, because I will have to come back empty."

I say, "It's only five minutes from here." He shrugs, so I say, "I'll walk."

Then, I decide to ask the rickshaw drivers in the front of the ashram. First, they say thirty rupees. So I say I'll walk. Then one says twenty-five, and I start walking away. Then he says twenty, and I step into his cool rickshaw. It has a bolted-on gate on one side of the rickshaw so you can't fall out. I always wondered about that, because it's wide open in the back where you sit. We arrive there and I give him twenty-five rupees. The bargaining is half the fun.

To enter Pune Central, I have to walk past a guard and go through a metal detector doorway like at the airport. I take the escalator downstairs where I buy a single scoop of chocolate ice cream. Then I take the glass elevator, with an elevator attendant, to the top floor grocery store.

It is interesting how our perception changes. The first time I went to this store, I felt amazed, confused, and thrilled at the differences of this store and the ones back home. I was aware of every step I took and everything I saw. Today, I walk through as if it is a grocery store back home. All I see are the similarities. I buy my groceries with no sense of awe at all. It's surprising what two months in India can do for you.

I'm so accustomed to the foreign-ness of the place now. Although I'll never be comfortable with the beggars, they don't shock me anymore. Their plight bothers me, but seeing them isn't the same as it was. The crazy traffic, the people, the language, the customs - - these are starting to feel like home to me.

I start walking back the same path I had taken to the store a month ago. There had been a man in a booth with a sewing machine, and I want to get a picture of that. His booth is closed today. As I walk down this narrow street, I see someone sleeping on the side of the road. This is not so unusual. But, he has some of his belongings by his head. On top of the belongings sits a big monkey, also asleep! I quickly grab a picture, although I always feel like I am intruding when I do that.

Although there is a policeman there, I don't cross at the light. It is still too scary for me. So, I walk down to the middle of the block where there is a median, and have no problem crossing. I run into Uncle Makeen and Zakir across the street from German Bakery. We talk for a short time, and then Sajeev shows up! I have been looking for him all day. After I introduce him to Uncle Makeen, I have him help me tell them something. Then, ex-roommate Bhava shows up! The three of us all hug (Sajeev, Bhava, and me - - not Uncle Makeen!) Bhava is just leaving town, so it is cool that we run into one another.

Sajeev is going to cash a check or something, and invites me to come with him. He, of course, crosses at the light. He takes my hand and says he can control me better. I gladly give it to him. I'm nervous after that experience with Jiadore when I stepped back into traffic.

On our way back, we run into Uncle Makeen again, and he talks Sajeev into a magic show. I stand to the side taking pictures. Afterward, something remarkable happens. Uncle Makeen lives up to all my great visions of him being a king and a master. He tries to talk Sajeev and a couple other guys into giving him money for the magic show. Finally, Sajeev comes up with fifty rupees. Uncle Makeen keeps talking in Hindi to Sajeev and the other guys, and I feel bad so I reach into my pocket to give him one hundred rupees. I put my hand out with the hundred-rupee bill, and Uncle Makeen pushes it away. He says, "You already paid the other day." Then he says something in Hindi to Khalid, which Sajeev translates later for me as, "She gave me more than I asked for a few days ago." He refuses one hundred rupees, which to these street people is much money! Uncle Makeen is a master, and I knew it! Tomorrow, he will probably ask for it back, but today, for that instant, the master appears.

I talk to Sajeev about it as we walk back to the ashram. I tell him my king and master theory about Uncle Makeen, and how sometimes he comes across as only a poor, old street magician. Sajeev says it is interesting how our energy changes from one moment to the next. He understands.

On an even more woo woo note, I meet Sajeev again after Evening Meeting to give him some acidophilus for a going away present. He tells me that before he came to the ashram, he had a dream of several people here. I am one of them! How cool is that? Talk about meant to be!

As cynical and critical as I have been of this place and the people in it, I freely admit that it has transformed me. The mandatory workshops that I attended changed me. They helped me through some personal issues that I had trouble dealing with myself. My experiences outside the ashram have transformed me as well. The people I have met, the sights I have seen, and the experiences I have had changed me so much that I will never be the same again. I am a different person than when I arrived. A better person. A more spiritual person. A more woo woo person. A person who has held a cobra in her bare hands! What more can I say?

Day Seventy-three – Celebration of Death

"This is not a good place for asking why." That's what Jiadore says she has learned in seven weeks of being here. That doesn't go with my personality. I always ask why. I want to know why. It's who I am, it's what I do - - I ask why. If this isn't a good place for it - - that reeks of dictatorship. But I guess that's what this is. And the dictator is Osho. Or it was, until his death. Now, his honchos make all the decisions. Osho doesn't even have a chance to say, "Oops, sorry. I was wrong."

Today is a death celebration. Someone told me when I first arrived there would probably be one before I left. I ask Devika's Indian husband why we have to shower and wash our clothes after attending the burning ghats part of the ceremony. He says, "This is how it is always done."

And being a "why" person, I ask again, "Yeah, but why?"

He gets angry then and says, "This is how it's done in India. It is not ritual, it is scientific."

They often use the word scientific here. They say the meditations are scientific, this is scientific, and that is scientific. None of this is scientific. Studies have proven that Transcendental Meditation is scientific - - but not Osho's varieties. It doesn't make it scientific because someone says it is - - even if that someone is Osho. If something is scientific, I want proof, I want a double-blind study, and I want evidence! There is none of that here, let me tell you.

They don't want you to ask why, because the real answer is, "Because Osho says so." Although, sometimes they say that, too. I prefer that to scientific. All this is so obviously not scientific.

The email I received said, "If you are going to join the Burning Celebration, please make sure to go and shower, wash your hair and change your clothes immediately afterward." It also gave a quote of Osho's, "Celebrate death, too, because death is not the end of life but the very crescendo of life, the very climax, it is the ultimate of life."

I speak to Prana and Adhanya about issues around the celebration. They also get angry with me. It shocks me when Prana yells at me about it. I'm not sure what it is, except maybe this is not the place to ask why.

After lunch, I change into my maroon pants and maroon shirt. Jiadore and I go to the auditorium. I hoped that I could get in without wearing my robe. No one says anything. The music blares again to ear-splitting levels. I run down several flights of stairs to the restroom, to grab some tissue to stick in my ears. When I walk back in, everyone dances around a table in the center of the room. Flowers cover the table. There

218

are several songs, several shouts of Osho!, and all of it punctuated by Osho quotes on death and dying. Osho is present everywhere. I do it all: dance, shout, and wave my arms. Today, I don't feel it is right to observe only. I celebrate her death - - her new freedom and her journey home.

Eight guys carry the deceased on a bamboo stretcher and place it on the table. The dancing goes on. A few people cry, but most celebrate. People in the crowd play instruments.

Next, they carry the stretcher outside to the sound of drums beating. The stretcher is barely outside the door, and the rest of us remain crowded by the exit sweating in the heat. Then everyone walks down the stairs amid more shouting, singing, and celebrating.

When the stretcher gets to the street, they stop and light fireworks. We dance down the street shouting, yelling, and celebrating. Periodically, they stop and light more fireworks. We cross North Main Road with the help of the guards, who stop traffic for us. Hundreds of Osho-ites dressed in maroon dance our way across the main street and down German Bakery Road. The shopkeepers come out to see what the ruckus is about.

Jiadore and I arrive at the burning area early and watch as they prepare it with wood. They line the bottom of the cement encasement with dried cow pies. Then, they place the stretcher on top and add more wood to her. With only her face showing, flowers and a red cloth cover her completely. The attendants also pour some flammable liquid all around. Then they walk around the body and with a torch, light the pile in several places. When they finish, they set off more fireworks.

As Jiadore and I stand watching the burning ceremony, I am about to turn to her to say something, when she says it first: "This could have been you." I was going to say the same thought to her! About me! We both think of it at the same time.

Before I went with Manik the other day, although I mostly trusted him - - I still had a shred of doubt. So, I wrote down all my last wishes in my own handwriting and gave it to Jiadore: no resuscitation if I were brain-dead; if I die, do not ship me back to the United States, have a death celebration here - - like the one we witness now. Luckily for me, nothing bad happened that day. Since that was only a few days ago, it is fresh on both of our minds.

While we watch, people continue to beat the drums while other people sway, dance, and sing. The fire feels hot even fifteen feet away.

Afterward, I dutifully go home and take a shower. I put all the clothes into the laundry, and even wash my sandals. I clear my camera and ID card with Reiki, since I can't wash them. Although I don't go along with all this, it doesn't hurt to do it. One never knows!

Then I call Phani to see if he will go snake hunting today. He says he'll pick me up in a half hour. When I go out there, he is already waiting, but with an empty rickshaw. He says the guy started walking, so we pick him up on the way.

The guy doesn't speak much English, but he shows me his wrist where a snake had bitten him. I show him my finger where a snake had bitten me. My scar isn't as big as his, but it is deeper. I remember in my youth when I worked with wild animals - - the person with the best scars received more respect and admiration. I was proud of my scars - - they were like merit badges or stripes in the military. My "conquests" included a chimp, a fox, a coatimundi, and a scratch from a tiger.

We go to the same place as last time, so I hope it is the same guy and same snake. It isn't. It surprises me how many different snakes I've seen. Every time has been a different snake.

While Phani and I wait for the cobra guy to bring out the snake, I tell him that I had been to the Death Celebration. I mention the whole shower deal. He disagrees with what everyone told me. He says since I don't have children and don't have a house, there is no big deal with showering and washing my clothes. But - - I'm glad I did it - - just in case! I wouldn't want any spirits following me home.

Suddenly, I notice that inside the rickshaw on each side of me, is a picture of Osho! I have been in that rickshaw many times and have never seen those pictures before. When I ask Phani about it, he says that I get in and don't look around. He tells me that he used to be a sannyasin! He says it isn't the same anymore since Osho left the body.

This is a bad snake experience. No, I don't get bitten. Worse. I'm burnt-out on cobras. The other snake charmers acted like they loved their snakes - - you could even see it in the photographs. This guy does not. He treats this beautiful snake badly. I feel so bad. When I try to hold it, he holds its head tightly and won't let go. He says it is poisonous, and he doesn't want it to bite me. But, when it tries to strike him, he doesn't look scared.

It breaks my heart seeing this snake. I think of cobras as royalty. This poor snake is all hooded up and beautiful, but there are flies on its head. You know how when someone you love has hair in their eyes, and you want to brush it lovingly away? I want to brush the flies away. The flies hurt his dignity. The whole experience feels bad. Beautiful cobra, bad experience.

I feel like a giant boa constrictor has crushed my heart. Between the beggars, the stray dogs, and cobras losing their dignity - - I'm ready to go home. My heart can't take much more of this. The sadness envelops me like a shroud.

Day Seventy-four - Divorce, Indian Style

This morning, Jiadore never shows up for our trip back to the burning ghats. Although someone told me not to go there alone, I have to. I refuse to waste a six o'clock wake up call. I feel too tired to do anything else.

When I get there, the fire still burns from yesterday's death celebration. I can see the flames. Devika said that after the fire finishes its work, someone takes the remains, called flowers, into Osho Teerth Park and puts them into the water.

Close to the burning ghats, there is a small area with a faucet that Jiadore used to wash her feet yesterday. Today, there is a man approaching the faucet dressed only in a large beach towel. When I leave, he still sits in that area with his towel on.

I walk down to the river and see some small white herons and a large rust colored bird. While I stand there, a painted stork flies by. Some pariah kites fly around, also. It's a good area for bird watching in the morning.

Rasha and I talk again today. Her mother now believes her all the way, but her brother still doubts her. She tells me that her uncle is jealous because his daughter had a "love marriage" instead of an arranged marriage. The other relatives have ostracized his family because of the love marriage. She says in India, you must have an arranged marriage. I ask if it bothers her. She says, "What to do? It's the way it is." That is a perfect example of "accepting the is."

I have often wondered what would have happened to me if I had grown up in this society. Would I still have become a rebel - - and would they have burned me at the stake or something? Or, would I have accepted it gracefully, as Rasha does? I don't know. I'm thinking the stake!

Although I had mentioned my divorce to her before, I bring it up again today. I say, "I told you I divorced my husband, although he is a good man. You can't understand that, can you?" She says she can't.

In India, Hindus can get divorced, but it is difficult for Muslims to get a divorce. She says if your husband is a bad man, you have to live with it. No choice. If he is a very, very bad man, then it is still up to your family and his family to allow the divorce. I can't imagine living in a society like this. Yet, if that is all you know . . .

We also talk about the Osho-sannyasins. How the Indian sannyasins' families often ostracize them because of their participation here. I find the whole conversation particularly engrossing. I'm sorry when someone else comes to her window and the it has to end.

My attitude about her uncle has completely changed. A few days ago, I hated him for his behavior toward Rasha. Now I find myself feeling sorry for him and his daughter. I know he wanted to do right for his beloved daughter - - she had fallen in love. How could he say no? Now, the other relatives ostracize his family because a love marriage goes against tradition. How sad is that? India has become full of sadness for me.

While I wait for Jiadore at lunch today, Prana asks why I am still there. She says, "That's nice that you have that friendship - - friendliness - - but remember that we're all strangers here. Be careful of who you are identified with. It's like marriage - - you know how that can be."

I say, "I had a good marriage before it got bad. I believe in marriage and disagree with what Osho says about it." Prana is so into all of this, that I always feel weird telling her that I disagree with Osho.

When Jiadore finally comes out of the meeting with Dwami, she says to me, "I'm jealous." She says that Dwami had gone on and on about me, how strong and tough I am. I find that intriguing. After I sent him the dog email, I felt sure that he had put me on his bad list. I worried that he was in with Sakra on how to get rid of a troublemaker like me. Surprisingly, my paranoia is unfounded.

While at Bukhara to eat lunch today, we sit at one of those little tables on the floor. It isn't comfortable for me. When I stand up, I accidentally tip the tray with my food on it. The soup goes all over my maroon robe, my leg, and my purse. The waiter hands me two little napkins to clean with. It remains all over the floor and me when I finish. It is awful and it is my only clean robe. I hope hand washing will take out the stains.

A quote from a Mumbai newspaper, *The Asian Age*:

I screamed at God for all the starving children, and then I realized that all the starving children were God screaming at me.
Anonymous

I see the little boy with one foot today. He walks on the street behind the ashram, close to North Main Road. He is so sweet, and only asks for money once. His beautiful brown eyes sparkle in the sun. I wish I could do something for him. He seems like such a good kid. It breaks my heart to see him.

Jiadore doesn't feel the same about the beggars that I do. I ask, "Why don't the beggars affect you?"

223

She says, "They don't act unhappy. In Czechoslovakia, I see people who have many material possessions, and yet they feel unhappy. I don't feel an unhappy vibe from the beggars." Although she has an interesting perspective, they still get to me.

Revatii approaches me as I walk back to the office carrying mail and packages. She stops me and paws through the mail until she finds her own. Without saying a word, she grabs it from the pile and keeps walking, although we both head in the same direction. Isn't it ironic that my friendship with Zakir, the street magician, is more substantial, more real, than my friendship with her? The moment in time with her felt good while it happened, but it was as momentary as a dandelion blown into the wind.

Later, I run into Zakir. He tells me a sad story that someone hit his son in the face, and now he needs an operation that costs forty thousand rupees. That must be the magic number, because Gowri once told me that her eye operation would cost forty thousand rupees. Then he talks about us being friends again, and how I can give him rupees when I leave. I'm tired of hearing that.

After work, Jiadore and I take a rickshaw, for twenty rupees, to Yerwada. Phani told me his wife goes here to do the grocery shopping. This place is totally awesome. It is the real India. We are the only Westerners here. This is India at its finest! The Indian people continue to amaze me. I stop to take a picture, and a woman walks right into the shot. It isn't a big deal because she didn't see me. But a man who did see me, asks her to move over for me! These people are so generous and kind!

This place is like a farmer's market and a flea market all in one. There are hundreds of stalls or little stores, and many carts with fruits and vegetables on them. The vendors display fish, eel, chickens, and more. Women fan them to keep them as cool as possible in this hot weather. The eels writhe around, and some chickens are alive, some dead. Fabric stores are everywhere, some jewelry stores, and some of almost everything you can think of.

Vendors line both sides of the narrow street. Rickshaws and motorcycles ply their way through. The sights and smells thrill me so much that I run around uncontrollably. Jiadore keeps pulling me out of the path of racing rickshaws. I say, "I feel like you're my mother."

She says, "I feel like your mother!" She is twenty years younger than I am!

The energy of the place astounds and delights me. We walk up and down each street in the area. I buy two watches for going away presents for Zakir and Uncle Makeen. Eighty rupees each. I would love to eat some of the fruit they sell, but I don't dare. Jiadore loves the place as much as I do, and we both want to return. The real India!

As we leave, I buy the second watch and receive twenty rupees change. A beggar woman stands right there with her hand out. I hate saying no. She follows us to the rickshaw with her hand still out. The driver starts driving away, and she says something in Hindi. I turn to Jiadore and tell her that I need to leave India. In Hindi, the woman had said to me, "I'm hungry."

Day Seventy-five - Osho Police Strike Again!

Although the beautiful garland that Jiadore got me has dried out, it still has a beautiful aroma. So, I guess this is a good time to talk about smells. There is something I like about Evening Meeting: no perfume allowed. Although, there are so few people here that wear perfume, it probably wouldn't make a big difference. How about odors? Of all my street friends - - vendors like Gowri - - and all the street magicians - - I have never once smelled a whiff of sweat on any of them. Conversely, I have smelled sweat on ashram visitors and Osho-ites - - including Indian Osho-ites. That strikes me as interesting. Indians are shiny clean, but as soon as they become Osho-ites - - the rules change. Someone in the room next to me just gave out a loud belch and doesn't say excuse me. The rules are different here.

Rasha and I have another conversation today ragging on the Osho-ites. I love talking to her about it, because we both agree on how tweaked they are - - sexually and otherwise. She also mentions the "father and daughter" team of Andre and Cathy.

As I walk out to get water today, I see a beautiful insect on the wall. When I show Jiadore, its beauty doesn't impress her. Varsha, the head photographer, walks by and thinks it is beautiful. Its wings are black and clear with a beautiful design. Later, I run into her outside Zorba restaurant, and she says that if I see anything to photograph to let her know. She says that she doesn't say that to everyone, but I have a good eye for it. That makes me feel good. I thank her.

After work, I walk up toward German Bakery again. Gowri isn't there - - most of the street vendors aren't there. I wonder if the police have been after them again. That has been worse lately. It makes it hard for those people who have no other way to make a living.

I walk down the road and go into a store to see if they sell t-shirts. Stupid me, I only bring one t-shirt to India. On the other hand, I brought five pair of wool socks. My sister-in-law had told me before I left that it had gotten down to fifty degrees one day. That scared me, so I brought long underwear and wool socks, but only one t-shirt. Another lesson learned. Now I'm boiling to death in long sleeves when my one shirt is in the wash.

They have a green t-shirt with an OM design on it for one hundred seventy-five rupees. I talk them down to one hundred fifty rupees - - four dollars. Then I go down the street and talk to Tanul, Manik's brother, for a while. I ask if Manik had said anything about our trip. He says in India men don't talk about their girlfriends. When I ask about infidelity, he says the culture is for one man and one woman, but most people don't go by that. I tell him in America it is the same.

My nodding yes to everything I don't understand gets me in trouble with Tanul today. I thought he said, "Do you want a chair," as we are about to sit, and I say yes. But, what he had asked was if I wanted chai tea. When someone brings it, I say I don't want it. It embarrasses me as I realize what happened. That is a communication problem!

Walking back to the ashram, I stop to talk to a woman street vendor who sits outside. Although she never looks friendly, I decide to see if she knows where Gowri is. Looks can be deceiving - - she turns out to be friendly. She asks me my name and tells me hers - - which is excessively long and hard to remember. We talk for a while, and then I start back to the ashram.

Jiadore mentions something about a long conversation with her boyfriend - - ten minutes. I relate how Sam and I used to talk for an hour when we were away from each other. Then I mention that it later changed into only five minutes, and how much that bothered me. That added to the eventual end of our relationship. I hadn't thought about that before.

I receive a wonderful telephone call today. They ask me if I would mind doing cyber cafe duty instead of gate duty tonight. They say it is an emergency and they can't find anyone else to do it. I've wanted to switch! How cool is this? Maybe they'll let me continue with cyber cafe duty. I thought maybe Dwami arranged it to get me away from the guards and the dogs, so I wouldn't complain anymore. That's acting paranoid again.

The cyber cafe experience is delightful. It is more work than checking ID cards and brushing away the mosquitoes, but I am happy to do it. It is a much more enjoyable experience. One entertaining event happened there, too.

When I first open the doors, a guy comes in wearing his white robe. An older gentleman sitting a few computers down immediately gets up and whispers to me, "He shouldn't be here in his white robe."

I say, "You are welcome to tell him that." He does! Osho police strike again! I think that's the end of it, but no, not for these Osho-ites. A half hour later, a woman tells me that I should not let him use the computer if he is in a white robe. She implies that it is my job to kick him out. I don't think so. If by chance they don't allow me back in the cyber cafe for not "doing my job," then that is fine with me, too. Although I like this job much better than gate duty, I will not compromise myself and become part of the Osho police.

Then, something worse happens. I tell Jiadore about what happened, and she tells me that she has been the Osho police in Evening Meeting! She doesn't say it like that, of course. But she tells me the night before, someone next to her coughed a couple times, and she had to poke them in the arm to get them to leave. Later, someone several feet in front of her sneezed, and she stood up, walked over to them, and asked them to leave! She says it made her ego rise - - she felt the power. I tell her that she has been here too long. She's scaring me. I've told her too many secrets for her to go Osho-police on me.

Tonight is the full moon. I've been seeing it coming the last few days, and I keep thinking, "This is the last full moon that I will see in India." It was only a few months ago on a full moon night that I decided to come to India. Now, here I am almost getting ready to leave.

Day Seventy-six - Shopping in the Real India

Early this morning, my brother's friend, Ramoda, comes popping into the office. He says, "You're still here? I thought you would have dropped out of the program by now."

I say, "No, I'm going to make it."

He says, "I don't think you are."

I say, "I only have three weeks to go."

He says, "It doesn't matter. You'll never make it." My brother probably gave him the idea to say that. Now I'm paranoid again wondering if he can arrange to get me kicked out! No, I should stop worrying: I forgot, I have Dwami on my side.

It still bothers me. When I talk to Jiadore later, she asks, "Why does it make you feel bad?"

I say, "It pushes the same buttons as my brother pushed when he said that."

Jiadore says, "This is a good place to play with it. You should have given him some grief about it." Now, I wish I had told him that I'm staying longer.

Later, Rishika asks, "What will you do after the three weeks?"

I say, "I don't know. I'm waiting for a sign from the universe."

She takes a piece of paper, writes in big letters, STAY HERE, PARVATI, and says, "There's your sign."

Then I ask her if it bothers her that men her age (she's in her forties) are with women who are twenty years younger. She pulls out a picture of her twenty-three year old boyfriend! She says that they are not exclusive, and they both sleep with other people. But, they have a good relationship.

What surprises me most about Rishika asking me to stay, is that she likes me. People like me! In the Inner Judgment workshop, one of mine was "worthless and invisible." I do feel invisible, but perhaps it's only at first. Maybe I'm like that beautiful butterfly that looks so much like a leaf. In the beginning, people can't see me. But, when they realize that I'm a butterfly and not an invisible leaf, they see how delightful I am!

After work, Jiadore and I walk toward North Main Road. The rickshaws there are usually cheaper than at the back gate. We meet that one little beggar boy that always gets to me. I see no other beggars around, so it's safe. What I mean by safe is that if you give rupees to one beggar and the others see you, the rest will overwhelm you trying to get money.

I want to give him twenty or fifty rupees, and Jiadore thinks I'm crazy. She sarcastically tries to talk me into giving him one hundred rupees. When we approach him, he holds up his leg without the foot and holds out his hand. I had already prepared the money to hand to him, so I did, but pointing to his foot bothered me. Although I'm sure he does it because it's effective, so I can't blame him. Jiadore still says that she doesn't have the feeling from any of these beggars that they are unhappy. She looks at it in a unique way, that's for sure. It doesn't make me feel any better, though.

We are about half a block from North Main Road when I see a motorcycle swerve sideways to scare a stray dog. I've never seen anyone do that before. I'm thinking the guy is a jerk, and next thing I know, he swerves right at us! I'm afraid I can't help myself and I give him the finger.

At North Main Road, we catch a rickshaw to MG road. Someone told me the MG stands for Mahatma Gandhi. MG road is a main shopping area near the ashram in Koregaon Park. I want to go there not for anything in particular, but because it is a "must see" place here.

I find a cool suede purse (Jiadore says it isn't suede) at a shop. They won't come down below two hundred fifty rupees, and I don't want to spend that much.

We leave and go through some of those "Indian malls" where the halls are narrow and lined with different shops. The colors of the cloth are beautiful, and we see so many different items for sale.

I keep checking my watch, because we have to get back in time for Evening Meeting. After I buy a t-shirt that says "England" on it, we catch a rickshaw. Jiadore always does the negotiating, because she's better at it than I am. But, it surprises me that it only costs twenty rupees to get back to the ashram. She says, "Oh, we're not going back to the ashram, we're going to Fashion Street so I can get some fruit." Oh my, it is getting late.

After spending ten minutes at the fruit stand tasting and picking out fruit, we walk away with Jiadore buying nothing. I ask her why she didn't want to buy it. The last time she had been there, she was with her Indian boyfriend and got it much cheaper - - significantly cheaper. I say, "You're a Westerner! Of course they're going to charge you more!" She doesn't want to pay that much more, so she walks away - - fruitless. The seller also offered me fruit to taste, but I say no to everything. Before I arrived here, someone told me that I shouldn't eat fruit on the street. I don't exactly understand why, but I've been too afraid to do it. Yet, Jiadore does it all the time and has not been sick.

Jiadore gives me a lecture today. We walk down this street in front of two older ladies. Even after Jiadore's strict instructions NEVER to stop on the street, a car swerves close to me, and I can't keep myself from stopping. These two women behind me don't know what to do. After they walk off, Jiadore says, "Look around. See how everything and everyone is moving? This system works. If you stop, it messes up the system and someone can get hurt. Don't stop in the street!" Meanwhile, every time we finish crossing a street, I put my hand on my heart, to check that it didn't stop beating from my intense fear!

Next, we go into a big one-story building that is the heart of Fashion Street, also known as FS. It's like a warehouse with vendors one after another in every direction. I can't tell where one ends and the next one starts, except the difference in products. They have shoes, jeans, purses, sunglasses, shirts, Indian clothing, and all manner of items. Everywhere you turn, there is a vendor. There is not one spare inch of space except where people walk. It is a maze of items for sale.

Neither of us buy anything; we walk around in awe. Again, we are the only "Westerners" here. I love it like that! The real India! While Jiadore buys a lemonade off the street, I search for a belt with a cobra buckle. I find a belt vendor and ask for a cobra belt. He brings out a belt made of cobra skin. Yuck! I step back, squeeze my eyes closed, shake my head, and say, "No, no, no! Just a buckle." He doesn't have one. What an awful experience!

By this time, it is way too late to go back to the ashram. During Evening Meeting, they lock all the gates so you can't get in. So - - we have two hours to spend in the real India - - at night! We could have gone to German Bakery to hang out for two hours, but the real India is much more fun! Although, I do tell Jiadore to keep the street crossing to a minimum. Crossing the street is terrifying enough during the day, but at night, it feels ten times worse.

We walk around, buy some bottled water, Jiadore buys some baked goods that I don't have the nerve to eat, and somehow we end up back at the store that has the purse. This time they start at three hundred fifty, and won't lower the price to two fifty. We walk out, and they catch us at the door. I get the purse - - suede or not.

Later, we go to McDonald's, have our picture taken with Ronald, and Jiadore buys a veggie burger. Then we walk down the street to some other restaurant, and Jiadore orders two faludas to go. A faluda is a desert with cashews and noodles and ice cream. She owes it to me because of a bet we had. I'm always whimpering about the stray dogs and threatening

to take them home. She bet that I couldn't bring them back to America.
With a little Internet research, I found that I could bring them back. A few
vaccinations, and they may as well be American. That's one faluda, thank
you very much.

Being in a rickshaw at night isn't much better than crossing a street
at night. Some of the rickshaws don't even have headlights, and I never
thought about checking before we step into this one. A few minutes later,
we are safe back at the ashram with all of our goodies.

Day Seventy-seven – Yelling Osho!

Part of my job consists of selecting some of the scanned newspaper articles and pinning them onto the Press Board at the front of the ashram. I've never done it myself. After the incident when Revatii and I became best friends, she said she would go over there with me and explain exactly how she wanted it done. Items to consider are: date, Hindi or English, different newspapers, etc. She never did go over there with me.

Today, she comes by and sees the press clippings on my desk. "Why haven't you done it yet?" She asks in her usual curt tone.

I say, "Neehara is coming over later to give me a lesson."

Revatii says, "You can't do it by yourself?"

I say, "Neehara will teach me the 'official' way of doing it." Sometime, I need to ask Revatii if she meditates, because she needs something in her life to calm her down. She is a sour old woman, and I still can't stand her. Before I leave, I hope I have the nerve to say something to her - - like maybe she needs some meditation or medication!

Neehara arrives later and we go over the whole board. She says something about me not wanting the job. I say, "I don't want Revatii's negativity."

She says, "Here, you don't get to choose what you want. We get it free!" Neehara also says that she loves doing the Press Board. She wants it looking good as if Osho was walking by. Whatever she does here, teaching meditation techniques or doing the board or whatever, she tries to do it the best that she can, because Osho spent thirty years developing all of this. I admire that - - perhaps more so because I cannot do it. Not here. I am too cynical about the demands and the rules forced on me. I am too much of a re-bel without much outlet to rebel.

Something makes me feel bad when I think about the death celebration. The other day, I wanted to be present and not be a witness. I thought the woman who died deserved that.

Mostly, I did that, aside from taking many photos of the festivities. But, something bothers me. Periodically, the crowd would yell, "Osho," like they do during Evening Meeting. I did it gladly - - one armed, because of the camera, but I still shouted it out. Why did I do that? Why did everyone do that?

It was a celebration for this woman's death - - for her peace, for her new life on the other side, for her homecoming. What does Osho have to do with it? The crowd mentality affected me, and I went along with everyone else. But, it wasn't fair to the woman. Although, if she was an

Osho-ite, and she probably was, maybe sharing the spotlight with Osho didn't bother her. It would bother me. If I were dead, though, I guess it wouldn't matter. Knowing that I was part of the crowd mentality bothers me, though. So much for the re-bel.

Day Seventy-eight - The Meeting Brings Clarity

The universe is making its intentions for me clearer and clearer. Today two happenings occur that point to me getting the hell out of here. Sakra has a nasty meeting for all the office staff, and the smog is so bad today that it hurts my lungs and gives me a headache.

So much for Indian time. This morning, Sakra calls everyone into his office. He announces that people have been coming in way too late in the morning and from lunch and breaks, and leaving too early as well. That will now stop. We must be here at nine in the morning; we are not to leave for lunch before one o'clock. We must be back at two o'clock and we are not to leave until four o'clock. And oh, yeah, no breaks. We may go to the plaza and bring back tea to drink here if we must. He also says that it doesn't matter if we have to work overtime. That is part of the job. You don't get off early to make up for it. These are the rules and if we don't want to obey them, we can leave. Period.

If we have any questions, he instructs us to go to Worker's Meditation. Chakori raises her hand and says she has a question. Sakra says, "No questions. Go to Worker's Meditation." It is hard, mean, and severe. And, he isn't smiling. He also says, "If anyone has to be anywhere else, they are to inform Parvati." If he asks me to start writing down if people come in late or leave early, I will refuse. I will not be the Osho police. Big brother is watching you.

The meeting is so cold, so uncompromising, and so unlike Sakra. Someone says that he didn't want to do it, but he had to do it. Although it is unlike Sakra, I'm not sure if it came from somewhere else. I wonder if my skipping work that day had anything to do with it, or if that's only a coincidence. The meeting is an awful experience, and I think - - I wouldn't want this job in the real world, why would I want it here? Why stay here doing something I don't want to do, and be a slave with these restrictions? Suddenly, it becomes so clear. Finally finding the golden cobra was esoteric and woo woo for a message from the universe. The meeting this morning is pragmatic and unambiguous.

And to make sure I see my path, the universe throws in a horribly smoggy day, which affects me badly. My lungs have hurt all day and so has my head. Okay, universe, I get it. I'm leaving India. I almost feel an urgency for this, and have no idea why. But, I imagine the universe will reveal it to me at right time.

Then, I am politically incorrect. I guess. Jiadore tells me not to do it, but I do it anyway. Sakra said to ask Worker's Meditation if we have any questions. So, I write them an email asking when we can get our money changed and how we can buy toilet paper. Those two places have the same working hours as we do. I even address it "beloved" and sign it "love." It's a legitimate question! Someone has to stand up for the peons, and somehow it always falls on me - - perhaps because I always volunteer! I'm okay with that. Someone has to do it! I'll see if I get a response or if they kick me out for acting impertinent.

I have another chat with Rishika this morning. She has been exceptionally honest and frank with me. She tells me how she started with Osho: she went to some Osho event and a little voice told her to get the hell out and never come back. But, something else made her stay. She says it was like getting on a ride and not being able to get back off again.

Rishika also says that she wants to get off the wheel of life and not reincarnate. That is a common thread with Osho-ites. They all want enlightenment so they don't have to come back again. Many of Osho's discourses address questions on enlightenment.

I think about Rishika telling me about her twenty-three year old boyfriend. Then qualifying it by telling me that they both sleep with other people. This might be my personal bias, but I think that you will never have that complete vulnerability and intimacy with many that you can have with one.

And I remember Prana saying, "We are all strangers here," and "Be careful who you identify yourself with." Why did Osho want to keep his disciples strangers? Because if they had no one else, they would turn to him? I find that particular piece especially compelling.

Tattva talks to me today after the meeting with Sakra. It is a pleasant and friendly conversation. Later, I run into her on the path somewhere. She looks at the ground as she walks by me and never looks up. I laugh as I walk past her. It feels so weird to me. Back in the office, as she talks to someone else in the reception area, she includes me in the conversation, even using my name. It surprises me.

After work, I stay at my computer to catch up on my journal. She walks by and doesn't see me in the semi-darkness. When I say, "Hello," she apologizes for walking in front of me. I tell her she is welcome to do that anytime. It is a curious exchange, but again she is friendly about it.

I know that I sometimes have people issues. It makes me wonder if this whole ashram deal is a mirror for me to see what I was or what I still am at times. Is it something to make me more aware when I am curt with someone?

Speaking of curt, Revatii is at it again today. While in her office to give her the mail, she wants me to take some newspapers. She starts separating them and telling me about the different articles in a soft voice in her strong Hindi accent. As I try to sort it out, I repeat what she wants so I can be clear. Then she says condescendingly, "Adhanya can't read Hindi."

That is so typical of Revatii. I need to be prepared to comment back. I always say I'm not good at that, but it is time to get good at it. In that Judgment workshop that I was in, Aasar said how effective spontaneity is. I need to be ready with a witty comment next time.

Although I am meant to leave India now, I feel like I will return one day. Perhaps not to Pune, but definitely to India. It has been a magical and intoxicating experience.

For lunch today, I walk to the thali place by myself. I've never done that before, but it works out well. They treat me good, and the lunch is great, as usual. For the first time, I tip the guy two rupees. It's funny how one's sense of money can change. I am so into paying thirty-five rupees for a great lunch - - under a dollar - - and anything more sounds so expensive.

The rules for tipping here aren't real rules. Jiadore rarely tips. Sajeev says that if the service is exceptional, he will tip. No one can give me a rule. I need a rule to decide if I can break it. Without rules, I am lost. So, I decide that I will make my own judgment. The waiter today is good, smiles, brings everything quickly, and so I tip him. I will do that from now on. I always felt weird not doing it before. Why didn't I start doing it before now?

On my way back to the ashram, I stop by German Bakery and buy a chocolate bar. They charge me thirty rupees. I'm almost certain that I paid ten rupees before. Stick it to the Westerner - - that's what often happens here. I can't blame them.

When I talk to Rasha, she never wants me to leave. If someone else comes to her window while I'm there, she whispers to me, "Come back!" Today I talk to her right before two o'clock. When I start to leave, she wants me to stay.

I say, "I can't! They'll fire me!"

She says, "That's okay. Let them fire you and come stay at my house!" Sorry, Rasha, I need to finish this commitment so I can show up my brother, among other reasons.

After lunch, I go in to Sakra's office to talk to him about tomorrow, cleaning day. I say, "I will be in late tomorrow morning because of the cleaning chemicals. I had put that on my original application in Worker's

Meditation. And, I told Mukta where everything is in case any one asks, so she will cover for me."

He says, "It is no problem, but you should teach her some of the reception duties in case anyone needs that. I'll arrange it so you can do front gate duty from nine o'clock until ten o'clock."

I wanted to go to the India Blossom restaurant and have banana pancakes. Wrong! Gate duty it is, but at least I get out of cleaning day! Although, I will miss watching Revatii clean the stairs - - my favorite part of the week.

Tonight, I still have a headache from the smog. My lungs hurt the way they used to when I grew up in a large, smoggy city. When I go to Evening Meeting, I ask Andre if I can sit outside during the dancing, because I have a headache. He says they don't allow that, and he puts his hand on my head. It is sweet. But, it doesn't help my headache. Once inside the auditorium, I put in earplugs made from tissues. The music doesn't hurt too much, because they had the base turned down. There is no pounding, although there are some percussion instruments.

The discourse is long and boring like I remember the other Zen discourses. Want to know why I haven't complained about going to Evening Meeting lately? Because my iPod has become my best friend. Tonight, without my iPod, it is a killer sitting here all that time. Then, the clapping at the end always gets to me. We have been hearing The Rebel series and there is no clapping with that. Now that we're back to Zen, I hate the clapping that goes with it. I think I'm going to develop a cough that appears right before the clapping. How long will it take them to catch on to that?

Day Seventy-nine – Locked In

My morning starts while it's still dark at four A.M. I wake up and am too wide-awake to fall back asleep, so I do my morning meditation. Somewhere in the middle of it, I get the brilliant idea to dress and check the gate to confirm that they lock us in at night. I pull on my tennis shoes, throw a maroon robe on top of everything, and out the door I go. No one is around. The air is soft and still. I walk slowly to the gate aware of any movement or sound around me. I step closer to see clearly. There is a half-inch gap between the two sides of the gate. In that gap, I see the big padlock locking me in to this madhouse.

There is a difference between hearing about locked gates and seeing them for yourself. I don't feel anger. I don't feel panic. I feel a certain disgust over the situation. Years ago, my mother and I visited Germany. While there, we went to see the concentration camp at Dachau. It had its share of horrors, to be sure. What I remember the clearest are the three tiers of barbed wire against the bright blue sky. The vision is still in my head. It haunts me. That's how I feel about the padlock that I see in that half inch crack - - something so distasteful, so wrong - - that it wanders around in your thoughts with no place to land.

They probably lock the gate not to keep us in, but to keep others out without having a guard at the gate. Whatever the reason - - the padlock keeps us in as well as others out. I remember a toxic spill many years ago that wiped out an entire village in India. The train tracks are near here. What if that happened here? A strong, thick padlock would keep us from safety and freedom.

I tell Jiadore about going to visit the gate last night, and my view of it in relation to the concentration camp. She says she has a similar view of it. She says that in Buchholz Concentration Camp, there is a sign built into the fence, which you can only see from the inside: "Work makes you free." Here, we are in the Worker's Meditation program. Fascinating, isn't it? She also says one of her concerns is what if there is an emergency in here - - someone needs an ambulance or something? Who would unlock the gate? Isn't it remarkable that independently, we each come up with a concentration camp reference when we think of the locked gate?

At nine o'clock, I report to the front gate per Sakra's instructions. There is no place for me. As I walk away, they call me back to break the guy at the Meera gate. I tell him to take his time, but he comes back in a few minutes.

While I sit there, I notice something that makes me sick to my

stomach. The stray dogs are gone. What have I done? I noticed a
"regular" at the back gate a week ago, and I thought that was strange
because I'd never seen any dogs there before. I sit at the gate, my hand on
my stomach, my thoughts racing, and plan to talk to Dwami.

When the gate guy comes back, I walk down the street to see if any
of the strays are still sleeping. I see the mangy one who I don't see often,
but no others. I walk to the street vendor down the street to ask if they
have seen the stray dogs in the last week. They say yes. Although still
concerned, I feel a little relieved. Before I confront Dwami, I need to ask
someone else about this, but I still feel badly. In trying to do something
good, to make a difference, did I hurt the situation - - hurt the dogs? I
don't know.

Since it isn't ten o'clock yet, I have some extra time. I go to the
bookstore and buy two Osho books and an Osho picture. Yes, it's true; I
did. Don't worry, though - - I still hear the electronic beeping, so I must
be okay. They haven't converted me - - not yet, anyway.

Adhanya and I have a conversation this morning about yesterday's
meeting with Sakra. She thinks that it is something all over the ashram,
not only in our office. Although, she thinks that Sakra is more serious
than most. She says he didn't want questions because that is beneath him.
He manages companies in the real world and doesn't want to bother with
his employees' dissatisfactions. According to her, this meeting happens
every year. I ask how long it takes before everything goes back to the way
it was - - people coming in late and having more freedom. She says a
week or two!

She also has health issues that prevent her from joining cleaning
day. Instead of going to Sakra, she went to the Worker's Meditation
office. They wrote it down. When I tell her that I had to go to the main
gate to work the hour, she says that she did work related stuff.

These people take this seriously. It makes me think they're
brainwashed. "Isn't this fun? You do my work for me, we'll call it
meditation, charge you to be here, and we'll all be happy! What fun!"
Have I gotten cynical again, or is this justified?

I also mention to Adhanya how bad the smog was yesterday and
how it bothered me. Although she has asthma and can't sit at the front
gate, she says she didn't notice. I tell her that my lungs hurt, and that I
recognize the pain from when I was a kid in a large, smoggy city. She
says that perhaps the pain yesterday was from memories of my childhood.
Let's not carry this analysis stuff too far, folks. My lungs hurt because the
smog was terrible yesterday! Because I had similar pain in similar

conditions when I was kid, doesn't mean they are in any way related. Smog hurts. Period.

I haven't mentioned Adhanya too much before, but she has affected me with her gentleness of spirit and non-obtrusive ways. She convinced me to be present at the Death Celebration - - not by telling me to do so - - but by a short conversation we had before the event. She may be a dedicated Osho-ite, but she is a good, soft-spoken person who always smiles. I will miss her.

When I mention to Jiadore my fears about the street dogs, she says she has seen them in the last couple of days. That gives me some relief.

After lunch, I am on my way to my room, when someone from the office asks if I'm doing reception. I say, "Yes, but not now." Hint, hint. He doesn't get the hint.

He says, "I know that, but I'm going to be out this afternoon, and someone is coming to meet me. Can you tell him that I'm in a session?"

I say, "I will try to remember that for the next half hour, but no guarantees."

He says, "I will leave you a note." Some things never change.

I receive a telephone call with great news! They permanently changed my floating work from the front gate to the cyber cafe! How cool is that?

After work, I walk up toward German Bakery and find Gowri. She introduces me to her nephew, a skinny forty-year-old Indian man. I give her some clothing that I don't want to bring back with me. She tries to sell me something - - I think she was going to give me a good deal, but I don't want anything. I still have more clothing to give her.

When I reach the ashram, I go out the back gate to see if my street magician friends are there. When Khalid sees me, he takes me over to where we always sit and introduces me to his wife and son. I have met his cute, little boy before. Khalid tells me that his son starts the English school tomorrow. He acts excited and proud about this. I take a picture of the three of them together.

At Evening Meeting tonight, I notice that Rishika and that big Indian guy, known as Buddha belly, leave early. Where did they go? Without him to grab my robe as I sneak out, I leave when Osho says, "Okay, Maneesha," so I don't have to listen to all that clapping nonsense. In the video, Osho doesn't clap. The audience in the video doesn't clap, either. Jiadore told me about a controversy over the clapping, and that some Osho-ites refuse to do it.

I walk slowly to the front gate, enjoying the silence of the night.

When I get there, the gate guy asks, "Is White Robe over?" I tell him it is getting close. I'm not sure if he will let me in, but he does. He asks because it is only eight-thirty, and the night before White Robe lasted until almost nine o'clock.

Later, I run into Chandra at the back gate. I ask, "Did everyone in the ashram get the 'on time' lecture?"

She says, "No, it's only a problem with that office. When I was there, I told Sakra about it repeatedly." Is this a pot calling the kettle black situation? Chandra was always late. Usually only a few minutes, but late is late.

When Chandra tells me about all the hours she has to work now, I moan. She says, "When you first sign up they take it easy on you. Wait till you come back."

I ask, "Does it bother you to work all those hours?"

She says, "What can I do?" But, I think she likes it. She's doing Osho's work. So many of these people are doing Osho's work and surrendering their own life. How would that sit with Osho now? What would he think about seeing the people missing the meditation piece of working, and only doing it out of loyalty to him?

I call Sam this evening to wish him happy birthday. When he recognizes my voice - - after I sing Happy Birthday to him - - he says, "Sweetie!" That surprises me. We have a good conversation. He says he is getting over me, and that makes me feel good. I want him to move on and be happy. He is a good guy and he deserves it.

Although, he tells me something sad. He says that when he read my blog at the beginning, and how awful it was for me, he thought to himself, as awful as that is, she would prefer to do that than be with me. He felt like he was a bad person. I tell him that my job was the awful part, and the reason we split up is that it wasn't good for either of us anymore.

He said that he might want me to help him with internet dating. When I tell him it will be good for him, he says he isn't sure if he is ready. I tell him that we had a good marriage for a long time; and I think we can each have that goodness again.

I enjoy talking to him and miss our interaction. He is still a good friend - - best friend - - and I hope we can keep that friendship. But, I don't have any thoughts of ever returning to him in a romantic relationship. That is over.

Day Eighty - Indian Culture

This morning when I go to pick up my clean laundry, it isn't there. My last two loads have come in a day late. This always scares me. The last time it was late, yesterday, I was t-shirt-less. I always have it planned to the day. When it doesn't work out, it's not good.

Rasha says that she and her mother went jewelry shopping yesterday. They bought a gold finger ring, an anklet, a necklace, and a necklace "for the boy." Rasha's mother wants to marry her off! My guess is the rumor about Rasha and her cousin scared her mother into pushing this. They have already picked out the boy - - a computer professional who lives in Mumbai. I ask, "Do you know if he's good-looking?"

She says, "My mother said he was very pretty."

The boy's sister met Rasha, and I ask, "Is the sister likable?"

Rasha says, "She is beautiful."

I say, "Yeah, but was she likable?"

She says, "Yes, she was likable. She is going to tell her brother that I am likable, too."

The engagement will become official in April, and the marriage will be in November in Mumbai. She wants me to come to her wedding. She says, "You have to come! I don't know anything!" I'm not sure what she means by that.

I say, "I don't have a job, and getting back to India is expensive."

She offers to pay for it. When I tell her that it is fifty thousand rupees, she realizes she can't. If I can figure something out, I will try to make this wedding. Rasha has been such a bright light for me on this journey.

Rasha's cousin told her that he became engaged because of her. He said that he wanted to marry Rasha. But, since he can't have her, he chose another woman. Rasha says that he always shared his joys and problems with her, but she had always considered him only a friend. What a sad story.

I find it ironic that in a country with the spiritual history of India, the culture discourages or doesn't permit love marriages. Perhaps you could look at it like a blind date. I always loved blind dates - - it was like a surprise package. It didn't matter if you liked the package or not, the surprise of it all always made it a pleasant experience. Only in this case, you can't say, "It's been fun, but I don't want to see you again." In this case, your surprise package comes home with you and you bear his children. No, I will never understand this arranged marriage deal.

Sakra comes in this morning, and I say, "The lights are on, and I'm here early."

He says, "Do you think you need to tell me that - - that I can't see it with my own eyes?" Well, at least he smiles when he says it, but it feels bad.

Speaking of feeling bad - - I walk into Revatii's office today to deliver her mail. She isn't there, but the office has the worst feeling to it. I wasn't thinking about it, but I suddenly felt it. It feels tangible and bad. Is she nasty because of bad vibes in her office - - or is her office bad because of her bad vibes? I think the latter is probably true.

Surabi calls this morning to tell me she will be late. She had been working on a laptop in her room - - Osho work - - and had gotten lost in what she was doing. She reported in so she wouldn't get in trouble. I tell her that I will fend off the Osho police for her.

Jiadore tells me that while walking back from breakfast at German Bakery this morning, she ran into the street dogs. She describes them all, in detail, so I feel much better now. Luckily, I didn't confront Dwami about them yesterday. Their presence here affects me so much - - I can't help it. Jiadore says that she even said, "Hello, doggie," to one. Then, her boyfriend said, "Don't talk to street dogs!" It's funny because she always laughs at me for talking to them, and now she did. Her boyfriend's response was funny, too. I'm happy the street dogs are fine, and nothing disastrous happened to them because of me.

I go to lunch with Jiadore and her boyfriend, Arjuna, today. We go to Bukhara. Arjuna pays for all of us - - one hundred twenty rupees for the three of us - - three dollars for a good lunch for three. We walk back and the street crossing terrifies me twice: once when I cross with Arjuna, and the second time when I watch Jiadore cross. I will not miss these street crossings when I leave here!

Partway down the block, we see some children playing on the other side of the road. One little girl comes over with her hand out. Then she starts doing cartwheels, stops and comes back over with her hand out. "Fifty rupees!" She won't leave us alone. She keeps saying, "Rupees, rupees!" Then I see my little one footed boy. He waves to me, twice. Another little boy comes over with his hand out, saying, "Rupees, rupees."

I say to the little boy, "No money, namaste," and he finally walks away.

Arjuna says to the little girl, "Bhago! Bhago!" and she leaves. I ask him what it means and he says, "Run, run!"

Indian people look at the beggars in a different way than I do. Arjuna says that you can go to public school free or a reduced price if you have a low income. So, I ask him why these kids are not in school. He says, "They live in the street. What would they write down for their address? Koregaon Park, street? No, no, they have to beg. It is their job."

Later in the afternoon, Rishika and I talk about Silent Sitting. I tell her how much I love it. More than anywhere, I can feel Osho's presence there. She says she hates it in there!

Rishika says that she always remembers something that Osho said, "Question everything I say." She was around when he was alive. He must have said it during a darshan, because I can't find it in any of his books. We also talk about Evening Meeting, because I want her take on the clapping part. She agrees it is awful. She says, "So many things are done in the name of Osho. If he was around now, it wouldn't be like this."

And I say, "He would have moved on." She agrees. That makes me even more certain that I want to title the book, What Would Osho Say.

The essence of life here - - in the name of Osho - - is "my way or the highway." Would he have changed that? He does act almost egotistical in some of the comments he makes. Even Worker's Meditation is so fallacious. In theory, we should be aware of every little movement, of everything that we say or do. But, how many people are like that? Is Revatii? I don't think so. It's good to aspire to that, but how many have achieved it? Few, I know. If there are any who have achieved that, they have moved on to a better situation.

I have mentioned a couple nasty comments that Revatii has made lately, but they haven't affected me like they used to. Although, they have affected me enough that I think I have to come back with a witty answer for my own sake. Now, I am waiting for her to give me another curt or rude comment. Will it happen before it's time for me to leave? I don't know.

After work, I walk to German Bakery. I run into Khalid the magician and his friend there. They tell me how bad business is. Then the friend, I think it might have been Uncle Makeen's son, asks me to buy him some tea. That always makes me uncomfortable, and I don't like it.

Day Eighty-one - Cost of Happiness

Before I leave my room, I glance at myself in the mirror and I look so at peace. I think - - not these exact words, but the meaning - - today is a good day to die. And, I have planned a snake appointment today. Although it feels weird, I am at peace with it. I've had this feeling before.

When I tell Jiadore about it, I say if anything should happen to me with the snake or getting hit by a rickshaw, to please tell my friends and family that I'm okay with it. She says she will, and that she has felt that way before, too.

This morning when I see Rasha at the stationery window, she asks why I didn't come to the laundry this morning. I feel like she is getting possessive with me, and it's not a good feeling. Another lesson for me? It's something I have done in the past, not only with men, but with women friends as well. It's not pretty.

She also asks what I had for breakfast, and what I did at the office this morning. I almost feel like it's my mother checking up on me!

During lunch, as I pass by the side of German Bakery, I run into Manik's girlfriend - - the one who went with us to Parvati Hill, and the one who showed me what to do at the temple. She recognizes me first, says hello, and shakes my hand. She tells me that Manik is in German Bakery area. I tell her that I have to eat, but I'll stop on my way back.

Continuing down the street, I see the man with the monkey that I had taken a picture of before. The monkey has a collar and leash on that I didn't see the other day. Unfortunately, I don't have my camera with me. I only carry it when I can slip it into the pocket of my jeans. My maroon robe isn't suitable for carrying a camera!

Then, Hassan sees me and calls me into his shop. I tell him that I don't have time and don't have money with me. He says he is going out of town for a few days, but I can pay his brother. I'll wait for his return on Saturday.

At the thali place, by myself, I sit facing the street at the table nearest the front. I smell the fragrant incense in the air and hear the beautiful Indian music playing on the portable stereo system. What a great atmosphere! Across the street from the restaurant, two men grind out the sugar cane on a cart. And, lunch is delicious as usual. It is a full sensory experience!

I have the same smiling waiter as I did last time. He brings me a coke without my asking for it. I don't want it, but it is so sweet of him to remember that I can't send it back. The food is always spicy hot here, so although I had decided not to have a coke today, it is great having it!

At the end of the meal when he brings me my bill, I pay and give him a two-rupee coin for a tip. He gives me the biggest smile, like I had given him something valuable. He is so happy and so smiling that it makes me feel good. Two rupees is less than ten cents. Happiness is so relative in this wide world of ours.

After eating, I stop at German Bakery and find Manik sitting at a table with a bunch of people. When I tell him that Sakra had yelled at me for staying away that day, it surprises him. We talk about the ashram briefly. Then, he tells me that he told his mother he would give her forty thousand rupees to help with his brother's wedding. He says he doesn't know where he will get it. I tell him I have to get back to the ashram so I won't be late.

Forty thousand must be a magical number around here. It's a thousand dollars. Gowri used to tell me she needed eye surgery that costs forty thousand rupees. Zakir told me that his son needed surgery that cost forty thousand rupees. Now Manik has told me that he needs forty thousand rupees for his brother's wedding. Forty thousand must be what they think a rich American can give without hardship. Trouble is, I am no rich American!

When I tell Jiadore the story, she says that when she was a kid, she had a friend who was a gypsy. Although the girl was only twelve years old, she knew how the whole scheme worked. She said that you never ask for the money directly. You make up a charming story to make the person feel like it would be charity to give the money. And if they don't, the designated story should make them feel bad.

I feel bad! This sounds like exactly what is going on with these stories with the forty thousand dollar price tag attached. I felt bad that I couldn't help Gowri and her eyes. But today with Manik, I'm not going to feel bad about his brother's wedding. And I didn't feel bad when Zakir said his son needed surgery, because I didn't believe him. Only Gowri was the most believable, but perhaps because she was the first to approach me like that.

Rushing back from lunch, I arrive at the office on time. I unlock the doors and switch on the lights just before Sakra comes through the door. He stops at my desk and says that he locked his keys inside his office. I say, "Bummer," like there is nothing I can do. He looks at me, not comprehending. I say, "Do you know what that means?" And he shakes his head, no. I say, "Too bad."

He walks to the side of my desk, because he knows I keep a spare set of keys there. A few minutes later, he comes back and hands me the keys. He says, "Not a bummer. It worked!" We both laugh. The moment feels good.

But earlier today, he angered me. He is so obviously different with young girls, that it annoys me. As some young blond walked out the door, he stopped her with a big smile on his face. He acts that way with Jiadore, also - - flirty and friendly. He acts differently, and the whole energy around him is different with me.

On the day I arrived at the ashram, he was the man who attracted me the most. It didn't last long, thankfully. When I realized the ways of the Osho-ites, I immediately lost interest. Still, this behavior annoys me. A man my age chasing after women half his age. It's disgusting.

I find men like that on internet dating sites. In their profile, it will say, fifty-year-old man looking for women eighteen to thirty. I look at that and although it annoys me, I wouldn't want a man like that. Would an eighteen-year-old boy interest me? No, it is distasteful. Would a thirty year old? Okay, okay, maybe! Still, I hate the whole May-December deal with men my age and young women. Perhaps part of my anger with it is there are many more opportunities for men like that than for women. Yes, Rishika has a twenty-year-old boyfriend, but how common is that?

Jiadore says that since my first cobra experience I look ten years younger. Perhaps my golden cobra was a magical cobra! How cool is that?

While on the way to get the afternoon mail, I see Phani and go over to talk to him. I ask if we can go see the snake today. He says, "Today?"

I say, "Not a good day? How about tomorrow?" Then he tells me that his rickshaw is broken, and that it will take a few days to fix it. It will cost four thousand rupees, and he has to pay for it himself. That part is a little hazy, but it should be fixed by Friday or Saturday.

At Evening Meeting tonight, I come up with a brilliant idea. The big Indian, Buddha Belly, is by the door, so I don't know how I could escape from the clapping. But, toward the end when everyone lies down, I start coughing a tiny, little bit, mostly to myself. When everyone sits up, I am holding it back in a loud way. He allows me to walk out without a word! I'm not sure if I can get out the gate, so I sit around for a few minutes. But, it is still worth it not having to sit through that infernal clapping.

Day Eighty-two - Conversations With Friends

I stop by stationery to pick up some paper. Rasha asks again, "Where were you this morning? Why didn't you go to the laundry?"

I say, "I didn't have any laundry today." Rasha frowns. I say, "If I feel like I HAVE to come see you, it will feel like a job to me. It would be much better if I see you with no pressure on me." I don't know if she understands what I mean, but she lets it go.

I have lunch again with Jiadore and her boyfriend, Arjuna. He sounds more opinionated than I am! I don't agree with everything that he says about the Osho-ites. But, he also says that everyone has their own truths.

He says that Osho was smart. He attracted the wounded people and kept them wounded. If he fixed them, they would leave. So, he arranged these "fake" therapies to keep them wounded. They are not all fake, though, because the last two workshops helped me. Maybe the other people taking the therapies were not receptive to recovering. Most of what he says, though, I agree with. Between the "get angry," "get happy," and the screaming at one another, much of it is all crap.

I also mention how the program takes up all your time. If you do the morning meditation at six o'clock, Kundalini at four-fifteen, and then Evening Meeting, that leaves no personal time. Arjuna says the idea is to keep people engaged so they won't get themselves in trouble. Now the seven day a week deal makes sense - - keep the masses out of trouble. That is the essence of life at the ashram.

I go to Worker's Meditation to find out when my last official day of work is. It is twelve days from now. I have one day off "as a gift." A gift and packing, whichever comes first! They also answer the question about breaks: you skip your tea that day and then you can hurry over to get your money changed. Essentially, you must stay in your seat for four straight hours. Those four hours are often tedious in the department where I work.

After lunch, I go see Sakra to tell him when my last day is. He asks, "Do you want to continue working from afar?"

I say, "Not for free."

He says, "You can pay if you want to." That's not exactly what I had in mind!

I ask, "When will I train someone new?"

He says, "Your last three or four days here."

It has taken me this long to discover that they train no one properly. When you arrive, they throw you into a job and leave you to fend for yourself. I thought Chandra was a bad teacher, but this is common. If you get any training at all, you are lucky.

The trouble is that this is one of my "buttons" - - I don't like looking incompetent. How else can you look with so little training? And then the regulars, who should be acting "meditatively" and "aware" in their jobs, get angry if you do anything wrong. That has been my issue with Revatii, but she is not the only one. Others expect you to know everything when sometimes you hardly know anything! If they were truly acting meditatively, wouldn't they understand that you weren't trained properly?

I hear Andre is leaving and I want to see him before he leaves. He has been my coach from the beginning, and I want to go full circle and finish with him. He asks, "How did you like the program?"

I say, "It was fine, but I didn't have enough time to myself."

He says in a slightly condescending but sweet manner, "That is what we all do. We separate ourselves. I do it, too."

What he meant was separating ourselves between work and play. That isn't what I meant. I want to read, I want to study, and I want to write. That is not necessarily play; it is just what I want to do. If you don't do what Osho tells you to do, then you're not doing it right, and there is something wrong with you. Still, it is a good meeting, and I thank him again for his help with the mosquito problem.

Jiadore tells me that she had a meeting with Sakra today, and that he cleared up something for her. He said, "Follow your heart." She says it is the answer she had been looking for. I tell her that I could have told her that! "Follow your heart" is the advice my mother always gave me. I'm not sure what it means for Jiadore, though. Although she is not an Osho-ite, she has been considering coming back here for one year. And she still hears the beeping!

Jiadore and I talk about Sam, and I say, "I want to find him someone."

Jiadore says, "No, you need to find someone for yourself first."

I say, "He should come first."

She says, "You need to be more selfish about this."

It makes me think that I'm not as ready as I think I am. I remember long ago when several friends and I were all single and looking. I used to hope for them to find someone first. Fear? Fear of intimacy? Aren't I over that? Is this fear or is this unselfishness? I don't know.

As I wait for five o'clock to meet Rasha, I find Jiadore and Arjuna at Zorba. I sit with them for a while. He touches her the whole time - - her hand, her arm, something. I like that.

Then I go out the front gate to wait for Rasha, and she doesn't show up on time. Gamel, the smiling guy from my workshops, is at the Meera gate. I go over to talk to him. He starts rubbing my back and touching me in a friendly way. I like this.

If I had any doubts about leaving Sam - - I don't and haven't, but if I did - - this place with all its affectionate people would have put a stop to that. There are men out there who are affectionate, and I want one. Soon, would be good, but if not, I'm okay with that, too.

Then I meet Rasha at the front gate for some pictures. We take a few, and then she has to change clothes. As a Sudexo worker, she wears a green sari. On the street, she wears her black Muslim clothing, called a burka. We arrange to meet at German Bakery, but I am waylaid on the way.

First, I run into Waseem right in front of Gowri. I try to take his picture, but he doesn't want me to. Then he and Gowri have this long animated conversation in Hindi, sometimes pointing at me. Toward the end of it, I recognize this, " . . . cobra pagal." Cobra crazy! I say, "I know what that means!" And the three of us laugh.

Then I continue up the block and run into Zakir. He says that he was off for several days for Muslim prayer - - somewhere ten hours away by train. Tomorrow, we will meet and he will sell me a cobra shed. He expresses concern if I can get it through customs or not. I hope it won't be a problem. He asks, "Where are you going to tell them you got it?" I tell him that I will say I found it - - because I did find another one right by the ashram. When I show him the pictures that I have of me and the other cobra around my neck, he tells me not to show it to anybody. He is more paranoid than I am!

When we talk about my leaving, he says something about a gift. At first, I can't understand him, so he spells it for me. I say, "Oh, a gift!" That embarrasses him - - he turns away and we both laugh. I say, "I think you should give me a gift." He says he will give me an Indian gift - - something for my hair. I already bought him and Uncle Makeen watches - - but I'll see how it goes.

After our conversation, I ask him to help me cross to German Bakery, as traffic is bad this time of day. So, I hold onto his elbow, and he helps me cross to the other side. These streets still scare me. I will feel lucky if I return with all my toes intact. Sometimes the cars and motorcycles get so close, I can feel the breeze of them on my toes. And, I

251

have my tennis shoes on!

  Working at the cyber cafe tonight isn't bad. For gate duty, I have to wear a maroon robe, but for all other night jobs, they allow regular clothes. That is cool. The other day when I wore my new t-shirt - - it was the first time in almost three months that I wasn't wearing maroon. The only t-shirt that I brought with me is maroon. At the cyber cafe tonight, dressed in jeans, it isn't bad at all. I talk to people, surf a while, and mostly enjoy myself. Definitely a step up from gate duty!

Day Eighty-three – Bathroom Roommate Woes

The air feels hot, stale, and thick today. I can almost feel it while I walk through it. My lungs don't hurt, but I have a headache. Maybe my lungs don't hurt because I'm not breathing deeply enough. That's why I have a headache.

My new bathroom roommate and I talk today. I tell her how to work the toilet or it will break.

She says, "You can call to fix it."

I say, "I was going to try to fix it myself."

She says, "Just call 472," like she has been here before.

I say, "It was fine before you flushed it."

Then she says, "I haven't used the toilet yet." It must have been Sudexo, then.

Now, she keeps opening the curtain to the outside. I never use the plastic curtain by the toilet or the one for the shower. They are too gross to touch. So we have been playing musical curtains - - she'll open it and I'll close it. It doesn't matter, though, because I'm almost done here.

I walk to the noodle place for lunch today. I cross the street by myself. The way to do it is to wait for traffic to clear on one side and then cross to the middle of the road. Then you stay in the center of the boulevard, which teems with traffic, and wait for the other side to clear. All the while praying that no one hits you. Cars, rickshaws, and motorcycles go over the centerline all the time. Sometimes as you stand in the middle, a car will be over the centerline coming straight at you, fast. You can't step back because there are cars screaming by behind you. You have to hope the one coming at you gets back in line in time.

Jiadore says that they can't afford to run over a Westerner. It's that kind of thinking that will get you killed. This brings me back to my mother's "dead right" comment. That's how I feel with this traffic. Yes, in a perfect, theoretical world they cannot afford to kill a Westerner. In the real world, they drive like crazy, and accidents happen!

Lunch is fine, but walking back across the street scares me more than before. While I wait in the middle, a big truck crosses the centerline and comes right toward me. Traffic has picked up behind me and traps me in the center. Luckily, the truck moves back in line in time. After it passes, I run across the street feeling happy to be alive! It would be a total bummer for a car to whack me in my last few days in India. If I have to die here, I would much rather it be by my golden cobra!

Evening Meeting didn't get out last night until almost nine o'clock, and I am afraid tonight is going to be another repeat. So right before Osho says, "Okay, Maneesha," I cough and walk out. No Osho police bar the doorway anymore. Maybe because the busy season is over.

My last days in India are disappearing as quietly as morning fog. I don't even see where they're going, and they're already gone. Although I am eager to leave the full-time-ness of this place, there is much to miss here, also.

Day Eighty-four - Sad and Confusing Times

When I say something to Sakra today in Hindi, he wants to know who's teaching me. I say that I have many Indian friends. Later, I say something else in Hindi, and he asks again. This time I tell him the street magicians. Later, when I am in his office, he says he asked because he thought it was my boyfriend. I say, "No, no boyfriend."

When I see Rasha today, I ask, "Where were you yesterday? I was afraid you might be in trouble from our picture taking escapade the other day."

She says, "I took a holiday to go to the university to take my tests. When I got there, they said I was a day too late! My mother yelled at me all night because it cost sixteen thousand rupees for the year!" She's hoping there's still a way to take the tests.

As the receptionist here, I receive all the stickers for everyone in the department. I didn't know that some people get vouchers as well. Inside the envelope, I find twenty one- thousand-rupee cards. Sakra gets one. When I hand it to him, I ask, "How do you rate that you receive this?"

He says, "I am poor." I heard a rumor that he was from a wealthy Brahmin family. Who knows?

Revatii knows I'm leaving soon and has been almost friendly toward me. Now that is scary.

I call Phani at three forty-five to see if he has his rickshaw back. He says not yet, and that he still needs two thousand rupees to get it fixed. But, he has a friend and they will pick me up in a half hour to see the snake.

While I wait for Phani, Uncle Makeen walks by. He holds out his hand when he sees me. Although I think he is asking for rupees, he only wants to shake my hand! We talk for a while. I want to tell him how honorable he is for not taking my hundred rupees that day, but I can't get the idea across to him. I'll have to have someone write it out for me in Hindi. Uncle Makeen tells me how bad business is and that he hasn't made any money all day. What a way to make a living. Free, but not free.

After Uncle Makeen leaves, I sit on this low cement fence around some wild growth. Workers sweep many areas around the ashram, clearing out the leaves and debris. Luckily, they miss this area. I think that it might be a good place for a snake to hide - - so I start looking. Right there caught in the leaves and foliage, I see a small piece of snake shed! Although afraid to reach in there, I do and pull it out. It's a fine piece. I wish I knew if it was cobra or not.

Then a rickshaw pulls up, and Phani gets out of the back and calls me over. Someone else who I've never seen drives the rickshaw. We go the usual way, and then the rickshaw stops and the guy from last week squeezes into the back of the rickshaw next to Phani. Phani is a big guy, so it's good the Indian guy and I are small. After pulling out the picture of me at twenty-five years old with my snake around my neck, I hand it to the guy. Then he and Phani have a conversation and all I understand is Phani telling the guy that it is an American cobra. The guy must have protested, because then Phani asks what kind of snake it is. Neither of them recognize "boa constrictor."

The rickshaw driver drops Phani and me off on the same corner as last week, and continues down the street with the snake guy. They return a few minutes later, and the snake guy carries the familiar woven basket carried in a pink cloth. He unwraps the pink cloth ceremonially. He opens the lid of the basket and taps on the side to get the cobra to hood up. The cobra hoods up and struggles to rise, but instead rolls over on its side. I say, "It's sick." The guy takes the cobra partway out of the basket, and although still hooded, it lies there, unable to even raise its head. I say, "It's sick. It's dying. It needs to go to a vet. I don't want this cobra."

I say to Phani, "This isn't right. It is like making kids do something when they are sick." Since I know Phani has little kids, I think it is a good analogy. From the little I can understand, Phani agrees with me, but the guy isn't happy at all. He had said that last week's cobra had died, and this is all he had. I tell Phani that I will not do anything with this snake. During their discussion, I give the poor snake Reiki to help it over to "the other side." That's the only place this pathetic thing is going. I feel so bad for it.

It's times like this when I ask myself - - what are you doing? These cobras would belong to these men whether I ever came to India or not. It is not my fault that they are poorly cared for and dying. Yet, a part of me thinks that it is people like me who create the need for such atrocities. Like ivory elephant tusks - - if no one bought them, there would not be the demand to kill the elephants. In my zest to find the golden cobra, am I partially responsible for this horror?

Although I find the situation appalling, and I hate the part of me that "needs" this, I can't turn away. I can't stop seeing the cobras. I can't stop wanting to hold them. I can't stop wanting to feel their power and energy in my bare hands. I can't help loving the sheer idea of holding a cobra. I can't help it. I am as much to blame as these poor souls who have much to learn about caring for snakes.

Finally, Phani convinces the guy that it isn't going to happen with this dying snake. So, the guy and the rickshaw driver take off down the road, and Phani and I stay there.

As we wait, I tell Phani that if the cobra bites me, that I would appreciate it if he would rush me to the hospital. It's only five minutes away, so no worries.

A few minutes later the guy returns with a snake basket. When he pulls out a large and beautiful cobra, I think he will hand it to me. Instead, he drapes it around my neck! I feel its muscles moving through my fingers. He keeps holding its head, and I keep telling him it is okay. Finally, he lets go, and I hold its head right behind the hood.

Some other guy there tells me not to hold too tight. But, he doesn't realize that I'm an experienced snake handler and I know exactly how to hold snakes - - even cobras. They're the same - - you can't hold tight - - you hold loosely and let them move through your hands as they will. So it moves through my hands and ends up with its head resting gently on my shoulder - - still hooded up.

Then, it turns around, looks at me, and gets so comfortable that it unhoods itself. But, it doesn't like the camera's flash and hoods back up. Its tongue comes out as it investigates me. Although it tried to strike the guy when he first took it out of the basket, around my neck it is not aggressive at all. It likes the warmth of my skin. And, it likes MY energy.

Several people watch this lady snake charmer with the cobra around her neck, and I see one guy taking pictures with his cell phone. It is amazing and fantastic! In search of the golden cobra, and I am finally living it. This must be a sign for me to leave India. I finally get what I wanted - - to hold a live cobra around my neck. I have completed my journey here.

He charges me five hundred rupees this time. When I talk to Phani about it, he says the guy is upset about all the "drama." I say to Phani, "Drama! That sounds so American!" The deal is that it costs five hundred this time, and the next times it will cost four hundred. I pay the guy and he walks back to his place.

Phani and I step into the back of the rickshaw and drive back to the ashram. Then he and I get out, and he starts giving me a sad story about his broken rickshaw. It bothers me. He wants a thousand or fifteen hundred rupees. That's about forty dollars. I tell him that I'm leaving soon and I only have enough money to see the snake a couple more times, and enough food for the rest of my trip.

I tell him that I am sorry, but I'm not a rich American. Then, I remind him of when he wanted twenty rupees to take me somewhere and he wouldn't come down to fifteen so I walked. I say, "Five rupees, and I walked!" I give him three hundred rupees instead of the usual two hundred and tell him I'm sorry. It is hard for me, but I tell him I have to go, and I walk away. He isn't mad, only sad.

This kills me. I'm considering giving it to him. Should I, or shouldn't I? I don't know. Life is so unclear for me here. In America, life feels much more black and white. Do this and don't do that. Here, everything is so hazy. Do you give the beggars money? Do you give your rickshaw driver this much money because you feel bad for him? Do you rescue the stray dogs? I would be a mess if I lived here. My strength of ignoring the beggars and the children and the dogs and my rickshaw driver - - is failing me. This is killing me; I can't face it anymore.

Osho told a story about a beggar approaching a rich man. The man gives the beggar a hundred rupees. When the beggar looks at the money in his hand, he says to the man, "No! You can't give me this!" The rich guy looks at him like he's crazy. Then, the beggar says, "I used to be a rich man and I gave beggars one hundred rupees. Look what happened to me!"

Although I have no job, I'm thinking of giving away forty bucks. Yet, when I think of what I said to Phani - - "I only have money to see the snake a couple more times . . ." - - I want to see the snake and Phani can't feed his family because of a broken rickshaw. That doesn't feel right. I am ashamed when I think of it - - and yet - - I don't know.

At Evening Meeting as I listen to my iPod and watch Osho with his Sanpaku eyes, I have to blink back the tears from today's experiences. At the end of Evening Meeting, I cough again so I don't have to sit through the clapping. Thankfully, I only have a few more Evening Meetings before I skip them completely. I step outside and enjoy the night sounds while I wait for another white robed figure to appear.

Later, Jiadore talks me into going to Celebrating Sannyas. It is a festive atmosphere with people "taking sannyas" - - committing themselves to meditation - - and Osho. Yet, I still find no one who actually meditates here. I ask Chakori, an old-time Osho-ite, and she says that Evening Meeting is a meditation. Yes, and my cobras love living in those little baskets instead of roaming free in the wilds of India.

Day Eighty-five - Osho-ites at Work

When I run into Adhanya today, we talk for a while. First, she asks if I had been to Evening Meeting last night. I say, "Yes, but I didn't listen." That much is true.

She says, "I had no idea that it was so hard for Osho to carry us like that. I felt so bad." She goes on and on about this, and I listen politely.

Then she talks about them making us come in on time and how it is okay. They only needed to raise the energy. When she mentions my working here, I say, "I have a hard time with the seven day a week deal. I don't have enough time to read or watch the birds or do what I want to do."

She says, "I have plenty of time to read. And I can watch the birds as I walk by them."

After asking if she has read Tom Sawyer, I give her my theory on people doing jobs for Osho. I say, "He has even said it in discourse - - how people like doing jobs for him." She frowns at that.

When I ask if she meditates, she says that everything she does is meditation. She talks about how aware she is and how much this place has helped her. She says that she's been here for thirty years. It's like peeling back the layers - - one by one her problems dissolved. They couldn't have dissolved too fast, if she's still here after thirty years! But, she is always friendly and smiling. If she says she's aware and does everything meditatively - - I believe her. She's probably the only one I could say that about!

When I tell Jiadore how ashamed I feel about saying that I only had enough money to see the snake a couple more times, when Phani couldn't get his rickshaw fixed to feed his children - - she says, "Everyone is involved in their own lives." I think that's true. He does what he has to do, and I will do what I have to do.

Jiadore's boyfriend, Arjuna, tells me there is a government place that cares for beggars, like the homeless places in the United States. He says they give them menial jobs, and the beggars receive food and shelter in exchange. But, they only stay a few days because they like the freedom of the streets - - and they make money in the streets. I understand the freedom part of that equation.

With Sakra busy in a group, Jiadore and I talk most of the day away. I hope they won't catch us or throw us out for this. All the rest of the people in the office are dedicated Osho-ites. You never know who the

Osho police are.

We talk about how after discovering the residential program, neither of us had any doubts that it was right for us. I find that intriguing. Now, neither of us have any regrets. She might even come back and spend a year. I may come back to India, but I doubt if I would come back to the working program. Although, stranger things have happened.

Meet Arjuna, my new therapist. Since he is Indian and grew up here, I run past him the story of Phani and his broken rickshaw. First, he says, "I think you like to think about it. Why don't you get another rickshaw driver?" He also says that if it makes me feel better to pay Phani the money, then it's worth it. Then, he adds there is a good chance that Phani isn't telling me the whole story; he might not even use the money to fix the rickshaw.

I can't get another rickshaw driver. Phani interprets for me, because the snake guys don't speak English. And Phani knows where to find the snake guys. As far as thinking about it - - I think he is exactly right - - I grew up with guilt. Although I have thrown off most of the leftover vestiges of it, India is the perfect environment to kick it into action again. Oh, poor me. It's my fault the snake is dying, it's my fault Phani can't pay to have his rickshaw fixed, it's my fault about the beggars in the street, it's my fault about the stray dogs - - ad nauseum. Well, the buck stops here. Or, I should say the rupees stop here.

Later, Jiadore comes back and tells me that after hearing the rest of the story - - about how much I give Phani for each snake appointment - - Arjuna says definitely do not give him any money.

After lunch, I take advantage of Sakra's absence and go to Silent Sitting again. I love it in there, and I always have a great meditation when I'm in there. It's my favorite place in this whole ashram.

I come back to the office after lunch and find Neehara sitting at my desk. She had the job before Chandra. Revatii has been asking her to do some scanning, so she has been in here often. Too bad that she is in here to see that I am twenty minutes late. Luckily, I have picked up my laundry and she sees it. She might think it is the office laundry, because when I get back I start putting out the cleaning supplies for tomorrow. Oh, well. Whatever happens.

After work, I walk to Pune Central - - the shopping center that has an expensive department store and a grocery store. I buy my last grocery purchases in India - - cookies, crackers, and cereal. I take the glass elevator to the top floor. The young boy already on the elevator steps off one floor before he wants to. I see him take the escalator up. Then a man gets on and stays at the opposite side of the elevator. "Westerners" must have bad reputations!

In front of Pune Central, I talk a rickshaw driver down from forty rupees to twenty. He turns the rickshaw around and drives the wrong way on a one-way street. That is only the beginning. The rest of the ride is full of honks and sliding into spaces that aren't meant for a rickshaw. But we do arrive at the ashram in one piece, thank goodness. This is my second worst rickshaw ride. The first was home from German Bakery one time, and the rickshaw went up on two wheels! That even scared Jiadore!

After Evening Meeting, I stop by the Buddha Auditorium because they have some special dance event. I open the door and see a handful of people dancing to ear-splitting music. The music is good, unfortunately. The song I hear sounds Celtic - - or maybe I'm just hungering for England! Even with earplugs, this music would have been too loud, though. So, I leave.

As I cross the street back toward the main gate, I see the street dogs in all their glory! It makes me so happy to see them that I could hug them all! But I don't; I walk past and continue to the main gate.

When I hold up my pass, the gate-watcher calls me over to him. Uh oh. This always scares me. He says, "It's allowed, but you have your shirt on inside out." Ah, he expressed that like a true representative of the Osho police. I am so glad the ashram allows me to wear my shirt inside out if I want to. That makes me feel so . . . so . . . free. Thank you very much. I'm leaving now.

Day Eighty-six - Out of the Ashram

This morning I check at the front gate to see if my name is on the list for gate duty. It isn't, so I am free! I walk to the India Blossom restaurant, and on the way spot all my furry stray friends. I also run into the smiling man with no fingers on his hands. He holds his bowl out as I pass, and I shake my head. He makes a sound - - not a moan, but a louder sound to get my attention. At first, I think that I will give him something on the way back. Then I realize that he is alone now and probably won't be on the way back. So, I stop, dig through my purse and drop a ten-rupee bill into his begging bowl. When I walk by on my return trip, he smiles and nods to me.

At the India Blossom, I have those delicious banana cinnamon pancakes and freshly juiced ABC juice - - apple, beet, and carrot. The juice costs more than the pancakes. I give the waiter a five-rupee tip. I'm getting into this, now.

On my way back to the ashram, I go in to German Bakery. They don't have the chocolate pie that I want. Since I arrive back at the ashram early, I go to my room and read.

At a quarter to ten, I go to the office and find that someone has already cleaned my desk. I do not vacuum or do the floors. They can wait. I pick up all the cleaning supplies and put them away. That's enough cleaning for me.

With Zorba closed, I have to eat at Meera. It is brunch day today. That must mean expensive, because it cost me a "fortune" to eat there today, and I don't even get any fruit. One hundred fifty-five rupees, for rice, beets, a cookie-sized piece of focaccia bread, and chocolate pudding. The pudding cost the most - - sixty rupees.

While I eat, I hear people laughing. On brunch days, they have these clowns out to entertain the people. He does some silly stuff with rubber chickens and balloons. Because of where I sit, I can't see too much. I have to hurry away, though, to make it in time for Silent Sitting.

Tomorrow may be my last day for a while. Maybe forever depending on this coming week. I'm only able to do this because Sakra is in that class.

While in the office, I hear the familiar "meow on a loudspeaker" call of the peacocks. I walk outside to see three of them there. These three always stay together. I watch them for a while, and then they fly up to a five-foot high wall. One flies almost vertically upward, but only five feet. Shortly, the one who had flown almost vertically, does it again; but this time to the top of the thirty-foot high building. It amazes me. Later, Rishika tells me to come back out and they are there again. She finds a tiny but beautiful peacock feather. I go to my room and bring back a cracker. The brave one pecks it out of my hand. They are so beautiful.

After work, I go see Hassan to pick up the jewelry I had ordered from him. He remembers the five hundred rupees! We talk about it. He says he even told his brother about it, just in case. I buy the cobra necklace; I couldn't leave it behind. It looks too unique not to buy it. When I finish buying everything, I have a hard time leaving his shop. There is a chance I will never see him again.

As I cross the street at my favorite "safe" crossing area, I realize the post that I thought would protect me if a car came my way is made of plastic. How disappointing that is! There is a low cement wall on the other side. Standing here is still safer than standing in the middle of the street with cars racing by on both sides. They still race by, but the cement wall would protect me.

I stop at the corner vendor to buy two more of those wooden cobras. I paid eighty rupees for the last one, talked down from one hundred fifty. Today, he wants two hundred fifty for one. In Hindi, I say "too much" and start walking away. He gives me another excessively high price. I ask how much for two. He won't come down much even when I say I had bought it before for much less. After walking off and him calling me back several times, we settle on two hundred for two of them. I also buy a beautiful peacock feather for ten rupees.

My bathroom roommate locks me out today after using the bathroom. She's never done that before. She is in there a long time, quietly. After she flushes the toilet, she goes straight into her room. She doesn't wash her hands! That makes me crazy!

At Evening Meeting tonight, the unthinkable happens. My saliva goes down the wrong "pipe." It is awful. It is at the beginning, and I don't want the Osho-police to send me to the mosquito-filled coughing place. So I do some deep breathing and pointed concentration, and it works.

The other evening as I meditated in my room, I had to cough. I thought about it carefully - - where am I? Can I cough? Is it okay? What are the consequences? I'll never cough again without thinking about it beforehand!

Tonight at the ashram, they have a mini-session fair. After Evening Meeting, I wander over. They have set up Buddha Grove with massage tables, floor chairs, and blankets. Candles burn all over and colored lights shine where the candles don't reach. Weird music floats through the air. Everyone receiving a session looks happy. The brochure says chakra balancing, divine healing, Tao face massage, and Tibetan pulsing. I go home and go to sleep.

I often hear fireworks at night. It's not every night, but often. Sometimes I hear loud booms that sound like bombs. It's so common around here that I ignore them.

Day Eighty-seven - Stray Dogs and Indian Marriages

It has been a slow, lazy feeling day. My last Monday on the job. I run into Revatii and she asks if I can do a black and white scan for her. I tell her I'll try. Later, she comes back after I have finished it, and I show it to her. She says it looks wonderful and leans over and gives me her cheek. So I give her mine! I say, "I'm learning how in time to leave."

She says, "Learning and leaving." She walks away smiling. My lessons with her are through.

This morning, I have an incredible synchronicity. Since I'm not listening to Osho's discourses at Evening Meeting, I read them at work. Today, I read about something that happened with Buddha and a rose. Later, on the Internet, I read a book excerpt from a new book by Eckhart Tolle. It has the same story about Buddha and the rose! It makes me look at Tolle differently now.

Tattva passes me by today with her head down, but I don't laugh as I usually do at the Osho-ites inability to make eye contact. Since Arjuna spoke about these people being "wounded," it has changed the way I look at them. Although I had the same idea in mind when I called them "damaged," that is a more confrontational term and unkind. Wounded makes me feel more compassionate toward them. I have to thank him for that new way of thinking. There should be compassion instead of laughter for these people. I feel bad for them.

Today Rishika acts weird. Some days she is friendly to me and other days she is distant or even cold. It's that whole wounded deal again. This morning is a distant day. Before lunch, she breaks down about some issues at work. I hug her and tell her that it isn't her, it is only the game. She isn't receptive to the hug, so I let her go and pat her on the arm. Poor Rishika. I feel badly for her. This teaches me a lesson though. Acting distant and acting friendly has little to do with me, and everything to do with her.

Later, she calls me outside to see a beautiful and huge grasshopper. The back of it looks like a thin leaf. When you look close and in the right light, the front of it looks all sparkly - - like the sun on the water or on the snow. I watch it for a while, and then the resident black cat comes over. She doesn't see it and walks on by. The silly grasshopper doesn't hop away, and that is a big mistake. Then, the cat comes back and says, "What are you looking at?" She puts her head down to the grasshopper and takes a big bite! All she leaves is a wing and a leg. (No prayer.) This is not my fault. This is nature, and you cannot take sides.

I meet Chakori at the front gate and ask how she is. She says, "I feel happy. I always feel happy around Osho."

Adhanya sees my new books today, including the one titled *Seeds of Wisdom*. She says it's good to hear his words before you go to sleep. The other day she said that it was this place, not Osho, that helped her so much. Yet she speaks of him in a reverential way.

When I run into Sakra before lunchtime, he asks what new Hindi I've learned. I say, "kall me-lang-ay," but, I pronounce it wrong. He says I should pronounce it, 'cull.' I say, "I know, but cool sounds much cooler!" Tomorrow, I'll have a great new one to give to him. Phani taught me how to say, "Blah blah blah" in Hindi. I can't wait to see what Sakra says about that!

Walking up the street from the back gate of the ashram, I run into the one-footed boy. When he sees me, he points to his missing foot with his other hand out. I say, "Not today. What's your name?"

He says, "Bala."

Then I ask, "Where do you live?"

He says, "On the street."

I ask him about his mother, and he points up to heaven. He keeps his hand out the whole time. I keep saying, sorry. Bala follows me as I walk down the street, but then a street vendor calls him over and he lets me walk on.

I had a thought to send this kid to school, but Arjuna is right. No address. No parents. How would he get money to feed himself if he was in school? Sometimes you have to leave matters as they are, as hard as that might be.

When I get to North Main Road, I run into Uncle Makeen, his son, Khalid, and several other guys. I sit next to Uncle Makeen. He wants me to buy tea for all seven of them. I say no. Then, he shows me that he needs his nails cut and wants to know if I have a nail cutter for him. He says a small one. I tell him I'll try to find him one.

Then, I go see Gowri. She wants me to sit with her, but she has a bunch of other women there, so I keep walking down the street. At the end of the block are a couple guys selling drums. I say I already have one, but one guy asks where I am from. Then he starts describing where he is from - - somewhere around New Delhi that is beautiful and has many tourists. The other guy with him wants to trade a small drum for my watch. The drum is worth about a dollar. I say no and point to the watch on his arm. He says it is an Indian watch that he paid twenty rupees for. And, I was happy paying eighty rupees for a similar one.

266

Then, soft heart that I am, I walk to the local Indian pharmacy and buy a small nail clipper for Uncle Makeen for twenty-five rupees. I run into Anderson on the way, and he tells me that Manik is upstairs at the coffee shop. On the way back, I stop and go in to say hello. He acts like he has no energy - - maybe he feels depressed. I don't stay long because there isn't much to say.

I stop at German Bakery to buy my wonderful chocolate pie. Tonight, I have to do the cyber cafe instead of Wednesday. It's too late to eat the chocolate pie, but I'll have it tomorrow instead.

I see Gowri again on my way back, and her women friends are still there. Gowri has me sit down, but then the women talk to her. It feels like they tell her to ask for money. That's the feeling I get, so I leave.

When I give the clipper to Uncle Makeen, he says it is too small. Although I try to help him cut his fingernails, he's right, it is too small. Oh, well. He wants me to go back and exchange it, but it's too hot to walk back and forth and back and forth. I want to get home.

The gate watcher at the pyramid gate talks to someone while I walk in followed by my favorite stray dog. I have something in my room to give him, but he goes the other direction. So, I hurry and get the focaccia bread from yesterday and come back down to look for him. He's by the silent area in the back. Someone sees me give him the bread and yells, but I turn around and act innocent. The dog snuggles into the foliage eating the bread. I walk away. When I look back, the guy who yelled has left. I say, give the dog a maroon collar and let him stay.

There are a couple ponds close to the front of the resort. When I walk by them at night, I hear the frogs - - though I've never seen them. Sometimes I'll make a clicking noise, and for a short time they answer me. When they realize that I speak a different frog dialect from them, they become silent. As I walk away, I hear them start their chorus again.

I pick up the keys for the cyber cafe at the front gate. While I unlock the door, a woman comes up and says they told her to work here for the evening. I admit that I still have lessons to learn. I act a little huffy and say they told me to work here, also. No way am I going to give it up, because I have already had more than my share of sugar and know I will be up half the night, anyway. But she is friendly and asks if I'd mind her staying there because she isn't sure she knows how to do all the procedures. She says her name is Jagrati and she would appreciate watching for a while.

Jagrati entertains me with many stories and gives me so much information about India. When she was child, there was a young widow

267

who lived in her neighborhood. The woman always wore white - - the color that widows wear. This woman had married at six years old. When children marry, they don't live together until their late teens. One day when the woman was twelve years old, her mother came crying to her, "Oh, no! You're a widow! Quickly, change into white!" Her "husband" had died of a childhood disease, and now she was a widow at twelve. In true Indian tradition, she was never to marry again. Nowadays, the government has banned child marriages.

Jagrati also tells me there are twenty-eight states in India and twenty-eight separate cultures. They are all a little different. She also says that although arranged marriages are still common, some families feel differently. She says her own father only wants his children to be happy.

Women in India should be submissive to their husbands. It is like Rasha. When I asked her if she would work after she marries, she said, "It depends on the boy." The man decides everything and the woman has no say. That doesn't sound like much fun to me, and not fair at all.

There is more stray dog activity at the back gate tonight when I go to my room. That same dog that followed me in is walking around, and the gate person asks the dog for his ID card. That's what I said! Put the dog in maroon and let him in! I run into Jiadore by my building. A few minutes later, the stray dog walks up to us and starts walking up the stairs to my room. I want to let him go and invite him in, but Jiadore calls him back down. When she goes to her room, the dog follows her and stays outside her door. Her boyfriend saw the dog and immediately said, "Oh, Parvati's dog, isn't it?" (The next morning, she found the dog still curled up outside her door!)

Many of these strays, including this dog, are "pariah dogs" - - an ancient breed that dates back thousands of years. I wondered why so many of them look alike. Not all of them are pariah dogs - - some are mongrels - - but many of them are. Jiadore still isn't impressed.

Day Eighty-eight - Hygienic Dancing

When I see Revatii this morning, she is cold as ever. These people run hot and cold faster than a broken faucet. That may sound like generalizing, but it is true more often than not around here.

Jiadore and I walk to the thali place for lunch today. On the way back, she placates me by crossing at the corner instead of in the middle of the block. She crosses first, and I have to wait until the traffic on my side stops. I confess to her my big fear of having a car hit me in the streets of Pune my last week here.

I tell her a story of when I was sixteen years old. A friend of mine had a condominium in a mountain resort in California, and she invited me up there to ski during school vacations. There we were - - the last day of vacation - - we had already paid for our lift tickets - - and I wouldn't ski because of my fear. I was so afraid of breaking my leg on the last day, I couldn't ski. It almost feels like - - I made it this far without incident, don't take chances now. So, here I am, my last week in India, and more afraid than ever of crossing the streets.

When I get ready for Evening Meeting, I have to put my white robe on carefully so the earphones land on my back. As I slide the robe on over my head tonight, the earphones slide to the floor. Taking it as a sign from the universe, I leave my iPod in my room.

I decide that I will be fully present for one of my last ever Evening Meetings. I dance during the dancing part and try to get into it. I'm not a dancer - - never have been. Although I liked ballroom dancing when I was a kid, the freestyle never suited me. In my youth, I'd go to dances and refuse to dance. It limited my opportunities!

This all changed when I was chosen to participate in a movie. They filmed the movie at a ski resort close to where I lived in New Mexico. I was in several crowd scenes - - where? The dance floor! AND, we had to dance without music! They added the music later. I wasn't going to lose my chance of being in a movie because I was afraid to dance - - so I danced. No one ever said I danced badly, and I had my ten seconds of fame. I got over my fears quickly. However, it's still not one of my favorite activities. But, I was present for Evening Meeting dancing tonight.

Next comes the sitting during the music/silence/music/silence part. That used to make me feel manipulated. Tonight, I sit quietly and listen to the music and the silence. Then the Osho discourse starts. When he comes on screen and namastes the audience, I namaste back. It's only polite, you know. The jokes at the end of the discourse include one of his many anti-marriage jokes. I have heard enough of that rhetoric.

There is no gibberish in this series of discourses, and I miss it. After the discourse comes two minutes of silence and then a few more minutes of lying down silence. Then comes my favorite part (heavy sarcasm here), the clapping. In the video there is little to no clapping, and in the background, they are saying, "Celebrate Bhagwan! Celebrate the love!" I stayed for the duration without a cough. I'm almost done here.

When my bathroom-roommate stops me on the way back from Evening Meeting, we argue. She asks, "Do you wear your shoes into the bathroom?"

I say, "Yes."

She says, "You can't do that."

I say, "I have to do it, because I'm not taking my tennis shoes off every time I step in."

She says she is going to complain to the space committee because it is unhygienic. Speaking of unhygienic, she never washes her hands when she uses the bathroom. If anything is unhygienic, it's that and it's gross. Thank goodness I'm leaving.

I meet Jiadore after Evening Meeting, and we walk to German Bakery. She has a veggie burger and I have a fruit salad and strawberry juice. The fruit salad tastes good, but the strawberry juice tastes almost as good as the chocolate pie.

We run into Bhava there. She is unfortunately back with her Indian boyfriend. He has stopped drinking, and she is trying it again. I feel bad for her and I hope that nothing bad happens. The guy is weird and scares me, so I'm hoping for a happy ending.

Back in the ashram, we go to the African plaza party. The music is African and sounds good. The dancing is pseudo-African. We are both tired, so we don't stay long.

Day Eighty-nine - Kissing the Golden Cobra

This morning, as I eat a papaya outside at Meera Restaurant (there is no inside eating at Zorba or Meera), my two peacock friends stop for a visit. They walk right up to my table like they recognize me from the cracker I gave them the other day. I hand the closest one a small piece of papaya, but he doesn't like it and spits it back out! So, I apologize for not having any crackers available today.

Suddenly, they flutter and fly away. Up walks a stray dog sniffing around where they had just been. As I say good morning to him, a sour faced woman staring at the dog distracts me. She makes some complaint about him, and I say he is only being a dog. She says something about chasing him out of there; and I say that I like his attitude. I should have said, "I like his attitude, it's better than yours." But, I don't.

Jiadore tells me today that she had thanked a gate guard. The woman asked why. Jiadore told her that she said good morning to everyone who came by and thanked them for showing their pass. Then Jiadore mentions all the grouchy people who check passes who never say a word. It's not just me! Jiadore feels the same way about them!

We go to lunch at the thali place again. On the way, we see the old beggar man with no fingers. He recognizes us now, which makes it even harder. As we walk by, he holds out his bowl as far as he can and makes sad, moaning noises. It still kills me, but Jiadore pulls my arm along so I don't slow and stop.

I have a long talk with Rasha today. She hasn't worked for days. I wondered what had happened to her. She says she had been sick, but she has a twinkle in her eye when she says it. Since there are other people around, I don't know if it's true.

Later, we talk about her upcoming marriage. She will be officially engaged in April. Custom dictates that she doesn't get to see the boy until the night they get married. He has already seen a picture of her. But, her mother will ask for a picture of him on the pretext to show a relative. Then Rasha can see the boy.

The wedding is in New Delhi, and she wants me to attend. Before my friend, Sajeev, left the ashram, he invited me to stay with his family in New Delhi. This could be a cool return visit to India in November or December.

I ask, "Will you go on a honeymoon?"

She says, "Yes, but I don't know where. It will depend on the boy."

I say, "I could never handle that because I hate people telling me what to do." Rasha nods her head, yes. I say, "And you seem like that, too!" She nods her head, yes, again. Then I ask, "How can you do this?"

She says, "I have no options." Yes, the rules are different here.

Rasha asks me to explain about my husband - - why I left him if he is a good man. I try to explain to her that he is a good man, but not good for me. It is difficult to understand when you are marrying someone you have never met, and you hope that you are lucky enough that he will be a good man.

I also talk to her about the Muslim women who wear black. Rasha is one of them! She calls it a robe, but later says something about a "nakab." I ask, "Why are some black, but there are many other colors, also?"

She says, "Black is the traditional, symbolic color. But, you are free to choose. I feel safe and secure in one. No one knows who you are." She tells me that you can take it off for members of your immediate family only. This starts when you are fourteen years old. During work, she has to wear a uniform; but she changes back into the black robe before she goes home.

At three o'clock, I walk across the street to pick up some supplies, but Phani waves to me so I walk over to see him. We arrange for a snake appointment, and he says that he will go get the guy and pick me up at 4:20.

He pulls up at 4:30 and shuts off his engine. I know something weird is up. He tells me a story about going to the train station to get the snake guy, and the police stop him and big trouble. They threaten to put him in lockup for three days. Phani has to pay them three hundred rupees. So he says. Somewhere in the story, he mentions his broken rickshaw. I'm sure this is to make up for the money that I never gave him.

I think that is the end of the story, but then he starts the rickshaw and we're off. He says that he only needs to find the guy. As we drive over there, I realize this is my last Wednesday in India. It gives me a weird feeling. I try to look at everything with "new eyes." I have been here so long now, the "alien-ness" of it has long worn off. I am accustomed to the trash in the streets, the people sitting or lying around everywhere, the piles of rubble, and even the beggars. No, I take that back. I'll never get used to the beggars.

Soon, we're there. We park over by where I saw the last snake. Phani walks over to those apartment buildings where the snake guys live. I sit in the rickshaw a long time before I get up and walk to the corner to see if I can see him down the street. Another rickshaw driver says that he saw him down by the apartments. While I wait, I try to meditate. Now that I know that I have Osho's picture on either side of me in the rickshaw, it makes it a little easier. Just kidding!

After what feels like forever, Phani comes back and says the guy will be here shortly. We wait and wait some more, during which time Phani tells me that we're like family. Yeah, right. He says, "I don't make much money, but inside I'm happy." That's more than many of us can say. He also talks about a Shiva festival tomorrow. If you go to it, your heart will be happy. Shiva is the Hindu deity pictured with the cobra around his neck.

Then another rickshaw driver that has something to do with the snake tells Phani the guy isn't coming. So, we take off. As we're driving away, the other guy yells something to Phani. He turns the rickshaw around and parks. The snake guy is coming.

This is another new guy that I have never seen before. I hear the snake hissing before he ever opens the basket. When he does open it, a beautiful, golden cobra is inside. It looks shiny and bright like it has recently shed. It stands straight up and tries to strike the guy. The snake opens its mouth! This one doesn't have its mouth sewn shut. Since the guy handles it, I am willing. I ask if he can put it around my neck, and he agrees.

This snake is lively. It does not like Phani snapping pictures with the flash going. I feel its muscles move in my hands. I feel its lungs fill with air, and then expel the air in a loud hiss. It is an incredible experience. Since it keeps having its hood facing away from me, I kiss it!

The snake guy puts it back in the basket and I wait to see what the price tag is. He wants seven hundred rupees. The other rickshaw driver and his friend say they need money because everybody gets some of this. I try to talk them down to five, but eventually pay six hundred rupees.

While we bargain, they say something about feeding milk to the snake. I try to talk them into feeding it proper food for a snake - - birds, lizards, rodents. Phani says, "The system is different here." Yes, the system is different here. That's why the snakes are dying. Milk does not sustain them.

Phani and I drive back to the ashram. As he's parking the rickshaw, I say, "You better have taken good pictures for eleven hundred rupees." I pull the money out of my pocket and hand him five hundred rupees spread out like a hand of cards so he can see them. I say, "Three for the police and two for you."

He has the gall to say, "Only two for me?" But, he doesn't look angry and he knows better than to pursue it.

The whole affair takes so long, that when I get home, I have to get ready for what I hope is my last Evening Meeting. My regular white robe is in the wash, so I can give it to Gowri before I leave. The only one I have left is the textured one my sister-in-law left me. But, they don't allow textured white robes, only plain ones. I'll give it a shot. I leave my iPod, my floor chair, and my white shawl in my room.

I run into Jiadore and Zona, another friend from our groups, in front of Buddha Auditorium and tell them briefly about the golden cobra. Then I voice my concerns about my robe, and both of them offer to lend me their shawl to cover it. That would spoil the fun, wouldn't it? I walk up the stairs talking to them, past the first set of guards, take off my shoes, give my name for the checklist, and make it past the last guard! No one says a word to me about it. Maybe I need to go back tomorrow to get a reaction out of them!

After Evening Meeting, I decide to try something called Awareness Games for Daily Life. They hold it in the same place as Silent Sitting. As I walk down the path, candles light the way. When I get to the glassed in area, I see everyone inside is wearing maroon. Oh, no! But, I ask and it isn't mandatory. White socks are mandatory, though. If you don't have them, they will lend some to you.

I walk inside the Silent Sitting area. A small handful of people sit in various places all around the room. It looks so unorganized that I ask the facilitator if it is Silent Sitting or Awareness Games. It is Awareness Games. I get comfortable, and they turn the lights down and close the door.

She says we will go through three of our senses: sight, hearing, and touch. We will start with sight. The music changes between each sense. Afterward, we will be silent and try to feel it in our center.

During the sight part, I look around the room. The walls have great slabs of marble with designs that look like a Rorschach inkblot test. At first, I think someone painted the amazing designs, but they are random, yet similar. The columns in the room are mostly black marble. I notice the floor has large slabs of marble fitted together. I read where they don't allow you to touch the floor because of the untreated marble. But, it's beautiful. What I thought was Osho's bed is instead a marble pedestal topped with a mirror. A bust of him sits on the shelf above it. Many panels of switches control the climate and lights in the room.

Next comes hearing with pleasant, soft music. After that is touch.

We are to touch our face, our arms, our chair, but not the marble floor. Then, the music stops, they turn the lights down even lower, and we sit silently for a while. And, I always enjoy being in that room "with" Osho.

I go to the plaza party after that to see Jiadore. While I wait for customers to clear so I can talk to her, who appears, but a pariah dog! It looks like the one who spent the night outside Jiadore's room the other night. He is happily wagging and going up to people. I call him over and he licks my hand and my face. He is a sweetheart.

Then Rishika comes over and asks for my help in making him leave. What could I do? At least she doesn't suggest beating him. So, I feel guilty but keep calling him out toward the back gate. We get him out there. Rishika walks off somewhere. As I walk back to the plaza, he comes racing up beside me, wagging all the while. Then Neehara sees him and starts trying to make him leave.

She said she doesn't want dogs here. I ask why there can be cats here and not dogs. It is a short but ludicrous conversation that ends with her saying, "I don't want pets here. I'm here to work on myself." I walk off, and so does the pariah dog, and everybody lived happily ever after.

Day Ninety - Shiva Festival

When I see Neehara today she asks me if I have pets at home. When I tell her about my beloved dog, Sheba, she says, "That's what I figured. That's why I backed off last night." How kind of her. She can be outrageously "Osho-ish" sometimes, but I think she has a good heart.

This morning, I ask Tattva if she meditates. She answers combatively, "That's a strange question! What are we doing here?"

I say meekly, "Meditation."

She says, "Do you go to Evening Meeting?"

I answer, "Every night."

She says, "That's the highlight of my day."

It's time for me to leave here, although I brought this on myself. Judging from her answer and her attitude, my guess is that she does not meditate.

Rasha wants me and Jiadore to come over for dinner Saturday night. When I tell her that Jiadore would have to skip Evening Meeting, she tells me about someone else who had come over and skipped Evening Meeting. She uses the slang word I use for skipping. It is so cute!

After work, we take a rickshaw to Yerwada to attend the Shiva Festival. Rasha told me about it when I saw her today. She called it Mahashivratri and said there would be "puja" - - worship. It is the coolest place. It is much more crowded than the last time we came. Most women we see are dressed in their finest clothes. Indian music plays on loud speakers, and we see more vendors than before. Many vendors sell novelty items, like those paper horns they have for New Years. Up and down each street, we hear kids blowing on them.

There is a small Shiva Temple with that red powder like when I went to Parvati Hill. Without a Hindu guide, I am afraid to go in and do it alone.

Jiadore says she will be glad to get back to Czechoslovakia so people will stop looking at her like she is from another planet. I don't mind it. Some of the kids today say "Hi" to us and love it when I answer them back. They probably don't get to practice English too often.

When we come back from Yerwada, Jiadore and I run into Sakra. He directs all the conversation toward her. I'm tired of this behavior and will be glad to leave it behind.

After Evening Meeting (which I skipped), I go to Awareness Games again. I think with a different facilitator, it might be different. A woman from my office, Mukta, is the facilitator. The whole format is different tonight! Much more woo woo! This time it consists of four parts. For the first part we meditate on our third eye. (I told you it was woo woo!) I visualize mine as a faceted crystal popping out of my forehead. It is cool. Next, we stand up and sway to the gentle music. I move my arms like a bird flying for a short time, but then sway from side to side until the end. After that we continue standing. We can also dance, although no one does. Mostly more swaying. Some people move their arms this way or that. The final part is silent sitting. Sometimes the instructions are hard to hear because of the facilitator's accent, or the sound system itself.

The whole experience is pleasant, and I'm sorry I didn't go to any of these earlier in my stay here. The wall behind the pedestal is a mirror and inscribed on it in white letters is: Osho, Never born, Never died, Just visited this planet between 1931 and 1990.

As I walk back from Awareness Games tonight, I look around and realize that I would not mind living in a closed community like this, as long as the people and the philosophies were closer to my own way of thinking.

Day Ninety-one - Reflecting on Friendships

My id card expires tomorrow. It only lasts for ninety days, and then you have to get another HIV test. This affects every person who is at the resort, including the Sudexo people. I asked Rasha. It costs her one hundred ten rupees. It cost me one hundred eighty rupees. Why the difference?

No matter how old you are, getting even a pinprick blood test is no fun. I thought of trying to get out of it, but the possible consequences scared me. I don't want them to kick me out a week before I'm scheduled to leave! You get the results from the test in fifteen minutes. If you test positive you cannot enter the ashram. I'm in.

I ask Rasha about the picture arrangement with her and the boy she will marry. She says that in the olden days (her words!) they did not allow the prospective bride to even see a picture of the prospective groom. The rules have relaxed some now. She says that it would be uncomfortable for all the relatives who want to see the intended to go to the family's house. Now, they allow a picture. Rasha can look, too, but her mother has assured her the boy is pretty.

Rasha says that her sister is getting married, too. Her sister saw her boy's picture and she is in love with him already! Apparently the boy feels the same way. I love a happy ending! Rasha says they will have a double ceremony.

Since Neehara does most of my scanning now at work, I mostly surf the Internet all day. Sometimes Sakra walks by. I don't know how he can't notice, but he never says anything. When I told him about my last day of work and asked when I would be training someone new, he said soon. I now have two work days to go and have not trained anyone yet. Oh, well, it's not my responsibility. Yes, two days to go. Two days and counting.

After work, I walk up past German Bakery to the sewing machine man on the side of the road. I stop to see Gowri on the way and show her my backpack. She looks at it and estimates ten rupees. That would have been the Indian price. When I get there the man says forty. I am happy that he can fix it. It's an old leather backpack. Part of it tore on my way here from me stuffing too much in it and carrying it by the handle instead of on my back. Having it fixed at all is a bonus.

The man says six o'clock or tomorrow. I can't come tomorrow and I don't want to wait until the last minute, so I decide I should come back and get it today. That means an hour and a half to kill. Walking up toward Pune Central, I enter the expensive looking store on the other side of the street. The prices inside are not that bad, and they have some cool pieces in there. All I bought, though, is a small bell and a miniature Bhagavad Gita.

I still have more time. When I cross the street to Pune Central, instead of going directly to the market on the top floor, I walk around to all the different departments. To give you an idea of how overpriced they are for India, there is a stretchy turtleneck shirt for six hundred forty-five rupees - - seventeen dollars. Name brand jeans, like Wrangler, are forty dollars. Their computer department is the same. There are some laptops there for a thousand dollars, but most cost more. After buying some cookies at the market, I leave.

I get back to the sewing machine man before six and he has already finished. He hands me the backpack, and he has done an outstanding job. It looks professional. After giving him fifty rupees, I say thank you in Hindi.

I stop on the way back to talk to Gowri again. Since I only understand one fifth of what she says today, it makes me wonder how I've been communicating with her all this time. When I tell her how expensive Pune Central is, she goes on and on about it. I think the essence of it is that for Indian people it's not that expensive because they charge them less. Phani said that, also; and Jiadore has experienced it when she is with her Indian boyfriend.

Then, as we talk about me leaving, she goes tells me about some guy with a couple kids and what a good man he is. At first I think she is trying to fix me up! That isn't it, but I never do figure out what she is saying. I tell her how beautiful she looks in her new outfit and she offers to give it to me! I will miss my friendship with her. She has been a pleasant part of this journey.

I run into Zona and she asks me about going out to dinner. I say, "I never eat dinner."

She asks, "What about going out to dinner with friends and not eating?"

I say, "I don't have many friends." After we part, I think about that. Why did I say that? Why don't I have many friends? What is wrong with me that I don't have many friends here?

That is always my conclusion when issues like this come up: there is something wrong with me. But, the answer is: nothing. At other places, I make friends - - perhaps not easily - - but, eventually. There are so few people in this ashram that I have a rapport with; it makes sense that

I only have a few friends.

Now that I have that out of the way, I have another question. Whenever Jiadore and I come across a person (it's usually male which might be the answer here) who has been in our groups from the beginning and who we both know, they always hug Jiadore and not me. What message am I sending out about not hugging?

Day Ninety-two - Dinner in the Real India

Last night I decided that I should sleep with the door open because my room was so hot. I felt nervous about it, but decided that was stupid. So, I locked the screen and fell asleep. My first dream was of someone opening my screen door and entering the room. I immediately woke up, turned on the light, and closed and locked the outside door.

Every once in a while outside my room, I hear a sound like a computer starting up. Tonight, with my door open, first I hear a loud beep and then the computer sound. I wonder what is going on here. They bugged the rooms in the Sheela-days, but I wonder about now. It's a curious sound.

This morning I wake up early so I can go to a class called Gurdjieff Movements. I have done some of it in a class that I took when I first arrived here. It's entertaining and good for the brain - - similar to brain gym.

First, we step around in a certain way. Then, as we are stepping, we have to "brush our teeth" with the wrong hand. Then we comb our hair with the wrong hand. After that we have to interlace our fingers not the way we normally do it. I believe all of it is to create new neural pathways in the brain.

Next, we line up and have to step forward a couple steps with a pause between each step, and backward a couple steps with a pause between. Then, we add in arm movements with our right arms. First out, then up, then to the side, and then down at your side, pause, and start again.

We do all of this while doing the fancy stepping. I can do it easily if someone is in front of me who I can copy. It is all with the right foot leading. When we come to using the left foot leading, I lose the rhythm. Many other people do, too. While the exercise calls for three lines of people, instead, we bunch together because most of us are lost. Had I done this earlier on in my stay - - I still wouldn't do it again! Although each class is different, and I've seen them do more stimulating exercises. So, I shouldn't judge by this one class.

Between a couple of the different exercises, my favorite peacock walks into Buddha Grove. He walks toward this large, freestanding mirror. I wait in anticipation to see how he acts when he sees himself. He turns away before he gets close enough, so I don't get to see his reaction.

At lunch, I leave early and walk to the thali place. On my way there, I run into Khalid and Uncle Makeen. I've talked before about

281

inviting them to lunch. Today I am alone and the time is right, so I ask. Uncle Makeen won't go! I think Khalid might have if Uncle Makeen said yes. But, Uncle Makeen smiles and says no. I say, "I'll pay!" That makes them both laugh. Holding out my maroon robe, I ask, "Is this why? It will hurt your reputation?" They laugh, but I'm not sure if they know what I mean.

Then Khalid says, "You go have lunch, and when you come back by, you give us the money." That's when I laugh, turn around, and continue down the street.

A bunch of men sit in the thali place having lunch. There is one other woman, and she leaves halfway through my lunch. A man who was sitting behind me drops an Osho tarot card in German on my table as he walks by. I try figuring out what it says, but I can't. Although I took two years of German in high school, it is mostly long forgotten.

Back at the ashram I attend Silent Sitting. I love sitting in there. I imagine Osho standing in front of me saying the equivalent of, "You go, girl!" And I'm about to go - - in only four more days.

When I talk to Jiadore today about the hugging, she says I give off a "don't touch me, leave me alone" vibration. She also says that sometimes I appear angry. I must not smile as much as I think I do. While I point the finger at other people like that, it must be because I am that way myself. Although I still have some work to do, it won't be here. I am ready to leave.

Jiadore stands by my desk at four o'clock today when the phone rings. She asks if she should get it. I say, "No, it's four o'clock." But, it keeps ringing, and I say, "Yeah, go ahead." It is Rasha! We had planned to go to her house for dinner tonight, and she wasn't at work today. We had both written it off and were going to go to MG road instead. Then, she calls to say she will meet us at German Bakery at 5:30.

We buy a cake for Rasha's mother, but there is no sign of Rasha. There is sign of a camel! I have to get a picture of me on the camel. So, Jiadore stands there with one hand holding this big chocolate cake and the other hand balancing the camera, and taking my picture. The camel walks up and down the street. Meanwhile, my little friend Bala, the one-footed boy, has walked up. I ask the camel driver if he will take him for a ride. This kid is so happy! You should have seen the look on his face. It is so fulfilling. I am glad I could give him this.

Then Rasha appears in her black robe. She has the face part pulled down so we can recognize her. Her cousin, who she agreed not to associate with anymore because of the rumors, has brought her here. She wants to introduce him to us, with a strict reminder not to say anything to her mother about him. He brought her on his motorcycle. Then we catch a rickshaw and are on our way.

The rickshaw drops us off, and we walk through an area that is so much the real India. Sacred cows, buffalo, and goats walk around everywhere. Especially goats. We walk down these windy narrow side streets, where there are shops and vendors all around. There are no other Westerners anywhere. When we get close to Rasha's house, little kids call out, point to us, and ask her who she has with her.

Finally, we arrive at Rasha's house. It is small with a flat roof. We only see three of the rooms. I don't know how many more there are. The first room is the kitchen, which has a small sink, a stove, and oven. The second room is a bedroom with one large bed, probably queen-size. The third room is a living room with a couch, some chairs, and a television. There are no screens on the windows, but I don't see many flies or mosquitoes.

We meet her mother, her sister, her younger brother, and her sister-in-law. Mostly, they talk among themselves in Hindi, and Jiadore and I sit there and listen. Rasha is the only one who speaks fluent English. Her sister speaks some, but is hard to understand. Her mother doesn't speak at all, but Rasha says she understands English. Her sister-in-law complains of a headache, so I offer to give her Reiki. She says it helps and she leaves shortly afterward.

After a while of visiting, they bring out the food for us. It is thali, and it is delicious. Rasha reprimands me when I put rice on my plate. She says I am to eat that later, not with the rest of the thali. I eat it anyway.

They also offer us water, which I am afraid to drink. I can't bring myself to ask if they had boiled it. So, although I am dry and dehydrated from the heat, I don't drink any. Luckily, her mother brings us some papaya juice. I hope I'm okay with that. I'd hate to get sick my last couple of days here. They don't eat. It is only Jiadore and me. Rasha says they usually eat at nine o'clock.

After dinner, we visit some more, and Rasha and her sister bring out their beautiful, fancy saris. They wear these for special occasions only. They are handmade with sequins and other sparkly designs on them. We take some pictures of a sari partially over Jiadore and me, and then take some other pictures of the family. Her brother had already left by this time.

After a while, we say we have to leave, and Rasha keeps asking, "Are you bored? Are you bored?" We assure her that we aren't bored; we just have to get back to the ashram.

After walking out of the residential area, we get to a marketplace that has everything you can imagine. This is way, way REAL INDIA. There isn't a Westerner anywhere. It is so cool looking around there. Many of the shops are closing by then, but still it is engrossing.

Rasha flags down a rickshaw for us. She worries, though, that they will try to charge more once we arrive. It costs fifty rupees; and there is no trouble when get to the ashram.

Day Ninety-three - Other Gurus, and Magician Friends

How can India be India if I don't get sick at least once? It is not a great morning for me. I get up early to go to something called "Divine Healing Movements," but I never make it. My stomach started hurting after lunch at the thali place yesterday, and it didn't stop. It still hurts a little now, but not constantly. I'll be fine.

I walk to India Blossom restaurant for breakfast, and it is wonderful again. While I am there, I hear the woman behind me talking to the waiter and she sounds American. Although I usually don't do this, the universe wants me to so I start talking to her. She invites me to join her. It turns out she lives in another ashram three hours from here. Her guru is Mayer Baba. He's famous by his own right, but not infamous like Osho.

She tells me that when she first went to her ashram, she thought that she could never bring her friends there because of the attitude of the people. It didn't occur to her until later that if they didn't act that way, then you could not learn forgiveness.

That is also part of the philosophy at the Osho ashram: that it is not your problem, it is their problem. The fallacy in that way of thinking is that if you allow these people to continue abusing others, it will only get worse. Let them be - - it is their problem. Meanwhile, they are affecting everyone else with their negativity.

As woo woo as my life has been since I arrived here, this woman is the most woo woo person I have met! Everything I say she wraps around her cosmic little finger and has a cosmic explanation for. She talks on and on about her guru and says that she and I were supposed to meet. Then, she gives me a picture of him.

I say, "He looks familiar."

She says, "Soul memory."

I'm thinking, "He looks like my Uncle Harry." Then, she tries to talk me into taking a three-hour bus ride one-way to see his Samadi (where his ashes are), and then three hours back. She says that once I get there I will understand. I've been woo woo-ed out, folks. Give me some loons, some eagles, and some herons and let me get my feet on the ground.

As I start walking back to the ashram, a rickshaw stops right in front of me. It is my friend, Chakori, and she offers me a ride. That is good, because I had stayed talking to that lady way too long.

When I get back to the office, Sakra and Jiadore are busy with Welcome Morning. I check my email, do a couple small jobs, and then go to the cyber cafe for their break. Almost immediately after I arrive, all the computers go down. It must be my vibes. I'm gathering all my energy for leaving this place, and it has affected all the computers."

Back at work again, I'm tying up everything for my imminent departure. I put away the cleaning supplies for the last time! Oh, I missed Revatii sweeping the stairs again. My last day of work has been uneventful. Chandra, who used to have my job, will have it again. It all works out.

I make a concerted effort today to be more huggable. This morning when I walk past the main gate and Gamel is there, I hug him good-bye. Then I hug the cyber cafe guy goodbye when I leave there. At lunch, Jiadore dares me to hug Ramoda. When he shows up later in the office, I hug him as well. This evening, when we return from the train station, I hug another friend at the front gate. I'm getting there!

Jiadore meets me for lunch at Zorba. She said that during Welcome Morning, Sakra said "If you are looking for the answer to a question, you will find it here."

I had asked her earlier if she wanted me to order a pizza for her, and she said, "Those pizzas are horrible!" Yeah, well. What choice is there? I leave her early to go to my last Silent Sitting. I have much on my mind today, and it is not as peaceful in there as usual.

Arjuna told Jiadore that he thinks there is a camera in her room. There are some weird objects in my room that could have a camera behind them, too. Also, I still hear the computer sound at night. Mysteries abound in this place.

After gathering all my cleaned and ironed "ashram clothes" - - robes, shawls, maroon pants, etc. - - I pack them into a bag. Today after work, I bring it all to Gowri. The drum vendor that I spoke to the other day is there. He and Gowri go on and on about me being snake crazy. Gowri tells me to show him the pictures, so I haul out the camera and scroll backwards to show my snake kissing pictures.

When I go to the bank to change some money, it turns out to be a guarded ATM machine. I ask the guard about a real bank and he says it is on MG road. Walking out, I see Bala with a couple other beggar kids. I ask, "Did you have a good time riding the camel yesterday?"

He says, "Yes," but then he puts his hand out for money. He waves it indicating the three of them.

I say, "Not now."

As I walk away, one says, "Chocolate." That always cracks me up in an unfunny way.

Then, I stop at the place where I change money from dollars to rupees, and change a big bill that I had. Next, another strawberry juice is in order! Mmmmm mmmm good!

After running into Jiadore when I get back to the ashram, I go out the back gate to look for my street magician friends. I find Khalid first. He says that Zakir and Uncle Makeen are sitting on the bridge by Osho Teerth Park; so I walk down there. Uncle Makeen doesn't have his white cap on, and I almost don't recognize him. I give him the paper where Arjuna had written something for me in Hindi. I wanted it to say Uncle Makeen is an honorable man, but it only said a good man. Perhaps there is no word for honorable in Hindi. And he doesn't grasp the part about me thinking he was a king. It would have gone over better if he were Hindu instead of Muslim. Hindus believe in reincarnation, but Muslims do not.

We hang out together for a while. Zakir kills a mosquito on my forehead, we talk about politics in America, and it feels like we are old friends. I will honestly miss these people. They have made this journey so much brighter.

I have my camera out to show the snake pictures. It's sitting beside me on the bridge on top of a postcard that I bought at German Bakery. Uncle Makeen starts saying something about the camera - - and he has asked me to give it to him in the past - - but today he tells me to put it in my pocket. He says, "If you put it beside you, you will leave it here. Put it away." What a kindly old coot he is!

While we sit there, Zakir looks at the postcard that I bought. It has much printing on one side of it, so he reads it all aloud. He tells me that he didn't learn English in school; he learned it from a German friend of his. That impresses me!

Zakir again arranges to meet tomorrow to sell me the snakeskin. Will he show up this one final time? He also says he will bring me a cobra, but I tell him that I don't have enough money now to see cobras. I'll see what happens tomorrow.

When Waseem talks about me buying everyone t-shirts, he counts to ten. Uncle Makeen turns to me and says, "No, not ten. Just four." He is such a good guy.

After Evening Meeting, which I of course skipped, Jiadore and I walk to German Bakery to catch a rickshaw to the train station. She wants to show it to me at night. We find one to take us there for forty rupees.

It is an engrossing place, but the guards there will not let me take any pictures. I see schedules printed in Hindi and English. People sit and lie everywhere waiting for their trains, with their luggage piled beside them. Little kids sleep on the ground. In the freight section, there are motorcycles partially wrapped up in burlap bags, with their destination written on the bag. I see boxes of all sizes stacked everywhere.

In the front, red-shirted bellboys sit on the ground waiting to help people with their luggage. There is a computerized list posted on a wall. That is the only confirmation that people get according to a man whom Jiadore met last time she was here. The train station stays open all night.

The dogs around the station are in poor shape compared with the strays at the ashram. It saddens me. When we walk around the neighborhood by the train station, we see many beggars as well as people sleeping in the streets. We walk up and down the immediate neighborhood. Again, we are the only Westerners around. After a while, we catch a rickshaw and have a scary ride back to German Bakery. Well, scary for me, not for Jiadore. She takes it all in stride.

And, I hate to disappoint all you conspiracy theorists out there, but you know that electronic beeping that I've gone on and on about? It's not! No, no, I still hear it, but it's not electronic! It's a bird! I'm trying to get the name of the bird from Arjuna, but he doesn't know the name in English. I'll have to do some research.

Day Ninety-four – Thee Lock

Last night, Jiadore and I got in late from the train station. We talk a while, then I work on the computer, and then I visit with Kanti in the office. I don't get back to my room until 12:30. Jiadore had told me that they lock the gates at 1:00; so I decide to stay awake until then. At one o'clock, I walk stealthily to the back gate and see the closed gate, but without a lock on it. Foiled again! I sit in the shadows in an inconspicuous place with my hands covering my white tennis shoes, and wait. Every time I hear a leaf fall to the ground, I flinch. But I see no one, including anyone locking the gate. I wait until 1:10 and then go back to my room to sleep.

With my "internal" clock set for five o'clock, I think if it goes off, fine, if not, that's fine, too. It goes off at 5:15. Silently, I pad down the stairs again, walk across the courtyard careful not to step on the crisp, noisy leaves, and arrive at the back gate. I take one picture from a few feet away, getting the whole gate in. But I want a close-up of the lock. So I step closer, focus with the telephoto lens, and snap the picture. Footsteps at the gate! Horrors! I turn off the camera, stick it in my pocket, and run away as silently as I can. When the person finishes unlocking the gate, I am hidden away. I'm hoping the pictures turn out, so I don't have to have another secret mission tonight. I'm exhausted!

At the back gate before eight o'clock this morning, when I show my pass, the gate woman asks me if I have a maroon robe. I'm wearing my jeans and blue t-shirt. I remind her the ashram doesn't require maroon until nine o'clock. One problem around here is that they don't train the incoming workers properly. Either that or she is a busybody. That's a possibility, too.

After that, I walk to India Blossom restaurant to meet Devika for breakfast. I have the delicious banana pancakes again. Then we catch a rickshaw to Jungali Maharaj Road. Devika tells the driver to use the meter. I've never done that before. Usually, they don't want to. The meter is tricky. When they installed the meters, the money was different. Now, you have to have a conversion card to figure out what you owe. Our ride costs forty-four rupees, but he drops us right at the gate of Pataleshwar Caves.

This place is cool! Carved out of a single boulder, it has a circular pillared area, and then the cave area has several different rooms you can walk through. We leave our shoes outside the cave and step inside another century. Hanging from above, a bell you can ring signifies awakening your consciousness. We walk inside one room where I see a large copper cobra. Above it, a device drips milk onto the cobra. Cobras in India supposedly like milk. Incense burns all around. It feels sacred and holy in here. It feels good. The whole temple area feels like positive vibes. I know that's a little woo woo, but honestly, it has a good, positive feeling to it. People all over kneel and namaste the cobra and other deities spread throughout the temple.

Then we walk next door to a temple dedicated to Jungali Maharaj. I don't know who or what he was, but people in here are kneeling, praying, and touching the feet of his statue. There is a mound in the middle with a blanket over it. We never find out what it is. We see people lean over the railing and touch their heads to the mound. Fresh flowers have been placed all over.

Although it is a hot day, we're early enough to walk to Lakshmi Road. It isn't that exciting. We walk down the street, avoiding the piles of rubble and large holes in the sidewalk, and eventually take a rickshaw. Although we head to Fashion Street so I can see it again, after twenty minutes riding in a rickshaw in thick traffic, heavy smog, and in the heat -- we both want out. We get out at Pyramid Mall, instead. It is too early to eat, but Devika wants to go inside to clear her ears - - the rickshaw and traffic are so noisy. I am having a hard time breathing from the pollution. That causes me to get a headache.

After a short while, we walk across the street to that Indian mall that I had visited before. Devika gently encourages me across by pulling my hand so I follow her. The mall has a downstairs! Down here in the coolness, I buy three Indian blouses for one hundred rupees each. I hope they are wash and wear, but I won't hold my breath!

Next, McDonalds! When I spoke to Kanti at the office last night, she said to be sure to try the Paneer Wrap and potato wedges; so that's what I have today. Plus a coke float. It is all good. Another great vegetarian eating experience at McDonalds.

The rickshaw ride back is scary. The driver has a one-liter container of gasoline at his feet in the front! And he is an awful driver, squeezing into places he shouldn't be squeezing, and driving crazily. I am ready at any moment to jump out and pull Devika with me if anything happens. Nothing does. He drops me off at the ashram and continues with Devika to German Bakery.

Between nine o'clock and four o'clock at the ashram, you must wear a maroon robe. Since it is lunchtime, I sneak into my office hoping that no one notices or complains about my blue shirt and jeans! It works!

I stay a while catching up on computer work. Then, Jiadore tells me that Rasha called and needs to see me now.

Rasha wants to buy me something for my trip home. She paid for the rickshaw ride the other day and she had her brother go to Lakshmi Road today to buy me a cobra belt buckle. Her family must have money, because she wants to buy me presents all the time, and her university costs sixteen thousand rupees. If not, she is the most generous person I've ever met. Regardless, she is a sweetheart and has made my stay here more pleasurable.

I go back to my room to start packing. What a daunting job I have to look forward to! On the way to India, I was twenty pounds overweight. On the way back, they don't allow you to be over at all. I'm hoping that everything fits without being over. I'll soon see!

At five o'clock, I've planned to meet Zakir at German Bakery for the snakeskin. I get there early, meet Bhava, and we say our good-byes. Then I walk down to Hassan's store and find a cool poster. Although I try to talk him down, he won't budge. I could push it, but fifty rupees means nothing to me and much to him, so I pay it. Hugging him good-bye, I thank him again for helping me that day.

Then I go to Manik's father's store. Shareef is in there, but not Tanul or Manik. We have a long talk about many subjects including war, politics, and marriage. He is a good man. I have enjoyed my friendship with him and his family.

I walk back to German Bakery at five o'clock, but Zakir is not there. Devika is, though, and I sit with her and order some strawberry juice. Devika wants me to mail a couple letters for her, but she hasn't written them yet. While I wait for her, Zakir shows up. We walk outside to a little alleyway - - I always feel like a spy with him. He wants everything secret and tells me not to tell anyone I saw him. He wants me to tell customs that I found the snakeskin on the street in Mumbai. The boy sounds paranoid!

He shows me this dinky, little piece of cobra skin that he wants four hundred rupees for. I say, "No way."

Zakir says, "Three." I offer two, and we settle on two hundred fifty. It is not worth that; but I'm done here, so why not. I had placed two watches on my arm and two in my pocket to give away today. I didn't want to just give one to them; I want them to ask for it so they feel like they are getting one over on me! So, when Zakir asks, I give him a watch.

Bala shows up while I'm with Zakir and sits down close to us. After I finish my business with Zakir, I dig into my pocket to get out a ten-

291

rupee bill to give to Bala. Walking over to him, I sit beside him on the curb. He points to the watch and gives me those gorgeous brown eyes of his. I pull another watch out of my pocket and give it to him. Then, I help him put it on his wrist. When I ask how old he is, he says ten. Then I see a tattoo on his inner arm.

This gives me a weird feeling. Many, many years ago in a large city, I had gone into a bakery to buy something for my mother. The woman in front of me reached across the counter to pay for her purchase, and I saw the telltale sign of a concentration camp marking on her arm. It made me sick to my stomach.

Seeing the tattoo on Bala gives me that feeling momentarily. I ask him what it is, and he says Bala. It must be Hindi for Bala. I hand him the ten-rupee bill. He takes it, cocks his head, and says, "Fifty." What can I do? I reach into my pocket and hand him a fifty. It will be my last association with this kid. Good-bye, Bala. We shake hands, and he hobbles off.

When I go to see Gowri to give her more of my clothes, she is asleep on the sidewalk in front of her wares. I hate to wake her, but the bag is heavy, and I don't want to carry it around. She says thank you, we talk a while, and then I hug her good-bye. I don't know if I'll get to see her tomorrow.

After entering through the main entrance, I walk through the ashram and out the back gate. Turning right, I walk to the corner, hoping to see Uncle Makeen. He is there. He knows I'm leaving "cull" - - tomorrow. When he sees the watch on my arm, he wants it. But he doesn't want the blue one; and I had already given Zakir the white one because I didn't know if I'd see Uncle Makeen again. Khalid asks if I have one for him, and I give him the other black one in my pocket. They trade. Uncle Makeen's son is there, and he wants a watch, too. Sadly, I have run out.

We talk about how many hours on the plane, if I'm returning, and how much I don't like the ashram. Uncle Makeen and Khalid both thank me and say they have to leave. Uncle Makeen says it is five or six kilometers to his house. We shake hands good-bye, and they walk down the street. I stand on the corner watching them walk away. Although I try taking a picture, the sun is going down and there isn't enough light. I watch until they are down the street, and then Uncle Makeen turns around and waves. I knew he would! Then Khalid and the other guy turn, too, and wave. They walk a little further and then turn around again. Those guys will miss me! Their cobra-crazy American friend.

Jiadore and I go to something called Shamanic Ritual tonight. Although I expect and want something woo woo, instead I get a mediocre variety show. We leave after the first act. We talk a while, and then I return to my room to pack.

Day Ninety-five - Last Day in India

I wake up at four fifteen today and sneak down to take more pictures of the lock. Mission successful. No one comes and no one sees me. I want to take even more pictures, but I'm afraid to stay out too long, so I go straight back to my room.

Jiadore and I walk to India Blossom for my last banana pancake breakfast. It is delicious, but they must have put more syrup than usual, because afterward I feel shaky. Either that, or I am nervous about my trip!

On our way to India Blossom, I gave money to that old man beggar with no fingers. For the rest of the day when he saw me again, he would always namaste me. And always with a smile. He is so sweet.

After doing some packing, I go down to print boarding passes. After that, I go in to see Sakra. We talk about the ashram experience. I tell him, like I told Andre, that I need more time for myself.

He laughs and says, "It doesn't matter what you do; you need to be present and aware of everything."

I say, "I like doing what I want to do, not what someone else wants me to do."

He says, "If you only do what you like all the time, then you will never grow." That makes sense. It is a good conversation, and he hugs me good-bye and asks me to keep in contact.

I say good-bye to Revatii. Then we hug and tell each other thank you for the lessons we learned.

For lunch, Jiadore and I take a rickshaw to the thali place. It isn't that good for my last thali experience. We have a different waiter this time. One little dish is cold and is usually hot, and that grosses me out. The sweet yellow stuff has something weird in it, so I don't eat much of anything. It's unfortunate it's turned out this way, but my last two meals at the thali place have been disappointing.

We walk up the street, and who is there but Khalid and Uncle Makeen on the side giving magic shows. Uncle Makeen tries to get Jiadore to watch, but we keep walking. If nothing else, they are salesmen.

Inside the back of German Bakery, I look for and find Manik. When he tells me that he sold his car, I ask if he did that for his brother's wedding. Manik says, no, he owed the guy money and he doesn't like debts hanging over him. We hug, and I give him my email address.

While I talk to Manik, Uncle Makeen's son keeps trying to talk to me from a few feet away. Mostly, I ignore him; but then feel bad that I treat him like he is invisible. But, he tries to get my attention while I am in a conversation with Manik. And, Manik is a friend.

I walk past Gowri's, and she isn't there. The vendor next door is, and I ask if he will give some clothes to her. He says to put it down by her other belongings.

Packing is a nightmare. I have much more than I thought I had; and I need to leave many items behind that I had wanted to keep. I manage to finish in time, and Rishika helps me carry my bags downstairs. Then Rishika and Mukta help me carry everything outside. Bhava shows up to say good-bye. That is a welcome surprise. Then Jiadore comes, and we take pictures of everyone.

Jiadore waits with me. The guy is a little late, but not too bad. It is a different guy and a different car this time. I sit in the front seat again, so I can take pictures. Unfortunately, I am too tired to even get the camera out of my pocket. After leaving the ashram, he drives down North Main Road, and I yell to Gowri as we drive by.

I watch the pariah kites soaring through the air until we leave the river areas of Pune. I see sign after sign for luxury apartments. Some of them are fancy and space age looking. Closer to Mumbai, I see several monkeys hanging out in the center median of the road.

We stop at a place that looks like where the other driver stopped on my way to Pune three months ago. This time it isn't scary at all. Whether that is because it's now daytime, or that I am comfortable being in India now, I don't know. While I wait for him, I go inside a building with public restrooms. It is so exciting! There is a stall with only a hole in the floor! How cool is that! Unfortunately, none of the stalls have toilet paper.

The rest of the trip to Mumbai is pleasant, but nothing special. Traffic jam after traffic jam slows us down, but there is nothing we can do. It gets nerve-wracking, but we arrive a little after seven o'clock. I'm glad that we had left an hour earlier than planned.

Someone told me there would be guys here to help me with my luggage, but there is no one. I ask the driver if he will wait for me to get a cart, and he says he'll get it for me. He puts my luggage on the cart, I give him a tip, and he drives away while I head into the terminal.

The woman in front of me starts talking to me and mentions German Bakery. I say, "Oh! Did you come from Pune, then?" She says, "I came from the ashram! I recognize you!" She had come into my office several times and recognized me; but I didn't know her. Surprisingly, she had left an hour later than I did, missed the traffic jams, and arrived before me. After we check our luggage, I lose track of her and only see her again once briefly.

The plane ride is fine, though long. Sitting by the window, I see stars, and that is cool. Otherwise, the flight is uneventful.

Everything about my journey home goes as planned. That is the universe's way of saying that coming back to America now was the right choice. Go with the flow, as they say. May the force be with you. Osho says, "You just listen to your own heart -- that is your only teacher." My Mom used to say, "Follow your heart." I say, "Where will this journey take me next?"

Afterward

It all feels like a dream now. Did I ever go to India? Was there really an old street magician named Uncle Makeen in my life? A cute beggar kid with one foot and beautiful eyes? A life of working seven days a week and forced attendance at a video showing of a dead Indian mystic named Osho? The golden cobra? Which life is the dream . . . this one in America or my life in India . . .?

I don't miss working seven days a week. I don't miss having to go to Evening Meetings. I don't miss hearing Osho rag on women and marriage, and I don't miss his many stories of arrests in different countries. I don't miss having to wear maroon. I don't miss not being able to drink the water or rinse my toothbrush out of the faucet. I don't miss having to pin numbers on my clothes before washing them. I don't miss the mostly unfriendly faces and weird attitudes of the Osho-ites. I don't miss the beggars who tore at my heart. I don't miss taking my life in my hands every time I crossed the street. I don't miss the pollution that made it hurt to breathe. I don't miss the dirtiness and unhygienic ways of daily life there.

I miss the unusual birds: the soaring pariah kites, the beautiful crested bulbul, and the other colorful birds. I miss the pariah dogs who were always smiling and wagging despite their personal hardships. I miss the street magicians who were every bit as colorful as the birds. I miss hanging on for dear life in rickety rickshaws, with Jiadore telling me to close my eyes. I miss the Indian people who were so friendly, helpful, and generous. I miss Rasha and her lessons, her stories, and her friendship. I miss my friends at the ashram who accepted me although I wasn't a "sannyasin." I miss the incredible peace I felt at Silent Sitting. I miss Osho's wisdom. I miss all the walking I used to do. I especially miss the Indian food!

Sakra says that if you always do what you want to do, you don't learn any lessons. It is in doing what you don't want to do that you grow. I see that. I have grown much in these past three months. Despite my complaints and frustrations while I was there, I would not trade this past three months for anything. Khush houn. I am happy.

Epilogue

How do I feel now after much reflection on my ashram experiences?

Despite the restrictive environment and my cynical attitude, the ashram was a growing experience for me. I learned many lessons that needed learning. Life at the ashram was a magical, transformative adventure.

I still maintain that Osho guided me on this journey. He guided me to the information I discovered, and he guided me in writing this book. He likes that I'm not a robot, and he likes that I questioned everything he said or did.

Would an enlightened person sexually exploit his disciples? Would an enlightened person always wear a hat to cover his baldness? Would an enlightened person talk about "my sannyasins?" I believe Osho was a wise and holy man. Much of his wisdom comes from an enlightened place. However, some of his actions and many of his words show little enlightenment. My conclusion is that he was often enlightened. He was a mystic with flaws. Learn from his wisdom and disregard the nonsense. Listen to your heart to discover which is which.

I can be your master only if I am not. If I am, then I cannot be a real master; then I can only be an egoist exploiting people.
OSHO

NOTE TO OSHO-ITES

Beloveds:

Before you condemn me for my audacity, remember this: Osho would have given this book his blessings. Remember the story he tells about giving his blessings to a book written about him that was filled with lies? You will find no lies in this book. You will find only my opinions, some of which may be wrong. The rest is reporting on events and happenings as I see them, as I experienced them.

Did you ever think that maybe if Osho were alive today he might want to change some of the policies at the ashram? Life is about change. It's time to admit the "experiment" isn't working. Do you honestly think that people who are meditative and aware would be constantly abusive and rude to one another?

Perhaps when you consider what goes on at the ashram today, you should ask yourself, "What would Osho say?"

Love,
Parvati Hill

Misery arises because we don't allow change to happen; we cling, we want things to be static. A man of awareness becomes courageous enough to accept the phenomenon of change.
OSHO

www.ingramcontent.com/pod-product-compliance
Lightning Source LLC
Chambersburg PA
CBHW051815090426
42736CB00011B/1490